T0303375

Learning from Difference

Learning from Difference

Learning from Difference
Teaching Morrison, Twain, Ellison, and Eliot

Richard C. Moreland

Ohio State University Press
Columbus

An earlier version of chapter 1 appeared as " 'He Wants to Put His Story Next to Hers': Putting Twain's Story Next to Hers in Toni Morrison's *Beloved*," *Modern Fiction Studies* 39 (Fall–Winter 1993): 155–80. © 1993 Purdue Research Foundation.

Copyright © 1999 by The Ohio State University.
All rights reserved.

Library of Congress Cataloging-in-Publication Data

Moreland, Richard C.
Learning from difference : teaching Morrison, Twain, Ellison, and Eliot / Richard C. Moreland.
p.   cm.
Includes bibliographical references and index.
ISBN 0-8142-0823-1 (alk. paper). — ISBN 0-8142-5025-4 (pbk. : alk. paper)
1. American literature—Study and teaching.   2. American fiction—Afro-American authors—Study and teaching.   3. Difference (Psychology) in Literature — Study and teaching.   4. Twain, Mark, 1835–1910. Adventures of Huckleberry Finn.   5. Eliot, T. S. (Thomas Stearns), 1888–1965. Waste land.   6. Race in literature—Study and teaching.   7. Ellison, Ralph. Invisible man.   8. Morrison, Toni. Beloved.   I. Title.
PS42.M67   1999
810.9—dc21   99-18510
                                                    CIP

Text and cover design by Ron Starbuck.
Type set in Apollo by G & S Typesetters, Inc.
Printed by Maple-Vail Book Mfg. Group.

The paper used in this publication meets the minimum requirements of the American National Standard for Information Sciences—Permanence of Paper for Printed Library Materials. ANSI Z39.48–1992.
9   8   7   6   5   4   3   2   1

To My Parents
Joe and Joyce Moreland

CONTENTS

CONTENTS

ACKNOWLEDGMENTS

I WISH TO THANK THE MANY STUDENTS AND TEACHERS from whom I have learned, in every case wishing I could have learned their lessons better. Elsie Michie, Dana Nelson, and Reggie Young gave support and valued advice on early drafts. Jim Catano, Bainard Cowan, John Duvall, Ojars Kratins, John Matthews, Wayne Parent, and Pat McGee all listened and responded more than once with a patience I appreciate. I also thank Barbara Hanrahan for her interest and confidence in this project from the beginning, Jerry Kennedy for his professional and personal support, and Donald Kartiganer, Carol Kolmerten, Stephen Ross, and Judith Wittenberg for giving me opportunities to test some of these ideas in public. I continue to learn from Mitchell Breitwieser, whose helpfulness and generosity as a teacher are legendary, and from Philip Weinstein, who has taught me about intellectual dialogue, both in his published writing and in his remarkably attentive response to my manuscript. Copy editor Elaine Otto gave me a skillful writing lesson, and Ruth Melville did what she could to keep me on schedule.

Susan, Gavin, and Luke have been my most persistent and forgiving teachers throughout the writing of this book. Learning from each of them has been both an ongoing challenge and something I love, similar to the intimacies and challenges of reading. Perhaps this book is an indirect attempt to understand what I have learned from them.

INTRODUCTION

Teaching Domination and Democracy in the American Literary Canon

THIS BOOK HAS GROWN OUT OF CERTAIN QUESTIONS that I and other teachers repeatedly face in teaching the changing canon of American literature. What is it I'm teaching? Am I passing down one literary tradition that tells us who Americans are as a nation? It has become increasingly apparent that this more traditional approach to teaching American literature runs the risk of overgeneralization. Certain dimensions of American culture and identity will seem underrepresented or even unwelcome in almost any one version of that tradition. Most teachers have therefore turned to some version of multiculturalism, especially the pluralist and oppositional versions of multiculturalism described by Gregory S. Jay in *American Literature and the Culture Wars* (103–6). Should I attempt to avoid overgeneralization and underrepresentation by adopting a pluralist multiculturalism? Should I emphasize the diversity of cultural traditions and identities within American literature as something to be appreciated and preserved against assimilation? One risk in this pluralist approach, however, is that I will lose my students and myself in a kind of consumer's vision of American literature—a potentially overwhelming menu of choices from which readers select their own recognizable cultural identities and perhaps learn to taste or tolerate others. This pluralism "emphasizes the characteristics of individual cultures rather than stressing the social or political relationships between them" (Jay 104). In its emphasis on separate cultural identities, it may also neglect differences within those identities. So should I instead adopt a more oppositional

multiculturalism, calling attention to the conflicts and differences in power that often perpetuate crucial differences and
tensions between these groups? I can in this way teach the dominant tradition along with the critical tools and the histories and
literatures that students need in order to read that dominant
tradition against the grain, to resist its cultural and historical
power. A risk in this oppositional multiculturalism, however, is
that its emphasis on the extensive, subtle power of dominant
economic and cultural structures tends toward determinism and
tends to undercut ideas of positive agency, change, and ethical
responsibility (see Jay 104).

My own suggestions about teaching American literature combine something of all three of these approaches. I would suggest
teaching an American literary tradition defined in terms of the
paired problems of domination and democracy, both in American
history and in the act of reading, including the constant process of articulating and asserting various personal, cultural, and
national identities, and the equally constant process of renegotiating these identities in our various interactions with others—personally, culturally, politically, and imaginatively. This
approach can tell us about who Americans are as a nation without ignoring the constant risk of overgeneralization and underrepresentation, since that political and ethical risk now becomes
central to the tradition. I would also seek to preserve pluralist
multiculturalism's sense of the importance of cultural traditions
in the process of forming and sustaining personal identities, not
only in the history of American cultures, but in today's classroom as well—in the act of reading, recognizing, and learning
about a diversity of cultural traditions in American literatures.
But oppositional multiculturalism is also crucial in its insistence
on the various effects that cultures constantly have on each
other, both when dominant cultures attempt to ignore or defend
against other cultures and when members of less powerful cultures attempt to resist or ignore such domination.

I would also suggest that American literature is an especially promising site for learning from such cross-cultural encounters, both as represented in the literature and as practiced in the act of reading and discussing our reading with others. Reading American literature becomes an occasion for recognizing ourselves, getting to know each other, but also for imagining and discovering in each other's experiences and identities unrecognized or unarticulated dimensions of ourselves. It is a chance to rearticulate and transform our own hybrid, overlapping, and interactive identities as citizens of a multicultural nation. Jay warns against "mistaking a common political arrangement for a common set of cultural beliefs," that is, "a widely shared commonality of convictions about religion, sex, nature, food, violence, sports, clothes, music, and art," a common culture that Americans do not actually share (176). But he argues that Americans do share a political ethos "predicated on the espoused, if not always realized, principles of cultural democracy, political rights, community responsibility, social justice, equality of opportunity, and individual freedom" (177). The study of American literature is an invaluable exercise in both observing and practicing this political ethos, articulating and asserting our own visions and identities, and taking responsibility for renegotiating these identities in our democratic and ethical interactions. This practice of democratic citizenship involves not only taking sides or counting votes but also entrusting ourselves to others and learning from each other in negotiations and decisions in which we risk being transformed.

The study of American literature may thus be understood as qualitatively different from either the study or the experience of American history. Literary study tends to be more participatory than the study of history, yet it is also more reflective than actual historical experience. The reader of American literature participates in a history that repeats itself in the activity and during the time of reading. We are drawn into making imaginative and ethical commitments that elaborate and explore the various identifications that constitute our identities. But we also know we are reading fiction and that we have a certain control over the pace, the intensity, and the interpretation of this experience. This relative control over our experience allows us to explore and reflect on encounters and identifications that we might not otherwise actively consider.

Reading expands our capacities both to shape reality according to our imaginations and to explore other versions of reality that challenge and perhaps transform our own. In a kind of transference, readers are encouraged to elaborate in the presence of another subjectivity our own (intrapsychic) idealizations and repudiations, identifications and projections. Like the analyst in transference, the literary text offers the promise of helping us to articulate, contain, and manage our anxieties and desires. But the literary text, again like the analyst in transference, also acts as another subjectivity, repeatedly surviving outside and intervening within our own imaginations, asserting its own identifications and projections. This other subjectivity reminds us repeatedly that our own thoughts and feelings, however psychologically real, are actually representations, fictions, for which we can take responsibility without insisting that they are the whole, or the only, story.[1] Whereas American history has in many ways persistently refused such an intersubjective model, American literature has been a site for troubled, anxious, sometimes eager explorations of such intersubjectivity. Readers of American literature thus actively participate in the dialectic of domination and democracy that also figures as a persistent challenge in American literature. Studying American literature in terms of domination and democracy is a valuable exercise in reflecting on a challenge that figures throughout our literature, throughout our political and ethical lives as citizens, and throughout our imaginative experience as readers.

The last few lines of Toni Morrison's novel *Jazz* call attention to a striking difference between her work and that of William

Faulkner, T. S. Eliot, Mark Twain, and many other European American writers. This difference also connects her work to that same literature and to the experience of a reader studying or reflecting on American literature.[2] What seems particularly different about her work but also connected to the rest of this literature is a certain readiness, perhaps a jazzlike or a democratic readiness, for unpredictable, transforming relationships with a second person, with the expectation that one's identity is actually made and remade in these relationships. It is a readiness that Morrison's narrator both models for and demands from her readers.

"If I were able," the narrator says, "I'd say it. Say make me, remake me. You are free to do it and I am free to let you because look, look. Look where your hands are. Now" (229). This voice suggests not only a readiness to enter into such a relationship, here with an unknown reader figured ambiguously as a lover, but also a pointed identification of the reader as someone already engaged in such a relationship, whether I as a reader have realized this before now or not. What seems almost embarrassing as an invitation is even more striking in this pointed reminder of my own actual position. I have long been holding the book, making and remaking the sounds and words that the narrator here admits she could not say aloud or make public or real without my presence and participation as a reader. And, of course, I could not have articulated these sounds and words myself without submitting my own unspoken voice and imagination to those of Morrison's narrator.

This passage and the novel it almost summarizes suggest a model of human relationships (including political, ethical, and imaginative relationships) that is more than a mere exchange or alliance or detour through another consciousness, or even a romantic union or fusion with another consciousness. Each of the major characters in the novel and each of us reading the novel has instead been made and remade in each other's interacting stories, often as an unintended, unpredictable consequence of our making and remaking each other into our own changing stories. Each of us has been "inward toward the other" (228), articulating ourselves almost inside out in the intimate losses and loves we bring to each other, and being remade again in the imaginative substitutes she says we are free to make of each other and become for each other.

Our selves and our freedoms are redefined here from their more common senses in American culture, or at least in European American culture, no longer as our individual freedoms from each other or from society as such, but instead as the rather daunting and potentially dangerous freedom to make and remake each other and to be made and remade, both in personal relationships and in our more "public love" (229), including perhaps the experience of studying a multicultural American literature. Instead of the radical individualism often associated with American politics, culture, and literature,[3] Morrison's work often suggests a model of human relationships that resembles Chantal Mouffe's description of radical democracy: "It is not a matter of establishing a mere alliance between given interests but of actually modifying the very identity of these forces" (235). Morrison's work not only differs from Faulkner's, Twain's, and Eliot's (at least in the way it is usually read, as variations on common American cultural themes); her work also engages with theirs in an ongoing debate about American political, ethical, and imaginative life. Her work acknowledges here and elsewhere that it is different from theirs, but also that it has been made and remade by theirs, as it also suggests that theirs has been made and remade by hers. And their work does look different when read and studied alongside hers.

This radically democratic model of human relationships suggests a useful reconception of American literature, at a time when literatures and cultures that have often seemed to compete for dominance over each other, or to be separate from or imperfectly the same as each other, seem increasingly and inextricably involved with and affected by each other. Henry Louis Gates Jr., for example, has influentially described African American literature in terms of its "signifyin(g)" on its own as well as other traditions, and Houston Baker Jr. has described much of the same literature in terms of its rhetorical strategies toward European American literature, including its "mastery of form" and "deformation of mastery" (49). Ralph Ellison often made similar assertions about the deliberate cultural eclecticism of his own work and that of jazz musicians. Critics such as Eric Sundquist, Shelley Fisher Fishkin, and Eric Lott, as well as Ralph Ellison and Toni Morrison, have called attention to the defining importance in European American literature and culture of an "Africanist presence," even when that presence is not an explicit focus. Such critics of African American and European American literature argue that writers and cultures may be most revealing about themselves in the ways they represent other writers and other cultures.[4] Homi Bhabha has elaborated this more general notion that personal and cultural identities are defined differentially, not by their essences or centers but by their various and dynamic boundaries with other identities (1–18). As in the passage from *Jazz* cited above, writers and readers of American literature increasingly seem to have been making and remaking each other from the beginning, whether they realized they were doing so or not.

Such interpersonal and intercultural relationships are an explicit focus in Morrison's work, as also in Ellison's work, and this explicit focus can be helpful in teaching a multicultural American literature, including work like Twain's or Eliot's where such interactions are more anxiously and indirectly addressed. These interactive relationships are represented in Morrison's work not only in third-person characters or in the past but also, more dramatically, in the first and second persons and in the present tense, unavoidably and unstoppably under way as characters or narrators speak or readers read. Morrison thus manages to combine the two implicit but often divided approaches to language that Meili Steele describes in recent African American (and much other) theory and criticism—the language of third-person critical explanations and the first- and second-person language that is more characteristic of most people's self-understanding. Steele argues that third-person accounts such as poststructuralism and radical genealogical critiques have been especially valuable for analyzing structural oppression and the internalization of those larger structural forces (as in Jay's description of oppositional multiculturalism), while first- and second-person accounts have been valuable for their attention to stories of personal and political agency and for conscious appeals to African and African American cultural resources (as in Jay's description of pluralist multiculturalism). Morrison's use of the first and second person in fictional and critical dialogue stresses this sense of personal agency and conscious appeals to cultural resources, but her use of the third and especially the second person in her writing also suggests a strong sense of historical, structural, and internalized constraints on the subject, even in intimate and lyrical passages like the last lines of *Jazz* cited above. "I" am not in total control of my speech or my identity even when speaking intimately to "you," but neither am I controlled only by large, impersonal, unmediated forces with which I cannot communicate or negotiate. This sense of our having various intimate, transforming holds on each other is in fact almost a constant in Morrison's work, even if some of us both within and outside her fiction may be strongly inclined to forget it.

Considered alongside Morrison's work, much of European American culture and literature seems inclined to focus on those who forget these various holds we have always had on each other, even when that literature is self-critical about just such forgetting. In Steele's terms, for example, William Faulkner calls his readers' attention to cultural, historical, and personal structures that repeatedly promote such forgetting. When I look for where readers' or characters' hands are in Faulkner's fiction, they are not already holding or touching other people, as suggested by the end of Morrison's novel. Whether readers or characters are involved, a hand's touch in Faulkner is represented not as an ongoing condition but as an event, if not a crisis. With regard to readers, Faulkner's language calls attention especially to our distance from his characters and his narrators. As Philip Weinstein writes about the language of *Light in August*, "agency [on the part of characters, especially] is shortsighted and vernacular, while awareness [on the part of narrators, usually] is speechless and poetic" (*What Else but Love?* 179), making it difficult to identify with either or to articulate that identification.

With regard to characters, I think of a scene near the end of *Go Down, Moses* where Ike McCaslin dramatically touches the hand of the granddaughter of James Beauchamp, the legally black and unrecognized grandson of Ike's own grandfather, the white dynastic patriarch who haunts the entire novel. What is dramatized in *this* touch, however, is not the making and remaking of Ike's identity in relationship to hers (although the absence of that possibility may be painfully obvious to readers, as it is to his interlocutor in the novel). What is dramatized instead is the *unmaking* of an identity that would tend to refuse, avoid, deny, or forget this touch, an identity Ike would have been widely expected to inherit from his grandfather and father. The unmaking of this patriarchal identity is sometimes represented in Faulkner's work as tragic, sometimes as ironic, but in either case it seems almost impossible that it could be remade or replaced, as might be more likely in a first- or second-person account. This patriarchal identity was apparently not even *made* (or constructed) in the first place. It just inevitably was, or at least almost everyone thinks it was. It is apparently not the expression of one possible world among other possible worlds, but the only conceivable world. Its loss therefore seems irreparable, at least to Ike.

Identity in Morrison, whether we imagine ourselves as characters or readers, is made and remade in our relationships to a second person, in the needs and losses we usually bring first to our mothers and to a complex series of others who bring their needs and losses to us in turn. We remake ourselves and each other in our acts of identification and projection onto others, and we repeatedly renegotiate these identities in the context of others' stories. For Ike McCaslin, however, touching this woman's hand is instead another reminder of the loss of Ike's own innocence and the failure of his legacy.[5] Losing this legacy means the loss of Ike's identity not only as a McCaslin but as a man. His McCaslin legacy, his identity, and his innocence all seem to have been lost at once in the act of incest and miscegenation that has revealed to Ike his grandfather's intimate involvement with and violent exploitation of his black slaves. The fact that Ike's kinsman has recently had an affair with this woman and is having Ike pay her off seems to confirm Ike's ironic sense that no one is ever made or remade, but only unmade, in such relationships. Ike himself has therefore virtually withdrawn from human contact long before this scene, and he recommends that this woman, too, try to forget that her affair with his kinsman "ever happened, that he ever existed." She replies that Ike must have forgotten whatever he "ever knew or felt or even heard about love" (346).

This woman is one of many characters—usually women and/or black characters—in Faulkner's fiction, as in much European American literature, who are given somewhat vague credit for knowing much more than Ike does here about being made and remade in their relationships with other people. Susan Donaldson describes these feminine figures in southern gothic fiction, including Faulkner's, as "semi-articulated." Considering these figures' semi-articulation in Faulkner's work next to the much greater attention they receive in Morrison's work suggests both cultural differences between the worlds of their fiction and different strategies toward such cultural difference. Faulkner's fiction leaves these figures semi-articulated in order to pay much more articulate and sustained attention to the *unmaking* of another sort of identity—the one constructed by and for white boys and men like Ike. In Faulkner's work, these men try unsuccessfully to forget and refuse any such mutual transformations in their relationships with others. When they cannot forget, they try to retreat from what seems an irreversible structural failure of their own identities, and they assume a third-person ironic stance toward anyone thinking to escape this structural failure, including themselves. They thereby ensure that they will get stuck repeating or dwelling on scenes of their own unmaking, rather than risk being remade in their relationship to someone else. These other characters, however, sometimes remain onstage as incompletely articulated expressions of other possible worlds and selves.

In another passage near the end of *Jazz,* Morrison sketches a brief genealogy both for this culturally powerful model of independent, masculine identity and for the "rogue" alternatives she explores in her own fiction. "I started out," the narrator says, "believing that life was made just so the world would have some way to think about itself, but that it had gone awry with humans because flesh, pinioned by misery, hangs on to it with pleasure" (227–28). Hegel and Freud are famous for versions of both these powerful cultural ideas, questioned and resisted here by Morrison's narrator. The cultural power of both ideas, however, as well as Morrison's critical and creative resistance to that cultural power, is apparent throughout her work. The idea that the purpose of life is the world's consciousness of itself suggests a model of one universal or representative consciousness reflecting on itself, but not interacting with or transforming either itself or any other consciousness. The other idea considered here, that humans might have turned out to be not the world's self-reflective spirit but afflicted flesh, subject to human misery and even clinging to misery rather than risk other unpredictable losses, suggests the undifferentiated *unmaking* of that same self-reflective model. Not just afflicted, the self here also clings to that affliction. Whether crushed, depressed, ironic, or self-destructive, this self effectively internalizes and repeats its own affliction in order to minimize its loss of self-control.[6]

Morrison's narrator adds, however, "I don't believe that anymore. Something is missing there. Something rogue. Something else you have to figure in before you can figure it out" (228). What the rest of her narration suggests is missing from both third-person models of self-reflective and self-destructive consciousness is the unpredictable, transforming role—the structurally inescapable but resistible and negotiable role—of the second person's unaccountably different consciousness, always already involved with our own. It is not a matter here of deciding whether or not to risk other unpredictable losses in interactions with other people, as Ike has attempted—unsuccessfully—to do. The trail of our losses leads us to other people and the stories in which we find our other selves, both those oppressive roles we may have internalized and those that offer us needed support and possibilities. We have brought our needs and losses to other people from the beginning and tried to make them into substitutes for those whose love we have lost and miss, while those we make into substitutes have been busy trying to make us into metaphorical substitutes as well. Each of us plays roles in each other's stories even as we script those others into our own, and each of us shifts unpredictably among our different selves as the writers of our own scripts and the readers and players within each other's. As Violet realizes and only slowly comes to accept and appreciate about her marriage, "from the very beginning I was a substitute and so was he" (97). What is especially "rogue" about this model of human relationships is how unpredictably we suffer, benefit, and change in the shifts among these different roles. Both the harm and the good that we actually do to each other in such relationships is often only obliquely related to our own intentions as the writers of our own stories, since these stories are always set inextricably in the midst of others. This harm or good that we do to each other can in fact so far exceed intentions that Morrison's narrator even imagines "the smiles of the dead left over from their lives" as having the effect of "brief benevolent love" on her character Golden Gray, even though these smiles were certainly not intended for him (161).

Golden Gray is perhaps Morrison's most Faulknerian character, providing another instance of Morrison's cultural difference from Faulkner as well as her readiness to explore such differences and interactions in her fiction. Gray's bid for his father's recognition is one of three scenes in *Jazz* that might be briefly compared to Charles Bon's several bids for his father's recognition in Faulkner's *Absalom, Absalom!* Like Charles Bon, Gray attempts to claim his identity directly from his father, man to man, but Morrison stresses neither the father's refusal nor the son's impotence so much as the cultural arrogance and personal possessiveness of the son's claim, as if to call into question this entire construction of father-son relationships. As Jessica Benjamin writes about Freud and Hegel, "the father-son relationship [as implied here by Golden Gray], like the master-slave relationship [in Hegel], is a model in which the opposition between self and other can only reverse—one is always up and the other down. . . . This reversible complementarity is the basic pattern of domination" (*Bonds* 220). In Morrison's novel, however, this particular bid for paternal recognition and identity is instructively interrupted and upstaged by the sounds of Wild giving birth and by the need to find a substitute mother for the baby who would eventually become Joe Trace. As Hunter explains to Gray, being a man, at least if you're black, means improvising and drawing "your manhood up—quicklike," and not just making a birthright claim (173). Instead of either successfully claiming his manhood as a legacy from his father or losing his manhood to his father's irresistible domination, Gray discovers the possibility of a different role for himself in his father's and his father's culture's improvised stories. It is perhaps in this sense that the "smiles left over from the dead" have their unintentionally benevolent effect on Golden Gray, in the way that he adapts and learns from their example of courage and humor against the odds.

Joe Trace will also ask for parental recognition, though in his case he asks his mother, and he asks in language that is again both different from and comparable to that of Charles Bon. "Is it you? Just say it. Say anything. . . . Give me a sign, then" (178). He gets no answer, exactly, and there is no reunion of mother and child of the kind dreamed of and attempted in *Beloved,* no unspoken reunion back before or apart from the interference of historical circumstances and other people. But Joe does find meaningful signs and traces. He has heard her singing and will later find her home, and he has learned from Hunter (Gray's biological father and one of Joe's substitute fathers) that even the crazy have reasons (even though Joe never knows what her reasons are). He finds his identity as a tracker and even his name— Joe Trace—in the traces of this and other lost relationships, traces he will make and remake in the tracks he sees in Dorcas's face and the redwing he imagines as he lies with Violet. His name and identity come not from his mother or father directly but from the various substitutes in the signs, memories, language, music, and other people in whom Joe makes and remakes himself and is made and remade by others as so many possible worlds. This freedom to make and remake each other is both a constant promise and a constant danger for which he learns to take personal responsibility, even though he can never take complete control.

The other bid for recognition in *Jazz* that I want to compare with Charles Bon's bid for recognition in Faulkner's novel is the passage with which I began. Morrison's narrator speaks to the reader as if to a lover, longing to say, "I have loved only you, surrendered my whole self reckless to you and nobody else" (229). Each of us knows as a reader we are not "the only one"— we are substitutes—but we play along. We have already long been playing along because, as the narrator knows, *we* have been making and remaking our own substitutes of this narrator and her characters. She makes a bid for recognition from me, and I make a bid for recognition from her, but the identity each of us gains from this recognition is neither our own nor the unmaking of our own, as it must be one or the other for Faulkner's Charles Bon. The rogue, jazz, democratic, intersubjective identity each of us gains instead from this recognition is the necessary ethical and political responsibility to make and remake ourselves in the shifts and negotiations between our identities in the stories we write and our identities in each other's stories, the stories in which we read, play, learn about, and negotiate with our less predictable selves.

When I try to imagine myself as a reader at about my students' age, I remember that Mark Twain's *Adventures of Huckleberry Finn* was my favorite novel when I was a junior at almost-all-white Baton Rouge High School in 1970, almost a century after the publication of Twain's novel and almost two decades before the publication of Toni Morrison's *Beloved*. In 1970, Baton Rouge High was about to become the city's token racially desegregated high school, and at least some of us were anticipating this change as a kind of adventure that seemed vaguely similar to Huck's inspiring adventures with Jim on the raft. We were inspired by the civil rights movement, as also by the antiwar movement and the women's movement, all of which were being represented to us in mainstream American culture in similarly flattering but problematic ways that seemed to echo Twain's famous novel. That is, these movements were being represented to us mostly as moralistic appeals to the individual consciences of "better" white, male Americans to distinguish ourselves (like Huck) from a bigoted past represented by easily demonized, working-class, "redneck" figures like Montgomery Sheriff "Bull" Connors and Twain's Pap Finn. In our less inspired, less adventurous moments, however, or whenever our moralism seemed overwhelmed by the puzzling indifference of vaguely larger, more powerful cultural forces, we might well have looked to the more "realist" dimensions of Twain's novel for an articulation of our apparent moral help-lessness. Had we looked further, we might even have found some consolation in T. S. Eliot's *The Waste Land* and its starker, more modernist elaboration of that same helplessness—as well as a sense of pathos and dignity in our apparent inability even to articulate or communicate that helplessness. We probably needed other cultural resources than these, however, resources and possibilities that figured only as vague frustrations and shadowy possibilities in our understanding of Twain and Eliot and the cultural currents they exemplified. Our situation called for something other than any of these heroic, helpless, or speech-less moralisms.

It seems to me now that my friends and I at Baton Rouge High were largely responding to what Toni Morrison has described in her nonfiction as the "solitude" and "separate confinement" of canonical American literature, especially as it tends to be read by a critical and cultural tradition that has emphasized its romance, its flight, its individualism, its exceptionalism, and its supposedly ahistorical, apolitical nature ("Unspeakable" 1, 12). Ralph Ellison has described similar tendencies in dominant American literature and culture as the American "tradition of intellectual evasion for which Thoreau criticized Emerson in re-gard to the Fugitive Slave Law," a tradition that Ellison considers to have grown "swiftly since the failure of the ideals in whose name the Civil War was fought" (*Shadow and Act* 36). Ellison's suggestion that African American culture is "older" than Euro-pean American culture "in the sense of what it took to live in the world with others" (*Invisible Man* 574), along with Morrison's comments on the "solitude" and "separate confinement" of the American canon, suggests an image of European American cul-ture and the literary tradition of the American romance as a kind of Robinson Crusoe character, as reinterpreted by Michel Tour-nier in fiction and Gilles Deleuze in philosophy. The Robinson Crusoe of Tournier and Deleuze is oblivious to the existence of other people and particularly to his servant, Friday. For his part,

Friday is not only more aware of Crusoe than vice versa but also (like the invisible man in Ellison's novel) aware of his own invisibility in Crusoe's view of the world.[7]

In more psychological terms, Jessica Benjamin describes a "loss of externality" that resembles this characterization of European American literature and culture, a loss of externality that "plunges the self into unbearable aloneness, or escape into merger with like-self beings, creating an identity that demands a destructive denial of the different" (*Shadow* 96). One question raised by such characterizations of the American canon—and by Friday's presence alongside Crusoe—is whether such relationships of blindness and domination can somehow yield relationships of democracy and cross-cultural learning, relationships in which, for example, Crusoe might learn from Friday "what it took to live in the world with others." This question of democratic relationships has been not only a question in American literature and culture but a repeated promise, however repeatedly deferred.

The work of Ellison and Morrison in both fiction and nonfiction turns the focus and the direction of American literary and cultural history back toward this deferred democratic promise. Their work retroactively emphasizes in the work of Twain, Eliot, and other canonical American writers a national work-in-progress of cross-cultural learning and democracy. For this reason, I will reverse chronology in the following paired chapters, looking at Morrison's work as a way of situating and questioning Twain's, then Ellison's work as a promising interrogation and interaction with Eliot's.

This project may be compared with that of Nina Baym's 1981 essay, "Melodramas of Beset Manhood: How Theories of American Fiction Exclude Women Authors." Baym's essay argued that the critics who so influentially defined "the American romance" were actually not defining an American "cultural essence" or a truly representative national literature so much as projecting onto the past a certain idea of their own national culture.[8] These critics described and canonized a group of male writers whose "membership in the dominant middle-class white Anglo-Saxon group, and their modest alienation from it" produced a "consensus criticism of the consensus" (129). Baym's essay demonstrates how gendered and exclusive this definition of a national literature was. It masculinized its hero and feminized not only the social impediments and entrapments from which he fled but also the beckoning wilderness toward which he turned instead. The essay also demonstrates how unlikely it was that women authors would produce work that would either fit this definition or be recognized when their work changed the gendered terms of the definition. Baym's essay thus calls valuable attention to the limits of this definition of American literature in accounting for women's writing or other American literary works that did in fact exist alongside the literature that was canonized. Her essay pays less attention, however, to the persistent cultural power of these ideas of Americanness, however limited their descriptive power or representativeness.

Mid-twentieth-century American literary critics such as Lionel Trilling did not completely invent and project onto the past their ideas of this American "consensus criticism of the consensus." Although they did effect changes in the canon, such critics did not have to look far for already prominent literary or cultural examples of these ideas, nor did these critics have to propose radically different readings of these examples. They may have largely ignored women writers in their ideas of the American canon, but that and other exclusions were crucial both in the dominant cultural tradition they described and in the response of other traditions to the power of that dominant tradition. By focusing less on the cultural power than on the descriptive limits of theories of the American romance, Baym's essay suggests almost a mutual independence in the relationship between male and female American authors (as in much of what Jay describes as pluralist multiculturalism).

Ellison and Morrison, on the other hand, tend to focus more

on the interaction between European American and African American literature and culture. Theories of the American romance may well have excluded most African American literature from the canon, but neither Ellison nor Morrison minimizes the importance of that exclusion within European American culture or the power of that exclusion to affect African American culture. Their work suggests that the promise of a national work-in-progress of cross-cultural learning and democracy may have been repeatedly denied or deferred by ideas like that of the American romance, but the promise was never completely forgotten. Morrison's and Ellison's place in the American canon does not simply displace Twain and Eliot. It allows us to understand better the particular character of their work and the traditions in which they wrote, not as the whole story but as undeniably influential ones in American cultural life.

In placing Morrison's and Ellison's work alongside Twain's and Eliot's, I do not intend to detract from the importance of Ellison's and Morrison's work within African American literature and culture, elaborating and institutionalizing these traditions in their own rights. Without such work on the *difference* between African American and European American literature, my focus here on the contrast and interaction between those traditions would hardly be possible. In addressing African American literary and cultural traditions, however, Ellison and Morrison also address European American cultural traditions, variously demonstrating the difficulty of segregating European American from African American literary and cultural studies. In addition to their roles as writers and critics of African American literary history, they have also helped define and redefine a national and cross-cultural literary and cultural history. In the latter respect, their work both analyzes and continues a national dialogue that might be described as a dialogue about domination and democracy in American culture.

Briefly, a tradition of domination, as influentially described by D. H. Lawrence, Lionel Trilling, Richard Chase, and again more recently by Toni Morrison, stresses the American individual's repeated declarations of independence from European feudal society and even from society as such. As suggested in Huey Long's slogan, "Every Man a King," this is a promise of unrestricted freedom that is nonetheless steeped in the tradition of domination against which it reacts. As mentioned earlier, Jessica Benjamin has described the father-son and master-slave relationships which figure largely in this tradition as "a model in which the opposition between self and other can only reverse —one is always up and the other down. . . . This reversible complementarity is the basic pattern of domination" (*Bonds* 220). Although this powerful current of American rhetoric usually goes by the name of freedom, it is profoundly shaped by the domination to which it is opposed and to which it often variously reverts.

Another less powerful but persistent current of American rhetoric focuses less on freedom from domination or from society as such than on democratic participation with other people in building and governing that society. In this tradition other people figure less as obstacles or rivals than as a given, crucial condition of human existence, so many expressions of other possible worlds, as in the following description by Deleuze of the other people Tournier's Crusoe lacks: "Filling the world with possibilities, backgrounds, fringes, and transitions; inscribing the possibility of a frightening world when I am not yet afraid, or on the contrary, the possibility of a reassuring world when I am really frightened by the world; encompassing in different respects the world which presents itself before me developed otherwise" (310). The cross-cultural idea of "double consciousness," for example, "this sense of always looking at one's self through the eyes of others," mentioned by Ralph Waldo Emerson, made famous by W. E. B. Du Bois (5), and elaborated throughout the African American literary tradition, has become an increasingly influential idea in the understanding even of European American literature, where "innocence" often names its absence. In the work of Morrison and Ellison, the double consciousness that Du Bois described is elaborated both as a social predicament and as a source of cultural wisdom and strength. Morrison and Ellison elaborate this latter tradition of American democracy in its tangled history with the powerful tradition of American domination. In short, each of these traditions has distilled and elaborated historical and cultural experiences, often articulating much of what other traditions leave relatively unexplored or "semi-articulated."

At the risk of vast oversimplification, I am suggesting that European American literature has tended to explore the idea and experience of individualism and a freedom from social constraints in works that also develop a sense of the loneliness of that tradition, what Morrison calls the solitude and separate confinement of canonical American literature. African American literature, on the other hand, has tended to explore more thoroughly the experience of what Du Bois calls "double consciousness," what Ellison calls "what it takes to live in the world with others," or what Morrison describes as being made and remade by each other. European American literature, in its solitude, often calls out for such different stories. And African American literature often calls out for stories of freedom and individualism in ways that look to European American literature and culture both for ideals to invoke and emulate and examples to guard against.

Needless to say, the mostly applauded innocence, moralism, and goodwill of a few adventurous white students at Baton Rouge High and similar schools in 1970–71 was not enough to dispel several centuries of variously institutionalized white supremacy in the United States.[9] Our goodwill was not enough, any more than Huck and Jim's goodwill was enough, any more than the apparent goodwill of the Emancipation Proclamation or Reconstruction or the Voting Rights Act has been enough without persistent legal enforcement and slow economic and cultural

change. Nor was the moralism and goodwill of the domestic antiwar movement enough to divert, much less to stop, the progress of American imperialism in Vietnam without a great deal of
political organizing, coalition building, and native Vietnamese
resistance. Yet these various demonstrations of innocence, moralism, and good intentions were precisely what American culture seemed most prepared to recognize and return. Feminists,
along with anti-imperialists and civil rights activists, would
come to be widely blamed in the decades of backlash ahead for
not being satisfied with countless featured gestures of more or
less official American good intentions.

Since well before Twain published *Huckleberry Finn* in the
1880s, many Americans have wanted to think that goodwill
would be enough, that an individualized change of heart, a moral
rebirth or conversion experience would be enough to make for
significant social change—or would be a moral substitute worth
as much as significant social change. This is a familiar, self-
congratulatory cultural memory of slavery, race relations, and
social change in American history and culture, especially for
European Americans, for whom it is all too often not a necessary
step but a sufficient alibi—a focus on individualized moral
change *instead* of the kind of democratic social change that would
require being made and remade by other people.[10] Twain's novel
has figured among the most persistent and prominent invocations of this ideology of American goodwill, although the novel
also shows this same ideology under considerable strain. Placing
Twain's work in the context of work like Morrison's and Ellison's
helps show the shape and the limits of the tradition in which
Twain's novel is usually read, as well as a certain troubled longing in Twain's novel and in his readers for an alternative to this
tradition.

Especially in its ending, *Huckleberry Finn* does dramatize the
predictable underside to this tradition's more flattering moral
memories and hopes, in the frustrating sense growing through-

out the novel that at least with regard to slavery and race, this prevailing "storybook truth about American history" is inadequate and therefore simply false: Americans did *not* leave feudal and clerical oppression and every other form of systematic social oppression behind in the Old World, to be confronted here instead only with individual moral problems (Hartz 3). But the culture that has read and canonized Twain's novel has often assumed too easily that the only alternative to such a "storybook truth about American history" is its *unmaking* in American society. What remains after that unmaking is the supposedly disillusioned, hard, cold, realistic idea (but the closely related idea) that while moral concerns may have had their place in the realm of the frontier past and surely still have a place in the nostalgic realm of sentiments and the home, or in the limited domain of individual behavior, the larger world of business, politics, social policy, organizing, and planning must be addressed instead according to Charles Darwin and Adam Smith. While moral responsibility is applauded at the level of the individual, and perhaps the individual's nuclear family, questions of wider social responsibility are considered best left to the invisible hand of the marketplace or even to nature's tooth and claw. To the naive, sentimental goodwill of American romance is opposed the political cynicism of American realism. Both are parts of the same tradition in American culture, and both have similar effects in American history, insofar as one often ignores and the other often capitulates before the mechanics and politics of social power. In another phase of the same cultural tradition, American modernism is more emphatic about both the necessity and the impossibility of wider moral and social responsibility.

In American history, the difference between black and white has certainly not been the only significant racial difference, nor has race been the only significant cultural or social difference. But I will be focusing in this book on the difference between black and white as a powerful and somewhat representative cultural difference in American literature and culture. Slavery and race have continued to raise some of the most glaring questions in American culture, questions usually inextricable from those of gender and class, about the wider effects of the national political rhetorics discussed above and about the corresponding literary rhetorics of American romance and its underside in American realism and modernism. According to these nearly mythic discourses, we are a nation of high-minded, adventurous, individualistic outcasts and entrepreneurs, attempting again and again to leave behind an alien, feudalistic, often feminized society. We seek to discover instead our naturalized, individualized identities in an unending series of "new world orders" where systematic social oppression either does not exist or is a minor—or "minority"—concern.

Repeatedly this attempt to leave such a society and its questions behind also entails a representation of that society's organization and laws as unassailable, unchanging, perhaps even finally inescapable. When the American romance of escape from that society is shown to fail, overpowered by greater social or natural forces, we tend to have American realism. When the romance of escape is shown to be inexpressibly and pathetically sentimental, we have modernism. The vision of a more or less inescapable, unchangeable society tends to be much the same in either case—as if the problem (or Hell, as Sartre's character says) is other people. In Jessica Benjamin's phrase, "the opposition between self and other can only reverse" (*Bonds* 220).

Most American readers of Twain's novel have tended to focus on Huck's individualized moral heroism when he decides to "set Jim free," but most have also had continuing difficulty dismissing the bitter taste of the book's last chapters. These last chapters offer tediously detailed evidence that this individual goodwill in which we tend to trust is not enough—especially when that goodwill is reduced to Huck and Tom's child's play at Jim's expense and Huck's trust in Providence and in the leadership of the middle-class Tom Sawyer. There is plenty of disappointing evidence here that Huck's moral heroism was not another final, clean break from America's past but is instead another repetition of a powerfully seductive discourse of American romance, and that this same discourse has probably been overruled here again by the equally American discourse of social and political cynicism.

Under the influence of the New Criticism in literary criticism, itself heavily influenced by the rhetorics of the cold war, critics have tended to dismiss this last part of Twain's novel as a moral or aesthetic mistake, the novel's failure to carry through and confirm the essential importance of Huck's individualistic, moral, and thus characteristically American vision (as in Trilling's famous reading). Or we have read the last section as a realist's prophetic glimpse of modernism's more thoroughly ironic disillusionment with any possibility of carrying Twain's moral or aesthetic insight into the "real world" (as in Eliot's famous introduction to Twain's novel). But neither of these influential critical judgments has quite settled most readers' questions about this novel's ending—or about the direction it seems to set for American literature. Neither judgment has allowed most readers of the novel's last chapters to forget the nagging, unresolved frustration of Huck and Jim's inability to articulate any effective protest against their middle-class leader in Tom Sawyer, who seems able to enlist their good intentions so effortlessly into his own cynical, self-serving version of their adventures (as suggested in Leo Marx's reading). Huck and Jim's example, so moving and also so frustrating for so many readers, remains somehow uncontained either within the realm of sentiment and nostalgia or within the related realm of ironic disillusionment. In this frustration on the part of readers (as exemplified in the essays recently collected in Leonard et al.'s *Satire or Evasion? Black Perspectives on "Huckleberry Finn"*), Huck and Jim's example continues to promise and actually evoke something more than only a moral gesture to save Huck's soul, and something other than inevitable, unassailable victory for Tom's tiresome cultural power.

In short, Twain's novel and its canonization certainly distill and elaborate powerful, persistent cultural currents in American society, but not without also evoking certain equally powerful, persistent, but largely unarticulated frustrations within those same dominant currents. It is as if Twain as an author, Huck as a narrator and character, and countless Americans as readers (especially European Americans) have tried and failed to imagine and learn—especially from the African American figure of Jim, and from the cross-cultural relationship of Huck and Jim—how to articulate and put into motion socially and politically effective challenges to these same dominant cultural currents. Among much other recent cultural and cross-cultural work, Toni Morrison's recent writing, along with Ellison's, has functioned as a kind of cross-cultural response to these largely unarticulated frustrations and questions in dominant American traditions. Work like Morrison's and Ellison's not only provides responses and alternatives to these traditions, but also ways of understanding the sense of frustration in reading a work like Twain's.

Like Ellison's, Morrison's work addresses these same dominant cultural tendencies and less articulated frustrations, even though she also writes, more clearly than Twain, out of resistance to that dominant culture. Ellison's and Morrison's work addresses what Edward Said describes as three main themes of much other such decolonizing cultural resistance throughout the world in this century. First, "the insistence on the right to see the community's history whole, coherently, integrally. Restore the imprisoned nation to itself" (215). Ellison's and Morrison's writing has worked to reclaim for African Americans cultural and historical territory that has been captured and charted more than once by works like Twain's, or largely ignored by work like Eliot's: their writing has worked to flesh out the words, thoughts, struggles, and histories of African Americans that have been obscured behind or beyond characters such as Twain's Jim or the silent, floating bodies of "dead Negroes" mentioned in passing in Eliot's "Dry Salvages." They have worked in this nationalist (or pluralist multiculturalist) direction to trace histories and values significantly different from those most emphasized in the dominant culture. Said describes this nationalist dimension of decolonizing cultural resistance as crucial but also necessarily insufficient and impure (224).

The second goal Said describes in decolonizing cultural resistance like Ellison's and Morrison's is thus "to enter into the discourse of Europe and the West, to mix with it, transform it, to make it acknowledge marginalized or suppressed or forgotten histories" (216). Works like Ellison's and Morrison's have challenged and encouraged the nation's dominant historical memory to take account of the marginalized, suppressed, and forgotten histories of African Americans and women. Their work in this more oppositionally multicultural direction offers a renewed and transforming look at histories that have been more often either denied or shrugged off as the unavoidable costs of a more triumphal national history.

The third theme described by Said "is a noticeable pull away from separatist nationalism toward a more integrative view of human community and human liberation" (216). Ellison's and Morrison's work thus also addresses the value of markedly different but also overlapping, interdependent, mutually constitutive histories in this ongoing cultural work of human liberation and community. In his introduction to *Invisible Man,* Ellison represents Twain's novel as a "raft of hope" in a longer American cultural and cross-cultural history. And *Beloved* takes up the question already explored by Twain of how a young, poor-white character like Huck might feel and act toward a runaway slave like Jim, how the runaway slave might enlist the white character's help, and how each might feel about the work of liberation and community that they somehow manage to do together "appropriately and well" in Morrison's novel (85).

Beloved examines at even greater length how the child delivered by these two characters eventually comes to reevaluate their cross-cultural interaction. This child, Denver, imagines the interaction between Amy and Sethe first as a miracle (as in American romance), then as a deceptive exception to the social rule (as in American realism), then as an incommunicable, perhaps unthinkably naive vision (as in literary modernism). But she eventually reconceives this same memory as representing a risky interaction with outsiders, a risk that is necessary before she can take any action beyond the steps of her own porch. The novel also examines how the local community comes to reconceive in analogous ways the relationship between its own most private and public acts, thereby making possible socially the interaction with outsiders on which the future of those within 124 depends. And the novel features a man and a woman with very different, representatively gendered histories in slavery and responses to slavery (Paul D's loving "small" and Sethe's loving "too thick," for example) coming to learn that they need to put their different stories next to each other's, in order to learn and gain strength from hearing and contemplating each other's different but overlapping stories.

The novel's work with these cross-cultural interactions, interactions with differences that are more than only personal differences, suggests an ethics and politics of difference, even a pedagogy of difference in reading, that is more broadly useful for reconceiving the relations between works throughout American literature. The interactions between characters within such works suggest that the works in which they figure may also speak from different cultures, yet they continue to address, listen to, and make and remake each other.

In chapter 1, I will attempt to show how Morrison's writing, especially in these dimensions of *Beloved*, both resists the dominant culture and also puts her own stories next to those works and traditions most canonized within that culture, effectively transforming the look and feel of the nation's ongoing cultural work in progress. In *Playing in the Dark,* Morrison suggests, for example, that American romance "made possible the sometimes safe and other times risky embrace of quite specific, understandably human, fears" (36). American romance made such more or less risky embraces possible by a kind of transference, in the way that it "transferred internal conflicts to a 'blank darkness,' to conveniently bound and violently silenced black bodies" (38). As her references both to internal conflicts and to violently silenced black bodies suggest, such transference allows for the articulation and elaboration of these internal conflicts and repudiations, but the self is also somehow faced with the actual bodies of other selves, whose bodies may be bound or silenced but who survive beyond the self's attempts at destruction and domination. By calling attention to its own imaginative distance from social reality, American romance thus made possible the contemplation of what was otherwise too combustible to explore, both the internal conflicts and fears that were otherwise repressed, disavowed, denied, and avoided in the dominant culture's most current terms and tropes, and the unforgettable presence of other bodies and other selves that called these dominant terms and tropes into question. Reminders of these other selves make the dominant culture's internal conflicts and fears seem more clearly both internal and dominant, and not the only possible version of their own or others' reality.

As suggested by Morrison's model (like Benjamin's model) of an unstable, "sometimes safe and other times risky" cultural and personal transference, I will attempt to show in chapter 2 how Huck's relationship with Jim in Twain's novel becomes an imaginative site not only for distancing readers (mostly European American readers) from the social realities of slavery, but also for allowing these readers to imagine in Jim's experience what would otherwise be more difficult to imagine and articulate.

What seems to be missing in the experience of Huck and Tom, who are both at least potentially (because they are white males) full members of the dominant culture, are assertions of friendship, loyalty, and love, along with the limits on freedom these may entail. These interpersonal feelings and commitments are regularly imagined and articulated at several removes from Tom and often at least at one remove from Huck, in the character of Jim and in occasional women characters. Also usually represented at several removes from Tom and at least at one remove from Huck are most recognitions of the need for practical strategies and plots for fleshing out good intentions, translating goodwill into ethical and political action, perhaps what Ellison meant by "what it took to live in the world with others" (*Invisible Man* 574). These assertions of friendship, loyalty, and love, and these recognitions of social and historical circumstances, are otherwise uneasily reconciled with the dominant rhetorics of American romance and realism, with their focus on ideals such as independence from social ties and the importance of individualized, moralized goodwill. It is easier to contemplate and articulate these divergent assertions and recognitions in the character of Jim than in Huck or certainly Tom, but this makes their articulation by Jim all the more important to Huck and to many of his readers, both for recognizing the limits of their own thinking and for considering other possibilities.

The question of imaginative projection in the dominant tradition of romance goes further than this, however. Certainly, these projections of inner conflicts and fears from within the dominant culture onto its variously institutionalized representations of subordinated or marginalized others such as African Americans distort and obscure countless features of actual and specific African Americans' own experience. Certainly, these projections function primarily in the service of goals other than fair and accurate representation of African American experiences. However, the cultural power of these representations also gives them a certain kind of truth. Such projections of inner conflicts and fears on the part of the dominant culture have of course functioned well beyond the realm of imaginative literature, not only misrepresenting social reality but also enforcing these misrepresentations in the organization of social reality.

The cultural work of imagining, articulating, elaborating, and actually living out ideals of friendship, loyalty, and love in all the contingencies of American society and history may have been disproportionately assigned to women and African Americans, and may have been disproportionately internalized and actually taken up and prized by women and African Americans, in a kind of cultural division of labor. Jennifer FitzGerald, for example, speaks of the "discourse of black solidarity" that "prevails among the marginalized African American community" in *Beloved* (671). Kaja Silverman stresses how differently our culture's Law of Kinship Structure inflects according to gender such "defining conditions of all subjectivity" as lack, specularity, and alterity: "conditions which the female subject is obliged compulsively to reenact, but upon the denial of which traditional masculinity is predicated" (50–51). Thus, too, it is only partly a projected, guarded fantasy on the part of Huck, Twain, and many of Twain's readers that they may need the help of a character like Jim to begin to imagine and address what is fearful, frustrating, lonely, missing, or just simplistically articulated in familiar rhetorics and traditions such as those of romance and realism.

Twain and his readers may need the personal help, experience, and resources of an African American character like Jim, resources developed in long and various histories of such experience with much of what the dominant culture otherwise avoids. Twain and his readers may also need the personal and cultural help and experience of women characters like Judith Loftus and Mary Jane Wilks and poor-white characters like Huck to explore and articulate what is more often denigrated or repudiated. It is in this sense that Twain's Jim is not only an Africanist, minstrel creation of a European American culture that warily subordinates and limits the significance and force of what an African American character might say and do. Twain's Jim also represents a problematic opening, an almost unavoidable form of address to African American culture then and now, a larger cross-cultural transference and interpellation to which writers like Ellison and Morrison have powerfully responded in their writing.[11]

It is in this sense that Morrison's work suggests that Twain's Jim might be read less as one writer's and one culture's caricature of another than as a wary, cross-cultural question. It is a question to which her own cross-cultural writing responds with its own equally wary questions and answers—as well as her own characters like Sethe who in some sense speak again for characters like Twain's Jim. Again, these are not the only questions to which her work responds, but her responses to these questions are crucial. Her work responds to these questions put by the dominant culture partly by drawing on histories and cultures different from but also inextricable from Twain's, and partly by understanding both cultures to be defined less by separate essences or centers than by their dynamic, contested, changing boundaries and interactions with each other.

Huck gestures toward what Jim and eventually Sethe might teach him about an ethics and language different from those he has known, including a love considered "too thick" to survive in American society, a love modeled on Jim's love for his daughter 'Lizabeth and Sethe's for Beloved, both of which depend not on escaping society but on reconceiving and reshaping social relations. Huck approaches these lessons by means of the discourse of American romance, with its emphasis on individual goodwill and repeated escapes from society. He follows this limited approach as far, perhaps, as it can possibly take him—as far as deciding on Jim's freedom but not so far as plotting Jim's actual escape into a different social future. Huck and Twain both finally seem to have given up on what they are learning from Jim, and they cede responsibility for their plots instead to Providence, to Tom, and to the discourse of American realism, as if to restore a more familiar kind of cultural equilibrium or sense of verisimilitude. But the questions surrounding Jim's presence in Twain's novel have lingered nevertheless, as if to be taken up again and elaborated in work like Toni Morrison's. Morrison's work retroactively makes Twain's work more interesting and promising than before.

Putting Twain next to Morrison helps readers understand the particular tradition of American romance and realism in which Twain largely wrote, as well as the difference represented by Morrison and the potential difference within Twain's work. Chapters 3 and 4 will attempt to demonstrate how T. S. Eliot's *Waste Land* and the tradition of American modernism it is often taken to represent are also better understood in the light of a cross-cultural encounter with Ralph Ellison's *Invisible Man,* which encourages both reflection on this dominant tradition and the exploration of alternatives to that tradition. As an example of canonical American modernism to be considered in terms of domination and democracy, Eliot's poem might seem a less obvious choice than a novel such as William Faulkner's *Absalom, Absalom!* which represents a range of cross-cultural encounters and poses explicit questions of social domination and democracy. But Ralph Ellison and many since have considered the explicitly social dimension of Faulkner's work as exceptional, not representative of the American modernist canon (*Shadow and Act* 164, 183). Eliot's *Waste Land* has achieved and maintained an exemplary status in the American modernist canon equal to that of Mark Twain's *Adventures of Huckleberry Finn* in the canon of American realism. For these and other more personal reasons on Ellison's part,[12] Ellison's *Invisible Man* addresses *The Waste Land*'s status (and *Huckleberry Finn*'s) in ways comparable to the ways Morrison's *Beloved* addresses the canonical status of Twain's novel. The relative exclusion from Eliot's poem of an explicit focus on American social and historical questions of class, gender, and race, along with the "exile" of much other American modernist literature to Europe, becomes a crucial issue of "blindness" and "invisibility" in the cross-cultural encounter between this modernist chapter of canonical American literary traditions, and novels like Ellison's or Morrison's that focus more explicitly on the history and meaning of such encounters.

Chapter 3 shows how Ellison's novel addresses a series of powerful blindnesses in Eliot's poem and in dominant American cultural history related to those of American romance, realism, and especially American modernism. Ellison's novel models for its readers not only the unmaking of these blindnesses but also the possibility of their being remade in a more democratic American history and culture, and especially in a more democratic, intersubjective experience of reading and interacting with other people. In this sense Ellison represents and responds to Eliot's poem as well as to Twain's novel as works-in-progress on a "raft of hope" in American cultural and cross-cultural history.

Chapter 4 will suggest a reading of T. S. Eliot's *Waste Land* in the context of Ellison's response. Instead of imagining and elaborating another bid for individual escape from one's own cultural limits, in the manner of American romance, or confirming the defeat of such efforts, in the manner of American realism, Eliot's poem seems to elaborate and effectively to universalize this tradition's apparently inescapable blindness to differences of culture, class, and gender, and to the difference involved in aesthetic and sexual experience, with the effect that almost all difference seems obliterated and all his characters threaten to "melt" into one (218n).

In terms of the two kinds of American loneliness sketched in *Beloved,* Eliot's poem steers well clear of Sethe's loving "too thick," in favor of several versions of Paul D's wandering and loving "small." Instead of doing what Paul D does, however, putting his more familiar story next to other stories that transform his own, Eliot's poem most often gropes toward such possibilities and insists on the incommensurability of such different stories, the impossibility of their communicating or interacting. When its

own cultural wasteland finally allows itself no particular transforming encounter with difference, the poem seems largely to
settle for the limited "pathos and dignity" of acknowledging and
effectively universalizing its own cross-cultural blindness, its
own indifferent but troubled blindness to difference. Whereas
Twain's novel might be understood to explore the helpless heroism of American romance in the face of cross-cultural encounters, Eliot's poem proposes a kind of heroic helplessness in his
extreme, modernist version of American realism. The poem remains dissatisfied, as it were, with the limited answers it finds
for its own lingering questions about difference, domination,
and democracy. Although Ellison would stress the movement of
cultural recovery, he would also appreciate Eliot's attention to
the moment of cultural breakdown, the necessary, repeated disruption of false cultural unities and reconciliations, including
the universalization of dominant traditions and the rigid and exclusive complementarities of self and other, male and female,
black and white. Ellison and others would also appreciate the
poem's jazzlike style, despite Eliot's own doubts about whether
such a music is "permanent or ephemeral" ("London Letter"
453), as if this "ephemeral" style is a cultural unmaking and a
defeat and not a promising cross-cultural opening and renewal.

A brief conclusion will return more explicitly to the subject of teaching American literature. Although my readings of
Morrison, Twain, Ellison, and Eliot will usually focus on characters, cultures, and writers as they interact, I am trying throughout to model a particular way of reading a multicultural American
literature, a way of reading that I propose we teach. This model is
different from the reading for self-recognition or tolerance suggested by some pluralist multiculturalism and identity politics.
I have also tried to avoid a reading so focused on structures of
power that it leaves no room for questions of personal agency or
ethical responsibility, as in some oppositional multiculturalism.
And the readings modeled here attempt to avoid defining one
canonical tradition of American literature except in terms of

the problems involved in defining such a tradition, especially questions of domination and democracy in the context of cultural and personal difference. Reading involves transference and transformation on the part of both writers and readers. To read American literature as an interactive ensemble of different writers and histories is to pay more careful attention to the importance of imaginative interactions across our various differences, including our interactions as we read and discuss these texts.

1

Putting Twain's Story
Next to Hers in
Morrison's *Beloved*

IN A NUMBER OF WAYS, TONI MORRISON'S *BELOVED* suggests a critical rereading and creative rewriting of Mark Twain's *Adventures of Huckleberry Finn*. This chapter will focus especially on the episode during Sethe's escape from slavery when she cautiously enlists the help of a poor-white girl, Amy Denver, who is escaping her own form of servitude. Morrison's novel considers both the limitations and the potential promise of their encounter and their respective attempts at escape. The episode raises questions about what each sees and responds to in the other, as well as questions about their larger social and historical circumstances—especially how far Amy will follow through on her good intentions and how far the larger society will allow Sethe to follow through on her own good intentions toward the daughter Amy helps her deliver, the daughter Sethe names Denver. This episode's potential relevance to questions of teaching *Huckleberry Finn* in a multicultural American literature is also suggested by its function within the novel as a familiar and powerful story that Sethe repeatedly tells her daughter Denver, who remembers and gradually reconsiders this story during the course of the novel. Her reevaluations of Sethe's story suggest how readers might reimagine and reevaluate Twain's story as well, and how Twain's work might be read and taught not separate from but next to Morrison's work and Morrison's work next to Twain's.

Denver's attitude toward the story involving Amy Denver strongly suggests its own version of the solitude and separate confinement described by Morrison in the tradition of American romance: "Denver hated the stories her mother told that did not concern herself, which is why Amy was all she ever asked about. The rest was a gleaming, powerful world made more so by Denver's absence from it" (62). Denver's favorite story, concerned with Amy's, Sethe's, and Denver's own magical heroism, is haunted by a sense of abject helplessness toward the rest of this "gleaming, powerful world," a world that appears as unchallenged in its omnipotence as the "miracle" of Denver's birth is in hers. Everything depends on whether Denver (or one of her idealized heroes, like her mother or Amy) is or is not at the supposedly all-powerful, magical center of this particular story's two-dimensional world, apparently as unconnected to any other as the raft on which Twain sets Huck and Jim adrift, its surrounding geography often relegated to a distant horizon.[1] Until she can draw on other stories and other ways to hear them, Denver's own story will alternate between the two kinds of American loneliness figured in Twain's and Morrison's novels.

Morrison's novel responds to Twain's by expanding on conflicts and fears just at the limits of *Huckleberry Finn*'s reach. For example, *Beloved* explores fears about personal limits, about the risks and responsibilities of making positive commitments to particular people and circumstances, such as in Jim's situation and in Sethe's "too thick" love. In effect Morrison inverts and reinscribes Twain's adventure novel, with its focus on the free white nation's ambiguously innocent moral heroism toward a vaguely exceptional slave like Jim, who becomes a convenient site for muted questions about the limits of that heroism. Morrison's novel focuses instead on the runaway slave, her family, and her community and how these figures actually managed to live and die under slavery and how some survived after escaping slavery. However "unspeakable" much of that slavery has been repeatedly deemed to be throughout American literature, it is represented here not as exceptional but as central to their American experience. These characters' experiences and memories of slavery and other people have required not just an individual mea culpa or declaration of innocence or freedom, but ongoing, practical strategies and struggles in the midst of others who need their help and whose help they also need.

Morrison's novel thus attempts to work through what Twain's novel sometimes reaches toward and sometimes keeps at arm's length, on the darkened underside of American romance and its frequent alternation between control and helplessness, heroism and abjection. At its limit, Morrison's novel describes this as the "loneliness that can be rocked. . . . It's an inside kind—wrapped tight like skin" (274). Her novel deals less directly with the conflicts and fears associated with the other loneliness she describes, the one that "roams," unplanned, unplotted, that "dry and spreading thing that makes the sound of one's own feet going seem to come from a far-off place" (274), the loneliness otherwise characterized by the practice of loving "thin" or "small" (162). But her novel does suggest how these two kinds of loneliness might interact to elaborate more promising forms of social relation, which her novel also explores. It is the roaming loneliness that characterizes Paul D and sometimes others in *Beloved* and that characterizes Huck and his drifting raft and most of the other white characters of *Huckleberry Finn*. Her novel repeatedly puts these two kinds of loneliness next to each other to form something else in their interactions.

One place to begin a close reading of such encounters is where Sethe's daughter Denver likes to begin, or where she and most of us have perhaps been taught to begin, although this is also where Morrison's novel emphatically does not begin. Denver has been taught to begin her own favorite story in "the details of her birth," with "two friendly grown-up women— one . . . helping out the other," so that "the magic of her birth, its miracle in fact, testified to that friendliness as did her own name" (29). Like a romance Hawthorne might have written, this one promises events, names, even miracles, carefully designed to signify moral qualities such as friendliness or even supernatural intent, such as Denver being, as Sethe says, "a charmed child.

From the beginning" (41). Despite this story's silences and shadows, it is a story whose ritualized magic Denver knows by heart and is careful not to alter or disturb:

> Easily she stepped into the told story that lay before her eyes on the path she followed away from the window. There was only one door to the house and to get to it from the back you had to walk all the way around to the front of 124, past the storeroom, past the cold house, the privy, the shed, on around to the porch. And to get to the part of the story she liked best, she had to start way back: hear the birds in the thick woods, see her mother making her way up into the hills. (29)

Everything has its ordered place here on Denver's path to the front porch and to the part of the story she liked best—liked best "because it was all about herself" (77). Only gradually will Denver learn more about the fears and desires that this story has helped her to ignore or control: for example, that she will have to leave this porch, even want to leave her own porch and approach other houses, learning to approach some houses by doors not at their fronts but in back (253). Other stories are marked by race, gender, class, and loss in ways that her story seems to invoke for now only to overrule or banish, lest her own story be unmade. She will remember and learn more of such stories later, but only insofar as she also learns to read this story and stories like it differently. For now, however, most of the rest of Sethe's past life has been declared "unspeakable; to Denver's inquiries Sethe gave short replies or rambling incomplete reveries" (58). For lack of, or for fear of, other stories, Denver remembers this incomplete reverie like an unalterable bedtime fairytale.

But again, Denver's story has been placed not at the beginning of Morrison's novel, nor at the end, but well within the context of other stories, so that its magic circle of safety is likely to seem to Morrison's readers not natural and inevitable or in the nature of romance or art but precariously and deliberately incomplete. It is a carefully, desperately guarded refuge that mirrors the very culture whose power it hypnotically flees, what Morrison calls the solitude and separate confinement characteristic of canonical American literature. But if some of these canonical writers do "have much more to say than has been realized" ("Unspeakable" 14), Denver's story, too, when it is placed alongside other stories, has more to offer readers and Denver than only its fragile illusion of charmed safety.

What Morrison says she was after in *Beloved*'s "abrupt" beginning, by contrast with Denver's story, "as the first stroke of the shared experience that might be possible between the reader and the novel's population," is that the reader should feel "snatched, yanked, thrown into an environment completely foreign," should feel "snatched just as the slaves were from one place to another, from any place to another, without preparation and without defense," "without comfort or succor from the 'author'" (32–33). This sounds like the totally unintelligible, frightening, helpless underside of Denver's nostalgic version of her own charmed delivery and birth, yet she needs both kinds of stories in order to begin to make sense of either.

Morrison's novel, then, includes two stories: the magically or heroically safe and the defenselessly unprepared. Yet her novel will suggest that the differences and encounters between these two kinds of stories are also played out within each. As she says in her essay, "Perhaps some [writers of the canonical romance] were not so much transcending politics, or escaping blackness, as they were transforming it into intelligible, accessible, yet artistic modes of discourse" (14), as she has elsewhere shown that the writers of slave narratives did for their own artistic and political reasons ("The Site of Memory" 299–302). In "creative encounters" with history, she says, "nothing . . . is safe, or should be": even in Denver's own romantic story, then, "safety is the foetus of power as well as protection from it" ("Unspeakable" 31), both a way to avoid and a way to consider what still seems unspeakable. Her story is a wary beginning in addressing her fears about the world. As for the more abrupt and dangerous, almost "unspeakable" story with which *Beloved* begins, it soon becomes clear, Morrison says, "that something is beyond control, but is not beyond understanding since it is not beyond accommodation by both the 'women' and the 'children'" (32). This novel shows how these women and children manage to transform the unspeakable into their own versions of "intelligible, accessible, yet artistic modes of discourse."

Both Denver's safe story and Sethe's more dangerous one, extreme versions of American romance and realism, are the kinds of story this novel challenges its characters and its readers to listen to more carefully "for the holes—the things the fugitives did not say; the questions they did not ask," and "for the unnamed, unmentioned people left behind" (92). And the novel demonstrates, I think, that this listening works best by putting distinct but linked stories alongside each other, the heroism alongside the helplessness it denies, and the helplessness alongside the heroism it disavows.

The story Denver remembers her mother telling her casts Denver as an "antelope" ramming and pawing in Sethe's womb, protesting at Sethe's thoughts of resignation and death. Sethe traces this figure of an antelope back to one of her few memories of her own mother, the antelope dance in which the slave men and women "shifted shapes and became something other. Some unchained, demanding other whose feet knew her pulse better than she did. Just like this one in her stomach" (31). Both Sethe's mother's antelope dance and Sethe's own antelope fetus connect her weakened pulse to that of a larger community and a particular loved one who are both demanding and empowering, capable of making and remaking Sethe beyond her power to do so herself. The irresistible social demand to which Sethe and the dancers respond in the rhythms of the dance is compared to an even more clearly irresistible social, ethical, and physical demand by the fetus within her, a demand on which both Sethe's own life and that of the fetus depend. By remembering her mother at this moment, Sethe suggests she realizes that her own birth once placed a similar demand on her own mother, who becomes an empowering example to her now. Neither individual escape (on the most sentimental model of romance) nor resignation (on the most cynical model of realism) is an option for Sethe here. She can be neither the triumphant, untouched master nor the resigned or stoic slave to this "demanding other" represented by both her mother before her and her daughter within her. This particular "demanding other" requires conceptual models of ethics and love different from those most obtainable in Denver's initial understanding of Sethe's story.[2]

The "demanding other" suggested by Sethe's situation has been relatively tamed in Denver's mirrorlike version of a story that is "all about herself." The "demanding other" for Denver is largely a certain heroic image of herself, although it will gradually also become her mother's example as someone distinct from either this heroic image or its repudiated opposite. Thus when Sethe remembers thinking she is "about to be discovered by a whiteboy" and be deprived of even an "easeful death," she can also laugh at how her hunger and shape-shifting imagination turned her into "a snake. All jaws and hungry," as if she could gobble the whiteboy up (31). In the face of apparent disaster, of being trapped on the wrong side of the romance complementarities of light and dark, male and female, life and death, heroism and helplessness, Sethe's story offers Denver the tempting idea of an easy escape, although her laughter also signals how simplistic this idea of escape is. The almost overwhelming demands on Sethe are represented in a form that is "intelligible and accessible" even for Denver, in the person of Amy Denver. What signals the part of the story "Denver loved the best" is that the whiteboy turns out to be not edible or black but at most "a girl" and the "raggediest-looking trash you ever saw," hungry like Sethe and looking for huckleberries (31–32).

It is a moment of almost comic relief in Morrison's novel to recognize Twain's Huckleberry Finn in girlface. We have seen him as harmless, transparent girl before, reminding us (as Myra Jehlen argues) that the gender constructions and roles of boys and girls (and perhaps even the racial constructions and roles of whites and blacks) are in fact constructions and roles, more learnable and negotiable than they often appear. We have seen him as a runaway apprentice, reminding us that the culture does have some sympathy for fugitives from servitude, most notably in the case of Benjamin Franklin but also in the slave narratives and to some extent in Twain's novel. And we have seen him put in his place by Jim as "trash," reminding us that his ideological identifications with the more powerful white middle class are fragile enough to depend on confirmation or dismissal even by Jim. Still, at the margins of Denver's version of Sethe's story is the fearful sense that "nothing is safe" in such encounters with history, either in Twain's novel or here, neither Sethe from this whitegirl, Amy Denver, nor Amy from Sethe's appeal for help.

Much of what Sethe remembers Amy Denver saying sounds dangerously insensitive. Amy uses the word *nigger* as easily and defensively as Huck does with Jim. She is no more committed by nature or in principle to Sethe's freedom or humanity than Huck is to Jim's, though Morrison makes this clearer than Twain did (judging from the many readings that stress Huck's good-heartedness or his eventually principled stand). In fact, such natural essences or moral principles, so confusingly and in-adequately articulated by Huck and for Huck by his adopted middle class in Twain's novel, never even seem to arise for Amy. It is as if Morrison's novel reemphasizes here the incompleteness of such racism *or* such antiracist moral principles in determining Huck's and Amy's subjectivities, next to a less systematic, more specific repertoire of emotions, gestures, skills, and activities— what Michel Foucault might call their "local, discontinuous, dis-qualified, illegitimate knowledges" (83).

Not by nature or in principle, then, but in the event of her cross-cultural interaction with Sethe, Amy Denver does find herself drawn, like Huck, unpredictably, almost unaccountably, into helping a slave escape. More than that, she will actually care for Sethe's swollen feet and beaten back and help deliver her baby. Yet Amy almost leaves Sethe lying where she found her in the weeds, as if there were nothing in either Sethe's or Amy's stories by themselves that would explain the work they eventually do together. That work depends on the transformative transference that takes place in their cross-cultural interaction. It depends on what each is reminded of by the other and allowed to address only through their dialogue.

At the prospect of "being left alone without a fang in her head" (32), Sethe asks for more of Amy's story—where she's headed, whether her mother knows—as if Sethe may want Amy's help to imagine a life for Sethe's own unborn child, or perhaps just to retain some hold on language and life at all as she struggles against surrender and death. And perhaps Sethe knows somehow that Amy might have more interest in their encounter than Amy admits or recognizes. "They slipped effortlessly into yard chat about nothing in particular—except one lay on the ground" (33). The one on the ground might well be listening that much harder, but Amy might have her own reasons to listen to Sethe. Amy might well recognize by a kind of transference with Sethe's present condition a version of Amy's own story, especially her mother's death just after Amy's birth and her own work since to pay for her mother's passage as an indentured servant. Sethe also listens to Amy talk again and again of velvet, which Amy describes as "like the world was just born. Clean and new and so smooth. The velvet I seen was brown, but in Boston they got all colors. Carmine. That means red but when you talk about velvet you got to say 'carmine'" (33). Amy has got it into her head somehow that the utopian answer to her losses and her desire is velvet, and she has learned somewhere—perhaps in the ads from the store in Boston, perhaps from a middle-class acquaintance like Tom Sawyer—that "when you talk about velvet you got to say 'carmine.'" Amy has learned this convention of her romance of class and velvet—a

personal, nostalgic, but also culturally constructed romance—
just as carefully as Tom and Huck have learned certain conventions of their romances, or as carefully as Denver has learned the
protective rituals of hers.

Amy has learned like Tom and Huck from the similarly polarized, naturalized American discourse of race that when she
talks about certain people she can say "nigger." But Sethe is listening harder than that, as if for other determinants or dimensions of Amy's overdetermined language, dimensions that strike
a chord with her own imagination and situation, other dimensions that may also account for why Amy does not simply leave
this "nigger woman" behind and continue on her way toward
Boston and velvet. For Sethe's part, she keeps listening and talk-
ing with Amy for reasons she cannot articulate: "Sethe didn't
know if it was the voice, or Boston or velvet, but while the
whitegirl talked, the baby slept. Not one butt or kick, so she
guessed her luck had turned" (33). Warily, she lets Amy know
how weak and injured she is, and despite Amy's racist insensi-
tivity, Amy responds with memories of her mother's and her
own helplessness, which she can address more bravely now at
one remove in Sethe's situation. Amy also knows how to treat
injuries caused by overwork and abuse. Her skills have been
developed under working conditions that overlap with Sethe's
despite the ideology of white supremacy that would minimize
such connections.[3] Memories of her own and her mother's helplessness are transformed here from something "beyond control,"
a powerlessness to be denied, repudiated, or projected onto
someone else, into something that is at least temporarily "not
beyond understanding since it is not beyond accommodation by
both the 'women' and the 'children' " ("Unspeakable" 32).

And at a moment when Sethe's strength is almost overwhelmed, Sethe can take courage from Amy's example (as also
physically from Amy's hands) or be reminded of her own strength
and courage at other times. Thus Amy encourages and walks
alongside as Sethe crawls, and "it was the voice full of velvet

and Boston and good things to eat that urged [Sethe] along"
to the lean-to where Amy "did her magic: lifted Sethe's feet
and legs and massaged them until she cried salt tears. 'It's
gonna hurt, now,' said Amy. 'Anything dead coming back to life
hurts'" (35).

By holding Sethe and by acknowledging and putting Sethe's
pain into language and even into an aphorism, Amy offers Sethe
not only her own physical and emotional help with bearing the
pain. She also offers Sethe the reassurance that her own present
pain has been borne, survived, recognized, and shared by others
in a universalized history and culture. This is perhaps a more
intersubjective, cross-cultural dimension of Amy's magic, since
Amy offers Sethe a vision of transcended circumstance that
tends to come more easily to European American culture than to
African American culture. This is a vision Sethe needs now,
whereas Sethe offers Amy in turn the recognition of circumstance and struggle that tends to come more easily to African
American culture than to European American culture. Such a
recognition of circumstance and struggle might be valuable to
Amy as a better way of addressing her memories of helplessness
than her obsession with velvet allows. Even if neither woman
can completely understand the other's position, each can appreciate that the other is now more capable of addressing what she
herself cannot, except in her interaction with the other.[4]

Denver's own rehearsal of her mother's story ends on a ring-
ing note of demanding but empowering, painful but also somehow magical resurrection—"Anything dead coming back to life
hurts"—which she recites as "a truth for all times" (35). Pain
and death are acknowledged here, but they are now more reas-
suringly associated with courage and even resurrection in Denver's guarded imagination, even if that courage and confidence
in resurrection are borrowed from someone else. Denver can
now better afford to return her thoughts to the uncanny sight-
ing that provoked her retelling herself this "told story": the
sight through a window of a dress kneeling next to her mother

in prayer, with its sleeve around her mother's waist. If the dress she saw with her mother was in pain, she figures now, it might mean another resurrection of the dead, or at least a risking of desire in the contingencies of history and interaction with other people: "it could mean that the baby ghost had plans" (35).

At its most reassuring, a romance like Denver's might represent such "plans" as an unthreatening secret thrill, part of "the downright pleasure of enchantment, of not suspecting but *knowing* the things behind things," the "safety of ghost company" (37). Such "plans" would obviously be designed to defend pleasure against a fear of pain, knowing against not knowing, and safety against danger. In this sense the function of "plans" (and fictional plots) in a romance would be to translate authorial or perhaps divine intention and principles directly into events, unimpaired by the disorder of historical contingencies or the interference of other stories. Thus Denver focuses here on the magic of her mother's story more than its riskiness, its heroism more than its potential helplessness. The story's more dangerous dimensions are largely left in the emotional keeping of Denver's mother, who has guarded this story's boundaries (and the boundaries of her experience) with a fearfulness proportionate to her desire for Denver's safety.

At this point in Morrison's novel, before Paul D's arrival and the renegotiation that his coming sets into motion with the past and future and with the rest of the community, plans of almost any kind are something Sethe avoids. Such plans seem like an invitation to disaster, a foolish tampering with an external fate so fixed in Sethe's own guarded imagination, so unapproachable from any other angle of time and space, that there are places where things that have happened to Sethe will always "be there for you, waiting for you. So, Denver, you can't never go there. Never" (36). Denver is aware that her mother "never told me all what happened" (36), but when Denver asks, Sethe says, "Nothing to tell except Schoolteacher" and his "book about us," and at that, "She stopped. Denver knew that her mother was through with it," and Denver both depends on and is curious about this deliberate silence about the world outside their yard and the other stories beyond Denver's own. Denver's story depends on that surrounding silence, but like the romances hers resembles, it is a way of both warding off and coming carefully to terms with other stories among which hers is set, both Schoolteacher's machinelike "book about us" and Morrison's ghostly renditions of "unspeakable things unspoken."

To Denver, Paul D's arrival at 124 seems initially to have destroyed this realm of safety and certainty and her solitude with her mother. But for Sethe his arrival and the stories he tells have set her thinking again about what the word *plans* could mean, the possibility and "temptation to trust and remember . . . to go ahead and feel . . . go ahead and *count on something*" (38), the possibility, in this case, of making plans that will not discount or dispel past experience or be certain of future success, but are either necessary or worth the risk of interaction beyond the self. The risk becomes worth taking because both the risk and the courage to take that risk are being shared with someone else, and she knows that safety and solitude are not viable options for either Denver or herself.

Sethe and Paul D will later remember the elaborate plans they made with others to escape from Sweet Home. Sethe warily begins to take such risks again, both by making plans and by remembering and telling Beloved stories of things "she had forgotten she knew"—as if it is only in the presence of this other that she can begin to remember what she has otherwise repudiated (58, 61). Overhearing these stories, Denver initially repeats her silent lesson that all such stories are dangerously off limits. "She clamped her teeth and prayed it would stop. Denver hated the stories her mother told that did not concern herself, which is why Amy was all she ever asked about. The rest was a gleaming, powerful world made more so by Denver's absence from it" (62). But Denver is also learning to consider such stories and risks herself by listening to her mother remember other stories and risk making new plans. By listening to these stories and imagining her mother's risk and courage as her own—neither as a hero in complete control nor as a powerless victim of circumstances—Denver takes courage from Sethe's example much as Sethe took courage from that of her own mother and from the other people involved in the plans made and risks taken in leaving Sweet Home. Denver takes courage not only from her mother but from a larger culture and tradition that are helping her plan and "plot" other stories and roles than those she has known.

When Denver next resumes her own version of her mother's story, she is beginning to learn what Huck Finn and many of Huck's readers never quite learned from Jim—how Huck's and Amy's alternations between imagined triumph and powerless abjection might make way for positively different configurations of desire and relationship. Unclamping her teeth and listening to the stories her mother tells Beloved, Denver begins to recognize that this "sister-girl," the apparent incarnation of the baby ghost's "plans," is a more "demanding other" than Denver thought, a companion not dedicated to Denver herself, as Denver initially hoped, but instead almost exclusively dedicated to Sethe, in ways that Denver can recognize more easily in Beloved than in herself. For Denver, then, this story of Amy Denver is no longer the story her mother tells that is all about Denver, no longer a private romance involving at most the two positions of idealized heroism and denied helplessness, a magical inside and an excluded outside, a second person only to affirm the first, but another story involving a more "demanding other." This less strictly protected story includes a mother who is coming to seem more than only an expression of her child's needs and desires, a mother who is also thus a first step toward others beyond the self. Seeing in Beloved perhaps her own possessiveness toward her mother, and seeing her mother as another subject interested in others besides Denver herself, Denver continues to work her way through a series of transferences that mediate her relationship to a world that includes other people. These transferences have included her temporary deafness, the baby ghost that haunted their house, her perfumed room in the boxwood bushes, and now the familiar stories she retells and embellishes for Beloved.

Swallowing "twice to prepare for the telling, to construct out of the strings she had heard all her life a net to hold Beloved" (76), Denver attempts to wean Beloved from an abject attachment to Sethe that resembles Denver's own. Perhaps at some level Denver also recognizes and emulates Sethe's own attempt to wean and hold Amy Denver's interest in something other than Amy's romance of velvet and Boston. The story begins to feel different now to Denver as she considers her former role in the story as a rescued but powerless victim, able only to identify gratefully with her heroic mother-protectors but unable to know either who these others are or how they did it: "She loved it because it was all about herself; but she hated it too because it made her feel like a bill was owing somewhere and she, Denver, had to pay it. But who she owed or what to pay it with eluded her" (77).

Denver wavers between an identification with her mother's supposed power and a repudiation of her mother's and her own powerlessness. She is beginning now, however, to recognize more self-consciously in Beloved's "alert and hungry face" both a mirror of her own desire to hold entirely to herself Beloved's (and her mother's) attention and the encouragement and support she needs from someone else to imagine and risk roles other than those of the imagined hero or the powerless victim, the complementary roles implied by her own most private stories and here again by Beloved's face. With the introduction of Beloved's subjectivity at a distance from her own, Denver begins "to see what she was saying and not just to hear it," "feeling how it must have felt to her mother," and adding the "fine points" and "details" that give "blood to the scraps her mother and grandmother [Baby Suggs] had told her," so that "the monologue became in fact a duet."[5]

As she recognizes Beloved's subjectivity apart from her own, she also begins to recognize her mother's subjectivity apart from her own, and her own favorite story becomes no longer the only story in a gleaming, powerful world but one among others, one for which she begins to claim ownership and responsibility. As she tells her story to Beloved, Denver begins to appreciate and share in her mother's similar risk and collaboration with Amy Denver, "how recklessly she behaved with this whitegirl—a recklessness born of desperation and encouraged by Amy's fugitive eyes and tenderhearted mouth" (78). Like Beloved's "alert and hungry face" for Denver, Amy's "fugitive eyes and tenderhearted mouth" are for Sethe a sign that Amy might recognize something of Sethe's own experience, and that the two of them might be able to address together what one is suffering now and what the other is trying to leave behind. That is, Sethe sees in Amy's face what Denver sees in Beloved's face, signs that the self might not be quite as alone and powerless as she fears, signs that some "unchained, demanding other" might both challenge her and lend her courage. Denver's safe story that she heard only as "all about herself" thus becomes a more challenging story she risks sharing with someone else, a story about her mother's own risky but also encouraging interaction with Amy.

Denver can imagine how Amy is "struck dumb for a change" when she sees Sethe's back (79), and how Amy's language careens then between two culturally recognizable but increasingly inadequate poles. On the one hand, Amy muses tenderly and perhaps ironically in a "dreamwalker's voice" of romance to describe Sethe's back as a chokecherry tree with all the significant detail of Hester Prynne's scarlet embroidered letter A and to wonder what God had in mind. On the other hand, Amy draws on the projected, muted "power of blackness" also figured in American romance to recall being beaten by her own master for as little as "looking at him straight," though never like this, as if this memory is itself something not to be looked at straight (79). But Sethe's groan is enough for Amy to "cut her reverie short," as if she recognizes that neither her dreamy interpretation of

Sethe's back nor her own present economic and racial safety from such victimization adequately addresses either her own memories or Sethe's present situation. Amy is moved to draw instead on another body of knowledge to shift Sethe's feet and gather spider webs to clean and drape on Sethe's back.

While she works, however, Amy slips back into using the same racialized discourse to draw a protective contrast between Sethe and herself: "You don't know a thing. End up dead, that's what. Not me. I'm a get to Boston and get myself some velvet. Carmine." But her contrast creaks under the force of their inter-action, although perhaps her contrast also works as a tempo-rarily familiar reassurance enabling that riskier interaction. She is reminded of "a old nigger girl" who "don't know nothing" like Sethe but who also "sews real fine lace," perhaps something like the spider webs Amy is using while she talks. This image of the lace and spider web and intricately circuitous yard chat sug-gests an alternative to the velvet Amy talks of otherwise. Amy's lace resembles that of someone who "don't know nothing," yet it is articulate and elaborate in addressing both Sethe's and Amy's own wounds.

Amy attempts the racial contrast again by remembering hav-ing had the leisure in Kentucky to "sleep with the sun in her face," something Sethe probably never has done. But then Amy remembers that this sense of leisure was a fantasy: it resulted in another beating of her own. So she turns her thoughts to Boston again, though it soon emerges that this is where her now-dead mother was "before she was give to Mr. Buddy," and here Amy asks Sethe for reassurance that Mr. Buddy was not her own fa-ther, as someone has told her he was (80). She asks for such re-assurance presumably for her sake but also for her mother's, in order to expand on the possibility of their past and future exis-tence aside from or beyond Mr. Buddy's domination. Perhaps her return to Boston is an attempt to imagine a new past and future for her mother as well as for herself. Otherwise, like Huck, Amy cannot risk thinking beyond heroism and denied helplessness, beyond herself and her mother in relation to Mr. Buddy, Huck's Pap, or Sethe's Schoolteacher, toward some conception of the world that makes interaction with other people seem worth risking. Her ability to imagine that world may depend on her first imagining her mother taking similar risks.

Amy and Sethe work both practically and imaginatively to provide for each other another world beyond oneself and beyond one's most nostalgic fantasies, another world that both demands courage and gives it back. In psychoanalytic terms, their imaginative transference with each other, as well as Denver and Beloved's imaginative transference with this story, is "predicated not merely on a boundary set by an outside other (an abstract idea of limiting the omnipotent self) but rather on a maternal subjectivity that is able to represent affect and hence process the pain of separation between the mother and her child. This maternal subjectivity will be the object of the child's cross-identifications . . . in the dialogic processing of loss, separation, aggression, indeed, negation in general" (Benjamin, *Shadow* 28–29).

In other words, Amy's talk of Boston and velvet, like her singing her "mama's song" to Sethe, functions here as another dream of infantlike safety haunted by the infant's inevitable loss of that safety, a loss of safety that has in her life, her mother's, and Sethe's often taken the form—not only the psychologically regressive form, but even the social and legal form—of a powerless surrender to the likes of a Mr. Buddy or a Schoolteacher. But this socially constituted and psychic image of helplessness can also be reconsidered and analyzed as only one among other possible articulations of a more or less inevitable sense of loss and danger, other ways for the mother and then any number of others through transference to help the subject "represent affect and hence process the pain." Whereas Amy's own socially constructed subjectivity (like Denver's) tends to frame this helplessness in terms of an infantile nostalgia for her "mama's song," Sethe's own losses and separations have been more socially and legally elaborated by the dominant culture and by her own African American culture. Not only is Sethe more articulate than Amy about both her own and Amy's helplessness, Amy is also less articulate about her own helplessness than she is about Sethe's helplessness. By a kind of transference, then, Amy's encounter with Sethe seems to give Amy the opportunity and the courage to address and rearticulate memories of her lost mother and of her own past abuse, memories that her dreamy talk of Boston and velvet usually keep more clumsily and fearfully at bay.

In addressing Sethe's situation, Amy can do something indirectly about an abuse and loss before which she may otherwise feel completely powerless. And by a similar transference, Amy's presence gives Sethe the opportunity and the courage to dare to think strategically of velvet, good things to eat, a tenderhearted mouth, and the "demanding other" of her own dead mother's antelope dance. She dares to think that death for herself and her fetus is not the only possible shape her story can take, placed though it now apparently is on the dark underside of a dominant discourse that is racialized, gendered, class-marked, and legally reinforced but never quite monolithic or unresisted. Amy's presence apparently helps Sethe regain the psychological distance and indirection necessary for her to imagine another story for a daughter to whom she will give part of Amy Denver's name.

Sethe's idea, risky for a former slave, that "there was a world out there and that I could live in it" (182), even love in it, risking a language and a community in which to articulate and thus to negate and renegotiate her danger and loss, is an idea that lasts only twenty-eight days, until she decides again there is no place for herself or her children in such a world. Eighteen years later Paul D arrives and tempts her to think again that "her story was bearable because it was his as well—to tell, to refine, and tell again" (99). What makes the difference, apparently, between her suffering from unspeakable depression and her having the courage to "bear" her story is the opportunity to reconsider that story critically with someone else, someone whose difference and distance from herself will demand that she take responsibility for telling, refining, and telling her story again, but whose related experience will also lend her the support to do so.[6]

When Sethe first tries to tell Paul D the part of her story he doesn't know, she overestimates the ease of that recognition on his part and the safety of that communication for her, thinking she sees in his smile or eyes "the ever-ready love . . . easy and upfront, the way colts, evangelists and children look at you: with love you don't have to deserve" (161). In "creative encounters" with history, however, as Morrison might remind her, "nothing . . . is safe, or should be" ("Unspeakable" 31). Paul D is not yet ready to address even in Sethe's story (through transference) these traces of what he has learned to repress in his own. So he falls back himself on the kind of racist distinction between humans and beasts that Amy Denver attempted between herself and Sethe. He will recognize later "how fast he had moved from his shame to hers" (165), how his absolute distinction between his humanity and her beastliness was based on a denied connection. But for the moment he is frightened by the vulnerability suggested by just how "thick" her love could be, compared with his own defensive practice of loving "small." He has also been disturbed by how Sethe and Beloved have both managed since he arrived at 124 to "move him" to do and to say things he "didn't know [were] on his mind" (114), "moved him. Just when doubt, regret and every single unasked question was packed away, long after he believed he had willed himself into being" (221).

Instead of acknowledging his own loss of his "red heart," thus translating that loss into a language with which he might interact with Sethe and thus gain some conscious, shared control over his loss, Paul D here draws on the more readily available discourse of a racialized and gendered romance to deny, repress, project, and transfer his loss onto her. His other option is the one Sethe seems to have taken, to disavow any such acknowledgment, negation, and communication of loss and sink into a deep depression. For a while, he and Sethe return to the two kinds of loneliness to which they are each inclined, as described in the novel's last pages.

Like Amy, because she is white, Paul D, because he is male, can better afford than Sethe to trust the dominant drift of their society and at least pretend to the self-sufficient hero's role, much as Huck Finn can speak of drifting naked on the raft for "two or three days and nights" that "swum by, they slid along so quiet and smooth and lovely," even as he and Jim drift farther and farther past Cairo into slaveholding territory (156–58). Paul D can identify with the role of self-sufficient hero on account of his gender (as if he "had willed himself into being") even at the risk (and especially to deny the risk) of using an associated racist distinction he also knows can be turned against him. Thus, too, Amy Denver's talk of velvet invokes class and race distinctions at the risk of having those same class distinctions turned against her as "trash."

Huck, Amy, and Paul D are therefore more prone to what the novel's last pages describe as the "loneliness that roams . . . alive, on its own. A dry and spreading thing that makes the sound of one's own feet going seem to come from a far-off place," the loneliness of the wandering hero or the supposedly invulnerable machine. Sethe and Denver, on the other hand, at least in their relations to the world outside their yard, are prone to a more abject loneliness, what the novel describes as the "loneliness that can be rocked. Arms crossed, knees drawn up; holding, holding on, this motion, unlike a ship's, smooths and contains the rocker. It's an inside kind—wrapped tight like skin" (274)—or, one might add, like the inescapable, incommunicable haunting of a ghost, unrecognized by others. The discourse of romance holds these two closely related kinds of loneliness in overly "separate confinement" from each other, relying heavily on cultural boundaries of gender, race, and class in ways that may reinforce those boundaries, but may also sometimes call attention to the limits of those same boundaries.

At this point Sethe feels she has no language or community beyond her own fixed and incommunicable "rememory" to help her remember the daughter she named Beloved. So she retreats again into this "inside loneliness" with Beloved, this riveting, unsupported, therefore somewhat compulsive romance of perfect safety isolated in unspeakable memories and surrounded by fears of irresistible danger and loss outside.[7] Denver knows from reflecting back on her own experience that Sethe and Beloved are "locked in a love that wore everybody out" (243). Any parent of an infant understands how much even such an intimate relationship also depends on wider social support. And Sethe certainly knows this from her experience in a context that denied that support, a context that gave her only the options of an indifferent, "small" love that could surrender her children to all the abuses of slavery or a love so "thick" it could not allow her children a life at all. As she thinks to herself, "unless carefree, motherlove was a killer" (132).

Sethe now attempts to reinstate that "too thick" love with Beloved. Like an infant in a relationship that is all about herself, Beloved depends on Sethe for everything, devouring her attentions, her time, her food, demanding absolute protection, accepting no excuses for Sethe's failure to save and protect her before. Both helpless and psychologically omnipotent in her demands on her mother, Beloved's role makes Sethe both psychologically responsible for everything and bound helplessly to fail, so that mother and daughter become almost indistinguishable from each other and their relationship becomes unworkable without others from the wider world around them.[8]

"Whatever was happening," Denver realizes, "it only worked with three—not two." So Denver "would have to leave the yard; step off the edge of the world, leave the two behind and go ask somebody for help" (243). Although Denver is unaccustomed to this role and is frightened to remember her grandmother's warnings that there is "no defense" against whitepeople's unpredictable and dangerous behavior, she also hears her grandmother ask: "You mean I never told you nothing about Carolina? About your daddy? You don't remember nothing about how come I walk the way I do and about your mother's feet, not to speak of her back? I never told you all that? Is that why you can't walk down the steps?" (244). Baby Suggs's imagined voice and laugh imply that such stories are just what Denver needs in order to understand not only the powerful truth that there is "no defense" but also what that truth by itself (like the violent beginning of *Beloved*) may seem to disavow about how Baby Suggs, Halle, and Sethe have dealt with loss and suffering. Such stories may be helpful placed alongside and thereby discovered and developed within Denver's own favorite story.

It is up to Denver now to appeal to a community that has in its own position of relative power denied its connection to Sethe for what she did and for disavowing her connections to them. In a kind of mutual transference, Sethe and Denver's situation now offers that community a borrowed opportunity and a borrowed courage to begin addressing memories and fears of their own that have been relatively unarticulated because denied, repressed, and projected beyond recognition (projected especially onto Sethe).

Stamp Paid, for example, is moved by Paul D's denial of Sethe to reconsider his own sense of moral superiority to Sethe and Baby Suggs: he acknowledges that he has himself nearly killed and then abandoned his own wife, Vashti, for having been sexually abused by their slavemaster. Ella is moved by Beloved's return to acknowledge having let one of her own babies die that was conceived as a result of a rape. Paul D slowly acknowledges having conducted a murder-suicide of his own in having beaten "the flirt called life" to death and locked his "red heart" in a box.

These members of Sethe's community are here reminded of losses they have themselves too easily denied or "stamped paid." Sethe's story offers them the chance to consider less directly in her case what they have been relatively unable to consider in their own language and society. This is also what Sethe considers all too directly, with almost none of the mediations and supports of language and society that they might offer her. Such characters need to put their limited and inadequate stories next to Sethe's story as much as Sethe needs their help in changing the shape of her own story, which otherwise remains isolated and unspeakably depressed—or locked in a deadly battle with her Beloved.

Denver gradually tells a much expanded version of her mother's story, not just to herself or Beloved, but to those in the local community whose help she seeks, a version that includes the most recent consequences of her mother's isolation since the "trouble" at 124. This less private version of her mother's story thus reminds at least some in that community of their part in Sethe's isolation, both after the trouble when they denied their connections to her and just before the trouble when they envied the largeness of the celebration and love at 124 and declined to send a warning of the slave catchers' arrival. In terms of the later and wider American communities reading Morrison's novel, Denver's gradually expanded version of her mother's story now includes the social and historical circumstances that often left people like Margaret Garner or Sethe and her local community no choice beyond the double bind of either a love too "thick" to allow one's beloved to risk living in a world of slavery or a love too "thin" to risk action, expression, or even memory on the beloved's behalf.

As the story Denver tells Janey Wagon at the whitefolks' house spreads in the local black community, there are "three groups" of interpreters, "those that believed the worst; those that believed none of it; and those, like Ella, who thought it through" (255). Even Paul D has at one point believed the worst of Sethe, reacting as many whitepeople would, with a version of their belief that "under every dark skin was a jungle," or that

Sethe, at least, has gotten what she deserves. Those like Lady Jones who "believed none of it" have more completely denied or repressed their knowledge of circumstances like those that have driven Sethe to do what she has. They have also denied or repressed their part in the silence and isolation in which Sethe continues to suffer. This group will accept Denver and maybe Sethe, but only on the condition that their past and its consequences be silenced and disavowed. Such interpretations yield a sanitized history without any place for slavery and a politics without any place for difference. Those who have "thought it through," however, learn how a jungle can grow "inside," not the jungle that whitefolks thought that "blacks brought with them to this place from the other (livable) place" but "the jungle whitefolks planted in them" which "grew" and "spread, until it invaded the whites who had made it. Touched them every one" (198–99). These interpreters recognize that U.S. whites cannot blame the violence of slavery on something blacks brought with them from the "other (livable) place." On the other hand, they realize that blacks cannot pretend to have been unaffected by these imputations of violence and by the actual violence of slavery, any more than the whites. Like any other configuration of power, the violence and domination of slavery exercises its repressive and constitutive effects both on its victims and its perpetrators. Thus Morrison describes racism's effect on both the racist and the victim of that racism as forms of the self's "severe fragmentation, . . . a cause (not a symptom) of psychosis" ("Unspeakable" 16).[9] To be able, then, like Ella, to "think through" stories as fragmented by slavery as Sethe's or Ella's own requires putting such fragmented, different stories alongside each other.

Paul D remembers Sixo explaining to him that the Thirty-Mile Woman "is a friend of my mind. She gather me, man. The pieces I am, she gather them and give them back to me" (272). And in the passage from which I have adapted the title of this chapter, Paul D remembers Sethe's "tenderness" about what he still calls "his neck jewelry. . . . How she never mentioned or looked at it, so he did not have to feel the shame of being collared like a beast. Only this woman Sethe could have left him his manhood like that. He wants to put his story next to hers" (273). By recognizing his shame and indirectly communicating that recognition, Sethe here helps him to understand and feel the tenderness and love that his own divided language of manhood and beastliness, like Twain's, almost cannot speak but is also maybe learning to speak from hers. His phrase "neck jewelry," for example, implicitly genders slavery as feminine, as if these spikes might become a woman more than they do a man, but the phrase also attempts the more tender language that he here appreciates in Sethe.

Paul D now has to persuade Sethe, however, that her "best thing" is something not wholly outside or wholly within herself, either in a parent's self-sufficient heroism or in an infant's unspeakable loss. Rather, it is in her ability to remember, articulate, and live out that desire and loss in and alongside other stories as incomplete, as lonely, and as potentially loving and supportive again as hers. As I understand it, this is not a fantasy of complementarity and restored wholeness for either individuals or cultures but a necessary and ongoing project of negotiation, an interpersonal and democratic project of making and remaking each other.

This last conversation between Sethe and Paul D is the first of what might be called two endings to *Beloved,* and it suggests again the possibility that the crisis of this romance may make way for a work in progress of imagination and love, not only in the interaction between Paul D and Sethe but more broadly between others divided or split along the fault lines of their culture's social and discursive structures. In the second of these two endings, the repeated refrain is that this "was not" and still "is not a story to pass on" (275), and indeed the novel has worked to imagine the echoes and circumstances of a historical incident rescued from near oblivion. It is an incident that must remind this novel's readers how many similar incidents have gone untold, because their victims were made into ghosts—not only by being violently denied a life at all (as in the novel's dedication, "To Sixty Million and More"), but also by being denied a role in the lives and memories of those around and after them. They remain ghosts when their individual, fragmented stories haunt memories but are never acknowledged by the living, whose recognition and shared memories are necessary to make those haunting memories real.

Even in this more chastened ending there is also the suggestion that these ghosts and stories are less unspeakably lost, less strange, and more uncannily familiar than we tend to think. They survive not as so many facts, identities, or single stories "to pass on" but only in the interaction or "fit" between identities and between dissimilar but connected stories. "Down by the stream in back of 124 [Beloved's] footprints come and go, come and go. They are so familiar. Should a child, an adult place his feet in them, they will fit. Take them out and they disappear again as though nobody ever walked there" (275). It is in just such interactions between fragmented but connected stories like Paul D's and Sethe's, Denver's and Beloved's, Sethe's and Amy Denver's, and Morrison's and Twain's that an American literature of cross-cultural interactions has a great deal to teach and learn. In the following chapter, I will attempt to read and learn more from Twain's *Huckleberry Finn* by placing its feet in the footprints suggested by Morrison's novel, footprints that seem both forgotten and strangely fitting in Twain's novel.

2

Huck Finn's Adventures
"Playing in the Dark"

IN *PLAYING IN THE DARK,* TONI MORRISON describes the primary function of African American figures in classic American literature: "Cooperative or sullen, they are Tontos all, whose role is to do everything possible to serve the Lone Ranger without disturbing his indulgent delusion that he is indeed alone" (82). Morrison also suggests, however, that the apparent insignificance of such a role for the Lone Ranger's Tonto may be a function of how such literature has been read. She has therefore recommended "the examination and re-interpretation of the American canon, . . . for the ways in which the presence of Afro-Americans has shaped the choices, the language, the structure—the meaning of so much American literature. A search, in other words, for the ghost in the machine" ("Unspeakable" 11). Morrison demonstrates how this ghostly presence might function in the American canon, particularly in Melville's *Moby Dick*. She mentions Mark Twain, Poe, Hawthorne, Cather, Hemingway, Fitzgerald, and Faulkner as examples of other canonical American writers whose works are "begging for such attention" (18). In the tradition of American romance and realism, Huck Finn is perhaps less deluded than some about being alone, but he is often read in terms of his striking out for the territories ahead of the rest, as if he were independent of all social ties in spite of his puzzling relationship with Jim.

Huck does sometimes depend on Jim for the service of representing at one remove some of what Huck has trouble recognizing about himself. Huck knows, for example, that despite his white male identity and his recent adoption into the respectable middle class, he is almost as defenseless as a slave legally, physically, and emotionally against his father's unpredictable rage and violence. He also knows he is often an unsophisticated dupe to Tom Sawyer. In this sense Jim functions to some extent for Huck as Eric Lott suggests that the tremendously popular American minstrel tradition tended to function for its nineteenth-century working-class and middle-class audiences—as an ambivalent but useful projection, staging and restaging Huck's own lack of power and middle-class sophistication.

Like other minstrel figures, however, Jim is not only a blackface character within Huck's all-white story, serving to hold certain uncomfortable subjects at arm's length. Jim is also an interlocutor who sometimes catches Huck off guard and leaves him and his readers at a loss for an easy response. This uneasiness is often signaled in Twain's novel by laughter, cliché, or silence. But Jim's interventions in Huck's solitude amount to more than an intermittent disturbance or negativity. Huck appreciates Jim's stories for their suggestive difference from Tom's stories, stories Huck tries repeatedly to dismiss as "Tom Sawyer's lies" (17). Jim's stories might be considered to function, then, as a kind of transference for Huck and for readers identifying with Huck. Jim's stories tend to articulate and elaborate on what Huck's own more conventional identities and stories often address only through projection onto figures such as Jim. Jim's stories help Huck to recognize the limitations of his adopted middle-class identity with Tom and to see Tom's tales as one kind of story to be compared with others. This comparison helps Huck begin to take responsibility for the stories he chooses as his own.

On the level of Twain's writing, however, Jim's stories are also drawn selectively and warily from African American experiences, misrepresented by but also affected by the dominant white culture, as suggested in Eric Lott's work on American minstrelsy and in Shelley Fisher Fishkin's recent writing in *Was*

Huck Black? on Twain's more particular sources for Huck's voice and for other dimensions of his work in African American culture. Twain's novel is thus already engaged in a cross-cultural dialogue to which *Beloved* later contributes. Morrison's attention to the difficulties and importance of placing a story like Sethe's beside those of Amy Denver, Denver, Paul D, and others helps to suggest both the limits and the potential promise of this and other such cross-cultural dialogues in American literature, notably that between *Huckleberry Finn* and *Beloved*.

As I have argued in the introduction, much American criticism of *Huckleberry Finn* has described either the ending or the entire novel as a moral or aesthetic mistake, a failure to carry through and confirm the essential importance of Huck's individualistic, moral (and thus characteristically American) vision. More recent historicist criticism, however, tends to redefine such a moral or aesthetic failure on Twain's or the novel's part as a "political symptom, the irruption into this narrative . . . of materials from the nineteenth-century political unconscious": a reason to "seize upon the text's inconsistencies and contradictions as windows on the world of late-nineteenth-century American culture" (Gillman and Robinson vii). Jim's characterization, for example, seems restricted by competing nineteenth-century stereotypes of the black male, evolving at the time Twain wrote "from the docile child of the antebellum paternal order to the black beast of post-Reconstruction" (xii). These inconsistencies and contradictions in Twain's work are not only windows on that historical world, however. They are also opportunities for cultural and personal reflection on the part of Twain and his readers. Like symptoms in an analysis in which the patient or analysand is recognized as a participant, these textual inconsistencies may focus attention on materials as they emerge from the unconscious into more conscious resistance and reflection, even if that resistance and reflection are still relatively indirect, inconsistent, and contradictory. These symptoms may thus tell us more about certain parts of nineteenth-century American culture than others, as middle-class European Americans, for example, both deny and reflect on certain dimensions and definitions of themselves and their democracy by means of contemplating images of African American experience. This is where previous moral, aesthetic, and historicist readings also suggest a model of reading American literature as cross-cultural transference, an opportunity to learn from each other's different experiences of our national history—as in the preceding chapter's attention to what Amy and Sethe learn from each other's stories, as well as what Denver, Paul D, and modern readers can learn from Sethe's story.

Beloved thus suggests an examination and reinterpretation of such cross-cultural encounters within Twain's novel as well as the place of such encounters in a larger cultural history. Inconsistencies and frustrations that are never explained away in the novel might be remobilized and reoriented to emerge somewhere else. I would like to think, for example, that there is at least some connection between the frustrations I felt in reading *Huckleberry Finn* as a high school junior, thinking in terms of moral and cross-cultural adventures, and my recent experience with labor and environmental actions in Baton Rouge. I have seen poor, working-class whites and blacks contend for a sentimental victim's role in which they have long been cast by David Duke and others. But I have also seen such whites and blacks become uneasy yet effective allies working for liveable neighborhoods and healthy jobs. They have built these alliances not on a trust in middle-class Tom Sawyer figures or in an economic or social system understood to function as the invisible hand of Providence, but on newly recognized common and overlapping interests (especially class interests) and a background of everyday experience and interpersonal encounters in some ways recognizable in those of Huck and Jim. Considered in this light, Twain's novel becomes an example of what Eric Lott has said of

American minstrelsy: such "popular entertainments in which race was foregrounded yielded up a sense of unrest waiting to be tapped at its class source" (87).

Huck's own intermittent sympathy for Jim's plight certainly stops far short of endorsing Jim's most radical, practical plans for escaping slavery and stealing his family from their owners if necessary. Yet Huck's transference and interaction with Jim does begin to elaborate a sense of unrest Huck seems to recognize in Jim but not in Tom, even if Huck never clearly identifies the class source of that shared unrest. Lott argues, "Minstrelsy's use of racial license to map class revolt was one gesture in the sphere of culture toward what remained undone in the realm of politics" (87). Even if Twain's novel remains unclear about whether class is the problem disguised by race, the interaction between Huck and Jim seems an example of what Lott recommends to the attention of U.S. cultural studies. Such "volatile engagement and internal self-differentiation of cultures, rather than consensus models of cultural assimilation or unity in difference, must become our focus" (92).

The realism of Twain's novel, however, often works against such "internal self-differentiation of cultures." In contrast to Morrison's novel, ghosts are simply not real in Twain's novel (except to Jim), and superstitions, sermons, circuses, dreams, and lies are all "frauds" that the novel's satire expects its nation of readers either to have outgrown since the 1830s when the novel is set or to reject as the stuff of unrealistic "sentimental" literature. All such frauds and superstitions are false to a dominant conception of reality that is assumed to be so overpowering and plain that only ridiculous sentimentality or wishful self-deception could be temporarily taken in by these—or any other—alternatives. Susan Gillman remarks that Twain "relies astonishingly often on the language of 'fraud' and its cognates—swindle, humbug, sham, pretense—to convey a vision of the broadest array of social beings, events, and conventions" (*Dark*

Twins 11–12). Thus even Huck's least conventional, most adventurous, and deterritorialized hopes are almost bound to be frustrated, repressed, or recontained in such fiction, at least in the way that Leo Bersani has described its typical function: "Realistic fiction serves nineteenth-century society by providing it with strategies for containing (and repressing) its disorder within significantly structured stories about itself" (*A Future for Astyanax* 63, qtd. by Hirsch, *Mother/Daughter Plot* 52). Yet Gillman also argues for an increasing capacity in Twain's realism for the self-reflection and cultural differentiation emphasized by Lott. Twain's "early reliance on literal, literary conventions of external, consciously divided identity becomes entangled with a social conception that treats identity as culturally controlled and then gives way to an imposture that is increasingly internal, unconscious, and therefore uncontrollable: a psychological as opposed to social condition" (*Dark Twins* 8). It is in this psychological condition that Twain's novel begins to sketch alternatives and possibilities that are left largely unarticulated socially or politically.

An important example of such realist tendencies toward containment and repression has been outlined in Laurence B. Holland's reading of Huck's story as a potentially disorderly, disturbing set of questions for its first American readers in the late 1880s, questions about "the flukish fact of Jim's legal freedom [as already declared in Miss Watson's will], and the failure of his world to flesh it out with the family, the opportunities, and the community that would give it meaning" (75). In Holland's reading, the novel resolves such questions in terms of a flatteringly well intentioned but childish "game" that this society plays again and again, since "the recurring necessity of freeing Jim . . . has become by this time [after the Emancipation Proclamation and the failure of Reconstruction] at once a moral imperative and an ineffectual routine" (67). Such potentially disturbing questions and imperatives are relegated to the largely feminized and infantilized realm of the sentimental. In this view, the function of Twain's novel is to invoke a flattering but relatively undemanding emancipatory vision in the recurring routine of a moral or cultural mea culpa, instead of setting into motion reorganizations and actions directed toward meaningful social change.

But even if Twain's novel repeatedly tends to contain and repress Huck's disorderly questions and hopes, the very repetitive quality of such containment might also signify a continuing, uncontained frustration, something driving that repetition other than a "moral imperative" that might well be satisfied by the dialectical resolution of a mea culpa ("I'm wrong. / You're right. / But I admit I'm wrong"). The mea culpa and the focus on real obstacles to difference or transcendence may be one "significantly structured story" about the society that produced Twain's novel, but the repeated inadequacy of this particular structure suggests that the "moral imperative" may not be the cause of the repetition but a symptom of something else, something that continues to upset or interrupt such attempted resolutions.

The suspicion of such potentially unarticulated unrest points mainly to the presence of the character Jim as the novel's almost exclusive representative of a group still not contained either culturally or politically between competing nineteenth-century stereotypes of the black male, evolving at the time Twain wrote "from the docile child of the antebellum paternal order to the black beast of post-Reconstruction" (Gillman and Robinson xii). Both categories are clearly inadequate to Twain's portrayal of Jim. Jim is never quite the docile child for whom the sentimental routine would be sufficient. Yet he never comes anywhere close to the inhuman beast who would make the sentimental routine seem irrelevant, so the sentimental mea culpa is likely to feel necessary but insufficient. That is, Jim is neither childish enough to make a white projection of internal conflicts completely safe and ineffectual nor threatening enough to provoke a strenuous defense of racial boundaries.

Twain's novel, then, generally speaks from a somewhat edgy

realist stance, satirizing the small-town southern past's outdated, defeated, sentimental illusions and hypocrisies, in favor of the post-Emancipation middle-class reader's common sense. But the novel's tone also leaves openings for Jim as an unemancipated slave and for Huck as a young and newly adopted member of the middle class to challenge not only their own past "siviliza-tion," but also that of readers positioned later in history and (usually) older in age. Huck's colloquial dialect, his background in the town's underclass, and the southwestern humor, "Bad Boy" books, and other genres of "lowbrow" writing these evoke no longer have the disturbing effect they once had on some of the reading public, but these features still suggest the presence of uncontained yet attractive difference in the midst of middle-class common sense. Students still sometimes seem tempted and disturbed, for example, by Huck and Jim's rationalizing of petty theft. Huck's presence invites his adoptive middle-class so-ciety to reimagine and appreciate its attraction to his difference within itself, a difference articulated especially in terms of class and age, but a difference which will remain incompletely con-tained even at the novel's end. Jim's presence is an analogous invitation played out especially in terms of race and freedom— an invitation for Huck and his readers to recognize an internal difference and to elaborate that difference in Huck's relationship with Jim. This transferential relationship with Jim is placed alongside less promising relationships with the Widow Douglas, Pap, and Tom Sawyer.

Having found riches with Tom and been adopted by the Widow Douglas into the middle class, Huck is being taught at the novel's beginning to shed the marks of his family history, but this process also calls his and his readers' attention to what his new identity asks him to deny. The "separate confinement" of his new identity thus also requires what Morrison calls his "playing in the dark" beyond the boundaries of that identity. Insofar as Twain's readers identify with Huck's uncomfortable new identity as a young adult and member of the middle class, they are invited to address their own unstable identities and to articulate more consciously than usual, through Huck, what their own identities or interpellations require that they deny. Even without the presence of serious ghosts in this novel, Huck's past with Pap Finn has a similar function as a lingering, unburied presence, returning both as a haunting fear and as a vague longing for the lifestyle he has left behind. Huck's past with Pap haunts him after his adoption, until Pap actually appears to take Huck back to the woods, where Huck would have settled back into that life were it not for Pap's beatings. As Huck and his readers learn from Jim on the novel's last page, Pap actually died early in the novel, so most of his returns to Huck's imagination seem even more ghostly in retrospect. Huck's conspicuous silence in response to this news is another sign of Huck's still unresolved feelings for Pap. And the sudden news of Pap's death may also make Pap less easily dismissed by readers behind the stereotype of the drunken and ignorant poor white.

Throughout the novel, Huck remains unsure that his new family and society offer adequate terms either to articulate or to compensate for what he has lost. Though freed of poverty and temporarily freed of abuse at the hands of his widowed, alcoholic father, he still feels "all cramped up" at the Widow's house. The defining borders of class and race and the conventions of church and school devalue his speech and practical skills. As noted by Neil Schmitz (107), the feeling of separation and confinement extends even to his new food: "Everything was cooked by itself. In a barrel of odds and ends it is different; things get mixed up, and the juice kind of swaps around, and the things go better" (2). Listening to Miss Watson's idea of "the good place" where her sort will spend eternity, Huck notices especially the absence of change and other people, until "I felt so lonesome I most wished I was dead" (4). As Huck summarizes Miss Watson's promises of a "good place" where "all a body would have to do . . . was to go around all day long with a harp and sing, forever and ever" (4), Huck imagines a sound quite different from these, as if this sound is what Miss Watson's music is drowning out: "that kind of a sound that a ghost makes when it wants to tell about something that's on its mind and can't make itself understood" (4). Huck is similarly inarticulate about his feelings for his past.

Huck has "lit out" for his former life before; he says he has returned only because Tom Sawyer has promised him adventures, perhaps a safer way of "playing in the dark" than he has known before. Such adventures offer Huck a way to escape "sivilization" and to explore unsettled dimensions of the self. As adventures, they would seem to promise, however, a certain safety against the danger of getting completely stuck in some black hole—for example, the unspoken area of his mother's death or the frightening scenes of his beatings by Pap. He apparently feels some attraction to these dangerous psychic territories, but has no language or strategy for confronting them. Tom's adventures promise Huck such a language, but it is Jim who most nearly delivers one. Citing Ellison, Lott analyzes a similar ambivalence of fear and desire in white American audiences' attraction to minstrelsy: "When the white man steps behind the mask of the [blackface] trickster his freedom is circumscribed by the fear that he is not simply miming a personification of his disorder and chaos but that he will become in fact that which he intends only to symbolize; that he will be trapped somewhere in the mystery of hell" (Ellison *Shadow and Act* 53, qtd. by Lott 25).

It is precisely Huck's unarticulated sense of the limitations on his own supposed freedom and safety at the Widow's that frightens him in his interactions with Jim's black mask and that he also recognizes and explores by means of that interaction. Because Huck does not feel as free of danger in the Widow's society as he is supposed to feel, he can almost automatically identify instead with Jim's more stubborn social predicament, as when he learns that Judith Loftus suspects their whereabouts and he announces to Jim, "They're after us!" Huck can make that almost automatic identification long before he can explicitly address the choice between Miss Watson's vision of heaven and the social "hell" represented by both Jim's lack of freedom and Huck's own sense of difference from his social betters: "All right, then, I'll *go* to hell" (271).

On the first of these promised "adventures" with Tom, Jim is the first person they meet. Tom quickly attempts to position Jim as the "bound" and "silenced black body" that will prove Tom the heroic master and Jim the helpless slave of the darkness in which Tom therefore safely plays. Tom and Huck watch Jim try to find them in the dark and then fall asleep against the tree as he tries to wait them out. Tom removes Jim's hat and hangs it on a limb over his head, after leaving five cents to "pay" for their stolen candles. These demonstrations of their greater awareness and control than Jim's, however, amuse and reassure Tom more than they do Huck. Huck therefore interrupts his narration of this first adventure with Tom to notice how resourcefully Jim later plotted his own version of the same events. Jim's story of being put in a trance by witches who "rode him all over the world, and tired him most to death," leaving his back "all over saddle-boils" (7), is certainly less heroic than Tom's. Like many of Jim's stories, it suggests a masked analogy with slavery, but it also places that condition within an elaborated folk tradition that is recognized and appreciated by his intended audience of other slaves.[1] From Tom and Huck's perspective, Jim's story lacks the social authority of realism ("every time he told it he spread it more and more" 7), yet Huck is impressed that Jim somehow makes a virtue of his social status as an always potentially "bad nigger." Huck writes that Jim's black audience paid to see his "five-center piece; but they wouldn't touch it, because the devil had had his hands on it" (8). Huck is learning how to tell this kind of story—like the story he will tell about himself as an abolitionist and Jim as an escaped slave—by telling us how Jim tells his own stories of danger overcome.

Unlike Tom's, Jim's story does not merely court danger or

contain fear by quickly projecting it onto someone else. Jim's story constructs out of his own experience and *survival* of danger and fear an imaginative and rhetorical social dignity, reinforced by a certain folk tradition, as suggested by his making the token coin from Tom into a talisman and a source of income for himself among his black audience. The dignity Jim constructs for himself in this story is not particularly heroic, authoritative, or idealized, but it is thereby more recognizable to Huck than Tom's. Huck's remark about this episode, that "Jim was most ruined, for a servant" (8), has at least some of the subversive humor of Frederick Douglass's reflections on his ex-master's belief that "learning would *spoil* the best nigger in the world" (78). This sense of Jim's surviving a "ruining" and "spoiling" depends on a division not between Jim and other people, as Tom's "mastery" does, but on a division within Jim himself, a kind of double consciousness of his assigned social identity as "servant" or "nigger" and the other identity he negotiates for himself in his storytelling. Though Huck will only gradually learn to articulate what kind of "learning" Jim might have that would spoil his status as only a servant, Huck is already beginning to recognize how Jim might well emerge not only as the servant, foil, butt, or "nigger" of Tom's (or Huck's own) adventures, but also as a source of stories for Huck's imagination and identification, stories he will slowly learn to appreciate more than "Tom Sawyer's lies."

Tom's adventures may seem like lies to Huck in the way they invent easily mastered threats to Tom's own idealized (and socially reinforced) heroism, denying and projecting any uncertainties about his own mastery onto easy targets like Jim. Huck feels less secure than Tom in his own new identity, however, and he knows Tom's stories can be turned against Huck himself as someone Tom says "don't seem to know anything, somehow—perfect saphead" (17), again with the backing of the town's assumptions about class and race. Huck may appreciate in Jim's stories, then, the possibility of a different kind of truth.

Jim's stories may not seem true in a realist sense, corroborated by dominant social assumptions as Tom's are. But Jim's stories do seem true to Jim's, Huck's, and others' less commonly recognized restlessness and fear. Tom's lies pretend to a conventional, mostly negative freedom from a darkness that remains vaguely defined, whereas Jim's lies might promise Huck a more positive freedom to articulate those fears he senses within himself.

Huck's own lies in the book's early chapters, while they might seem only doomed denials of social guilt (to the Widow, for example), or only defensive maneuvers designed to protect his and Jim's temporary distance from the surrounding society (by offering only what will pass for a realistic truth in that society), can also be read as reflections on the fictions in which we imaginatively participate as Twain's readers. Huck's lies challenge his society to bend and stretch its own dominant truths or lies—especially the truth or lie about its relation to Jim and Huck as criminals—in ways that are promisingly and frustratingly close to the ways he and Jim are trying to stretch that dominant truth themselves. That is, these lies come close to articulating a language and a praxis for their relationship and what they are trying to do.

Huck tells a series of such "stretchers" to people whom he would not expect to help a runaway slave but whom he does expect might help a runaway apprentice (in the story he tells Judith Loftus), a pair of murderers (in the story he tells the ferryman to get him to go check out the sinking *Walter Scott*), or a victim of smallpox (in the story he tells the bounty hunters). In this last case (and I may be stretching things a bit myself), his challenge amounts to an unspoken gamble that if these slave bounty hunters would risk their lives to help someone with smallpox (as he supposedly is), they just might be moved (affected or even infected, as suggested by the terms of his lie) to help Jim out of a similar danger, as Huck finds he himself is still unaccountably trying to do. It is as though he thinks they, too, might do in the event what they would not do on principle. He pretends to invite and welcome others' help and participation in his and Jim's endeavor by appealing to their sympathies, but he seems to know their sympathies' limits better than he knows the limits of his own.

In a more psychoanalytic, individualized (intrapsychic) reading than this one, Peter G. Beidler has read Huck's lies, especially his identification of himself as Charles William Allbright in the raft episode, as symptoms of Huck's "identification with suffering children and his desire for refuge in death" (20). Such a reading is plausible given Huck's (and Jim's daughter's) particular experience of child abuse, an experience represented here as almost unspeakable, at least by Huck and Jim. More historicist readings like Lott's, however, suggest ongoing historical trends in how such supposedly unspeakable experiences were nevertheless conceived and represented in mid to late nineteenth-century American culture. Huck's lies thus have not only the psychological function Beidler suggests, but also a historical, rhetorical function. Huck's lies make a rhetorical appeal to his interlocutors in the novel and also to the novel's readers for a recognition of workable articulations of his and Jim's changing experience.

Lott cites William Taylor on the cultural importance that had been attached to children's experience in sentimental literature earlier in the century: " 'To attribute to someone the simplicity of a child, . . . especially in the middle of the nineteenth century, was a compliment of the first order, and dangerous, too, if the child were to be mistreated and sympathy was not the response sought for' " (Taylor qtd. by Lott 305). The simplicity of a child implied a human nature and a "good heart" shared even across races before the corrupting and divisive effects of adulthood and "real world" environments. Lott attributes to the persistent cultural power of such sympathy for children much of "the somewhat backhanded power of black characters in *Uncle Tom's*

Cabin and, in a more vestigial way, *Huckleberry Finn*. And yet," Lott adds, "such a racial philosophy very quickly fell into one of white supremacy."

Romantic racialist thinking, George Fredrickson notes, "was one aspect of the retreat from environmentalism and the Enlightenment view of a common human nature" (Lott 125). This shift from environmentalism and from the idea of a common human nature (also important in nineteenth-century evangelism) can be seen in the frequent tendency of Twain's novel to portray Jim's childish simplicity, despite his age, in his companionship with Huck, whereas Huck, with "as good a heart as ever any boy had" (*Mark Twain's Autobiography* 2 : 174), is represented as if he might develop further as he continues to learn the ways of the world.

This historicist reading, however, while it may represent dominant historical trends in which this novel certainly participates, is not the only possible result of such cultural sympathy for children as potentially transferrable to blacks and the poor. Huck's dialogues with Jim also explore the more tentative possibility that Jim has managed to carry and develop his own "good heart" beyond the spheres of childhood and the sentimental into an adult stance with which Huck may in some ways identify and from which he might learn valuable lessons. Critical attention to the novel's representations of "suffering children and death" therefore needs to draw on both historicist and psychoanalytic readings, since these supposedly unspeakable subjects are likely to function as placeholders for what dominant discourses both historical and psychological seem inadequate to articulate.

This is also the place where a dominant discourse sometimes turns toward cross-cultural encounters either to fend off or to learn about what it does not already know. As Felix Guattari writes, "The unconscious remains bound to archaic fixations only as long as no assemblage [or praxis] exists within which it can be reoriented towards the future" (2). Thus also Michael Ryan has argued for the potential political value of a differential, variable conception of the private sphere and its position at more or less distance from a society's dominant discourses. While that private sphere's independence may have been overemphasized in the criticism that canonized the "American romance" and individual acts of ironic understanding in reading, many historicist reactions against such readings may also have underestimated that same private sphere's independence and variability: "If we continue to think of the private negatively as a realm of ego imaginaries, we lose much of value politically in the process. If the private is a precipitate of interpersonal relations, shot through with mediations that tie it to public structures, it is also a gateway to that world, a way of refiguring its supposedly systemic laws" (231–32).

Thus Huck looks to Jim's narration of 'Lizabeth's experience for ways of articulating Huck's own experience as a suffering child, having been himself like 'Lizabeth effectively deaf to his own father's authority and punished like her for that same deafness. His dialogues with Jim, like Amy's with Sethe and Denver's with Beloved, become an occasion for imaginatively exploring undeveloped personal and cultural possibilities. Having lost his mother, with only a violent father to take her place, then only a society Huck imagines to be in violent pursuit of him and Jim to take that father's place, Huck might well be expected to turn back deafly (as Denver does) toward the inarticulate but imaginatively inviolate, archaic psychological territory of infancy and death (as suggested in Beidler's reading). But Jim's story about hitting 'Lizabeth restages Huck's memories and fears of being beaten in a way that offers Huck the chance to understand his own memories differently. Jim's story adds especially the apologies and regret that Huck's own memories lack, perhaps indirectly reassuring Huck that he was not responsible for his father's violence. Jim's story also adds his future plans to make specific amends for his own and others' abuses of 'Lizabeth, again suggesting a different understanding and a different future direction for Huck's own story.[2] Jim's story is still recognizably related to Huck's own experience, but it suggests the possibility of a more loving, less violent father and society than those Huck has known.

The feelings usually relegated by the dominant discourse to sentimental literature, maternity, and childhood are imagined here as having a possible extension and articulate plotting into a life beyond fantasy, maternity, and childhood—though Jim's status as an adult and a father remains ambiguous. His character is not so adult and free as to be unbelievable to Twain's readers, but it is also not so simple and enslaved as to be entirely predictable by those readers or by Huck, who is often taken aback and provoked to serious thought by what Jim says. What the dominant culture has regretfully left behind or left unexplored in its own childhood, it can also perhaps imagine may have been more fully developed and articulated in another culture such as Jim's. If it cannot usually take that possibility seriously itself, it can more easily do so through its identification with Huck, who retains just enough of his elders' defensive racism to hold their attention while he listens to Jim more intently than either Huck himself or his elders could easily explain.

The problem with which Jim helps Huck is not only that he cannot get away from his society (as many have argued, in the tradition of the American romance) nor only that he cannot escape his society's escapist past and confront its current realities (as in a "realist" reading). Huck is also attempting to articulate a language to account for and a plan to follow through on his own growing sense of connection to Jim. Holland stresses the way Huck's negative dream of freedom—as an escape *from* civilization, *from* the six thousand dollars, *from* Pap and other would-be parents—struggles throughout the novel to articulate itself in relation to an antithetical and less easily elaborated dream of a more positive freedom in Jim's "longing to escape from slavery and enter *into* the civilization that chafes Huck; Jim's . . . desire *for* the money, the eight hundred dollars, that would buy freedom for his family; [and] Jim's longing to be reunited with his wife and daughter and to *assume* the role of husband and father" (70).

Jim's more positive notion of freedom is more culturally supported and more easily recognized and articulated in Jim's culture than in Huck's, Twain's, or the dominant cultural traditions with which they are most familiar. One historically persistent, dominant discourse in American culture (and modern bourgeois culture more generally) names both these dreams as "freedom" and either expects or promises that the second freedom of which Jim speaks (a freedom both negative and positive) will follow somehow (never mind how) from the first—from Huck and Jim's minimum legal freedom *from* domination. This American bourgeois conflation of negative and positive freedoms may be largely true to the experience of the "victors" who have written much of our history. These victors have tended to represent their success as a heroic escape from Old World domination or from old-fashioned New World traditions and not in terms of the practical costs of their own society in the domination and exploitation of native Americans, Africans, and indentured servants. This American bourgeois conflation of negative and positive freedoms attempts to mediate and contain what remain nonetheless important social differences signaled in Holland's distinction between Huck's negative discourse of freedom and Jim's more positive one. To think of Huck and Jim simply as two people seeking freedom from society and domination in another American romance or even realist fiction is to miss the significance of there being two of them from different cultural traditions, involved in ongoing negotiation over the meaning and purpose of their flights. To articulate their differences is to appreciate not just a resemblance but a more positive connection between Huck and Jim, especially an interactive opportunity for Huck and a rhetorical opportunity for Jim, opportunities which are difficult, mostly frustrated, but all the more important.

The aimless, slippery quality—the negativity—of Huck's flight (like the "loneliness that roams" in *Beloved* 274) is especially useful for finding possible openings in others' weaknesses and getting himself and Jim out of dangerous situations. However, Huck's lies and escapes *from* civilization, money, parents, and bounty hunters are repeatedly accompanied by his own countervailing feelings—less articulated but strong feelings—of weariness, fear, and loneliness, a more positive loneliness *for* some kind of human companionship or society. This loneliness is perhaps most dramatically clear when Huck climbs out of a tree on Jackson's Island and is so delighted to find Jim.

Jim figures here as a kind of substitute and transference for the different forms of support and companionship Huck has only ambivalently rejected in the Widow Douglas and Miss Watson, then rejected again in Tom's adventure plots, and then again in his familiar lifestyle with Pap in the woods. Floating down the river later with Jim, Huck is increasingly critical of, or at least uneasy with, the various forms of domination directed at him, Jim, and others. But Huck tends to feel and articulate that need only in the negative, defensive, vague terms of escape, individual heroism, or abjection. He lacks what John Brenkman calls a "critical hermeneutics" that would enable him both to criticize existing structures of identity and relationship—"the forms of domination which imprint the production and reception of culture, past and present"—and to seek more positively "to clarify social changes the need for which is articulated in the symbolic domain of culture and the realization of which lies in the direction of political self-organization and action" (229). The faltering steps he takes in this direction result primarily from his imaginative transference and interaction with Jim.

Huck's erratic progress toward imagining and articulating different kinds of freedom and connection become even more frustrated (both for him and perhaps for Twain, if we can judge from the three-year hiatus in his writing) as his predominantly negative, somewhat naive vision of freedom carries the raft past Cairo in the fog and even farther into slave-holding territory— apparently farther from even the minimum legal freedom for Jim. It becomes increasingly obvious how a notion of freedom conceived as individual heroism and escape from difficulty fails to account for the need to plot how they will meet and address political and historical contingencies that cannot simply be escaped or overcome. It is not enough to be fleeing with Jim on the drifting raft or to think of himself as being pursued with Jim. Huck also needs to develop the personal and cultural resources to resist the current of his historical circumstances, the kind of resources he may suspect Jim and others already have.

The gap between their negative freedom on the raft and the positive freedoms they also need as two equally necessary strategies of addressing domination widens dramatically at this point in the novel. Huck has gone about as far as he can in mimicking his society's dominant discourses of freedom and adventure, a hero determined to outwit and escape those who would dominate him and Jim. Stories placed earlier in the novel might suggest an eventual evolution of his and Jim's negative potential freedom into a more positive reality. The runaway apprentice story Huck tells Judith Loftus, for example, evokes a classic American promise that running away might lead to the social acceptance, even the social acclaim of a Benjamin Franklin. But the difference of Jim's presence as a runaway slave has complicated that classic promise, or perhaps Jim's presence has exposed the blind spot on which much of that promise is based, which makes it an ideological promise whose only guarantee for many—both socially and psychologically—is its outright denial to others.

Toni Morrison's *Playing in the Dark* calls attention to how Huck's own sense of freedom depends on a contrast with Jim's lack of freedom. "Freedom has no meaning to Huck or to the text without the specter of enslavement, the anodyne to individualism, the yardstick of absolute power over the life of another" (56). This limited conception of freedom by contrast with Jim's situation may account for what Morrison calls "Mark Twain's inability to continue, to explore the journey into free territory" (*Playing* 55). But Jim's presence both calls attention to the limits of Huck's sense of freedom and holds before Huck the example of Jim's more positive, less individualistic concept of freedom.

Jim's presence keeps alive for Huck and his readers not only the possibility of escaping the kind of society and family Huck has known, but also the possibility of developing a different kind of society and family in his relationship with Jim. It is a possibility that remains incompletely realized in Twain's largely realist novel, but the novel does show Huck imagining the possibility, and Twain invites a similarly imaginative transference in Huck's second-person address to his readers.

Repeated escapes from society to the raft seem to result less and less in any real progress for Huck and Jim. Even Huck's lies become more hollow, static, and dilatory with repetition, unable to articulate or plot the more positive possibilities for which they only suggest a groping need. The creative heroism of Huck's smallpox lie, for example, which Jim admires as Huck's "smartes' dodge" (128), functions both practically and imaginatively as another restaging of their dilemma. It suggests the quarantined isolation of Huck's idea of the raft as a floating haven, a freedom that is temporarily hopeful but also extremely limited, fragile, and short-lived. Again, though Huck pretends to welcome the slave hunters into their raft society, he can also count on the slave hunters' own interest in a negative freedom from obligation to keep them away.

Beyond a certain point, however, the pull of Jim's predicament seems to Huck as irresistible as a contagion, even if Huck is still unable to explain the attraction. Huck has largely yielded to that attraction, as suggested by the terms of his lie, when he calls Jim his father. But Huck leaves unmentioned the fact that his still powerfully internalized "conscience" about slaveholders' private "property" has just bullied him into setting off in the canoe to turn Jim in. The entire episode also comes just after the mock heroics of the Raftsmen's Passage (where Huck tells another lie representing himself as the dead victim of another murderous parent) and after Huck's intense confusion in the fog.

It is in the fog that Huck has begun to feel the full disorientation of his rapid movement away from relatively stable social, psychological, and natural markers, without any corresponding sense of where (or toward whom) he is moving, or how his story relates to the social or even the natural world around him: "If a little glimpse of a snag slips by, you don't think to yourself how fast *you're* going, but you catch your breath and think, my! how that snag's tearing along. If you think it ain't dismal and lonesome out in a fog that way, by yourself, in the night, you try it once—you'll see" (100–101). Huck's description here of his loneliness and disorientation in the dark without any markers other than his own perceptions resembles a philosophical description by Deleuze of "what happens when Others are missing from the structure of the world." For Michel Tournier's Robinson Crusoe, once he has lost his sense of a structure inhabited by other people, "The known and the unknown, the perceived and unperceived confront one another absolutely in a battle with nuances. 'My vision of the island is reduced to that of my own eyes, and what I do not see of it is to me a total unknown. Everywhere I am not total darkness reigns'" (Deleuze 306).

Deleuze describes this world without Others in terms that also recall Toni Morrison's description of the terrifying whiteness that haunted Melville's Ahab and Poe's Pym and that Morrison associates with the doctrine of white supremacy: "When Others are missing from the structure of the world . . . there reigns alone the brutal opposition of the sun and earth, of *an unbearable light* and an obscure abyss: the 'summary law of all or nothing'" (Deleuze 306, emphasis added). Huck's experience in the white night fog is a nightmarish taste of where he might be without the world of other people he sometimes thinks he can do without, the world whose attractions and necessity Jim has largely come to represent.

When Huck finds Jim and the raft again after this terrifying night on the river, Huck acts out his own apparently giddy relief by attempting, like Tom Sawyer, to deny and project his own fear and loneliness onto Jim. He attempts to make Jim think that their separation in the fog was only a dream and that Jim's interpretation of the dream in terms of plausible warnings about the social forces working against them was only a foolish mistake (104). Jim's well-known reply, however, "Dat truck dah is *trash;* en trash is what people is dat puts dirt on de head er dey fren's en makes 'em ashamed" (105), is an example of how this transferential relationship can work when the other actively intervenes in the transference. The supposedly safely bound and silenced black body survives Huck's attempted domination, actually talks back, and is at least partly heard.

Jim then reworks his interpretation of their night apart in the fog. First he acknowledges the "plain" realism of Huck's question about the trash on the raft—by stressing within Huck's lie that material otherness which Huck has attempted to throw onto Jim and which Jim can throw right back at Huck as a class epithet. But Jim also compares Huck's realism with their usually unspoken feelings and actions toward each other as friends.

Huck feels the force of Jim's counterinterpretation, but Huck's difficulty in navigating and articulating his own departures from dominant, romantic constructions of their relationship (as one or another form of domination, heroic conquering, or freedom *from* domination) shows not only in the fifteen minutes it takes him to apologize, but also in how he describes that eventual reaffirmation of friendship in terms of his having to "humble myself to a nigger" (105). His language here suggests only a double-negative freedom *from* a familiar discourse of domination (not-mastering a nonmaster), a deliberate, strained inversion of that familiar discourse, but not quite an alternative.

He is still mostly steering clear of the frightening fogs, dreams, and interpretations surrounding those more positive possibilities of other discourses of freedom and connection that Huck has increasingly glimpsed "tearing along." But such interactions with Jim encourage his self-consciousness about the limitations of Tom Sawyer's style. In such interactions he becomes unsure whether he can rely on his own perceptions or whether he needs to attend more carefully to Jim's perceptions as well.

As if those possibilities of a positive freedom must either triumph heroically as planned at Cairo (becoming "real") or become unbearably disorienting, sentimental, and unreal to Huck and his readers, all or nothing, the steamboat soon comes "smashing straight through the raft" (130), driving these alternative possibilities almost wholly beneath the novel's increasingly bitter and realistic surface. When the steamboat bears down on the raft, Huck dives deep, but when he resurfaces and hears no reply to his calls, even students reading the novel for the first time notice how he does not even mention the presumably drowned Jim again for eighteen pages and how he seems almost eager to embrace "sivilized" life again with the Grangerfords. But it is also possible to trace in the ripples even on this most conspicuously smooth and "realistic" surface Huck's (and Twain's) continuing, frustrated attempts to create ways to articulate Huck's grief, both for what he has apparently lost in Jim and for what he has almost lost of himself in losing Jim.

One example is Huck's introduction of himself to the Grangerfords by means of another lie about the gradual disappearance of his family, the circle of people who might be expected to address his particular losses. Never mentioning his mother, he says that his sister married and ran off "and never was heard of no more," then a brother went looking for them "and he warn't heard of no more," then "Tom and Mort died," until "there warn't nobody but just me and Pap left, and he was just trimmed down to nothing, on account of his troubles; so when he died I . . . started up the river" (135). With a little displacement, this is a fairly accurate account of the narrowing of Huck's social options from the society of the sisterlike Widow and Miss Watson, then Tom's society playing in the dark, haunted by the vague fear of "Mort" or perhaps Pap's Angel of Death, then Pap's society in the woods, then the society he found on the raft with his new companion and potential father in Jim, who is now, too, apparently dead "on account of his troubles." The whole story is a shrewd lie, of course, as Huck and his readers know, but here again the terms of the lie suggest at least a psychological effort on Huck's or perhaps Twain's part to articulate indirectly the emotional history of a relationship Huck is unable to describe in either the realistic or sentimental terms his audience would expect.

Another indirect discharge if not articulation of Huck's grief for Jim is his preoccupation with the young Emmeline Grangerford's sentimental pictures and poetry. Again, Huck's own emotional interest in Emmeline's art seems impossible to accommodate within the terms of the sentimental mode in which she works—she would never have written a poem mourning the death of a runaway slave. Nor does his quite emotional response to her pictures and poetry match the more realistic, satiric humor Twain provokes at her expense—Huck's readers may laugh, but Huck never does. Under the cover of Twain's satire and Emmeline's conventionality, however, some of Huck's own concerns approach the surface of his transference with her. He quotes her poem about a drowning victim, then tries to write one himself for the poet who apparently died for lack of a language for her grief, an emotional situation oddly resembling his own—though Huck may not notice the resemblance.

Still another inarticulate symptom of Huck's emotional separation from Jim is the doubling of both Huck and Jim while they are separated. Both Huck's double in Buck and Jim's in Jack are much more at home in "sivilization" and the identities it assigns them. Perhaps the most telling symptom, however, is the uncanny shock Huck gets at the sight of Buck, lying dead at the edge of the water. It is just the sort of narcissistic image that he and many readers have repressed throughout these pages. Looking at Buck's face, Huck can see a reflective picture of himself, as well as a more composite picture of both himself and the other main figure of his transference in Jim, the other part of himself he had earlier thought was drowned without even admitting it to himself. He can see the civilized double of himself in Buck who would never escape the expectations of his society, but he can also perhaps begin to recognize the other face he nearly lost in Jim, the face that promises Huck a new perspective on his society's expectations and a way to address the feelings he has begun to develop in their relationship. One paragraph later Huck raises a yell again in the spot where the raft was being repaired in the swamp, and this time he does hear Jim's reply: "It was Jim's voice—nothing ever sounded so good before" (154). Not only does Jim reply to Huck's call, he also goes on to articulate his own earlier grief at the news of *Huck's* probable death. Huck's silence suggests again Jim's ability to articulate what Huck cannot, in a way that Huck can appreciate and learn from in his own renewed transference with Jim.

In psychoanalytic terms, this speculative encounter between Huck and his mirror image in Buck's dead face at the river's edge, as well as Huck's hearing Jim articulate the grief Huck himself tended to contain, may be compared to the narcissistic scenes Kristeva suggests are still now in contemporary discourse emblematic of a crisis of signification and, at best, a work in progress of imagination and love. According to Kristeva, a narcissist like Huck vacillates between "two absences in contemporary discourse" that, between them, leave Huck without "his own territory," his own "psychic space" (*Tales* 375). Without "a secular variant of the loving father," such discourse is "incapable of assuming primary identification—the substratum for our idealizing constructions" (374). The social symbolic and its constructions seem to offer no attractive compensations or substitutes for the loss of the infant's maternal relation. On the other hand, "he loves nothing because he is nothing" (376). Without some secular version of the Virgin Mother, without some representation within the symbolic of the semiotic that otherwise drives and exceeds symbolic representation, without some figure of a loving mother who is also another subject, the narcissistic subject is pulled back with "fascination and disgust" toward an archaic mother who is "neither subject nor object, an *'abject'-mother,* a place of [impossible] warding off and differentiation, an infection" (374). Modern American narcissists such as Huck are both socially and psychologically split between these two unbearable absences—of loving father and otherloving mother, responsive reality and expressible desire, negative and positive freedoms, spaces for criticism and spaces for anticipation.

But if this is the crisis that makes love almost impossible, as Kristeva claims, if "the old psychic space, the machinery of projections and identifications that relied more or less on neuroses for reinforcement, no longer hold together," then "it may be because another mode of being, of unbeing is attempting to take its place," less an established psychic or social machinery than an intersubjective, cultural work in progress. The important psychoanalytic work in progress this suggests for a work like *Huckleberry Finn,* as taken up again in *Beloved,* might be neither to rebuild "a solid, introspective inside, master of its losses and wanderings," nor to "follow, impel, favor breakaways, driftings," neither to recontain disorder under the rule of a new Father nor to "free" a disorder confined to the subordinate, perhaps gendered and racialized realm of a Holy Mother, but to help such modern narcissists "to speak and write themselves in [the] unstable, open, undecidable spaces" (*Tales* 379–80) of their relationships with each other, for example, in words and acts of imagination on a raft on the Mississippi, or in the transferential reading of books about such rafts.

If realism tends to restrict itself to the sovereign norm, the only alternative, both irresistible and impossible, may appear to be delirium and lies. In Buck's dead face, Huck can neither forget what he has almost lost in Jim nor quite recognize and articulate that loss. So he largely continues to swing between two equally unsustainable, oscillating phases of obsessive, hollow heroics, imitations of the conquering Father's supposedly irresistible mastery, as with the wrecked steamboat, or later in Tom's "evasion" schemes and, on the other hand, paranoid hysterias and delirious intoxications, as in the fog, or later in the generalized fright and "brain fever" at the Phelps's farm. As Jim and Huck's raft drifts farther into slave-holding territory, Huck is still occasionally impressed and manipulated by the overpowering but hollow and uninspiring mastery of figures like the King and the Duke or Colonel Sherburn. And he occasionally comes close to identifying with his own abjection in drunks like Boggs or Boggs's irresolute champions in the mob or in the intoxicated wish fulfillment of the circus drunk turned conquering hero.

But again, the trace of a positively different, less isolated social relation does appear in the next chapter, when Huck attempts to convince himself and Jim that there is nothing for them to do about the King and the Duke, since they are "all alike" (199)—all the men who were taken in by the one-upmanship of the Royal Nonesuch and the reaction it provoked. It is against this background of empty heroism and powerless abjection that Huck hears Jim's story about hitting his daughter 'Lizabeth to make her mind her father, which almost fits these patterns, except that Jim's story suggests that he learned something from his daughter's silence in the face of his own attempted mastery. Jim's story insists on a positive difference in identities and relationships, not only in Jim's regret for "treat'n her so" but also in Jim's positive plans to set her free in a different sense than Huck might tend to expect. Jim would set her free from her slave masters, from his own abuse, but not from a changed relationship to society or to him as a changed and loving father (202).

Here again, as in the chapter in which Jim articulates the

grief Huck does not, the chapter ends with no corresponding comment from Huck, yet Jim's story has offered for Huck's imaginative transference (and that of readers at least partly identifying with Huck) a different plot for narratives that Huck (as realist) has almost decided are all alike. Huck's abuse by Pap, for example, has seemed a narrative from which Huck's only escape was a real or a convincing death, as suggested in Huck's escape from Pap's cabin and again in Huck's story of Charles William Allbright. Huck automatically identifies with this infant choked into silence by his father, floating in a closed barrel and recognized by his father only in flashes of lightning at night. I cannot be sure, of course, that Huck's silence in response to Jim's story about 'Lizabeth means he is actively considering or imagining the alternatives evoked for me by Jim's story, but Huck's silence does suggest opportunities for his or a reader's transference, especially once such missed or unexploited opportunities are placed next to similar, more developed opportunities in a novel like Morrison's *Beloved*.

Huck's ambiguous silence in response to Jim's apparent drowning and his stories may be compared to Denver's deafness, the baby ghost, and the "live green walls" in Morrison's novel, where these are all more obviously reflective, narcissistic shields against confusion that help keep Denver's head just above abjection. Each is a reflection on and indirect articulation of her own loneliness, projected onto the surface of her "real" social circumstances. But Denver gradually recognizes and sees beyond each of these reflections as a functional but not unalterable barrier against the "gleaming, powerful world" outside herself.

Each of these reflections is both privately desirable and potentially connected to other stories, both critical and anticipatory. As Morrison explains her use of these and other instances of the supernatural in *Beloved*, "one of its purposes is to keep the reader preoccupied with the nature of the incredible spirit world while being supplied a controlled diet of the incredible political world" ("Unspeakable" 32). Whereas Twain tends to stress the blinding or hypocritical function of the incredible and the supernatural for most of his characters, Morrison articulates and emphasizes its potential function as one way of coming to terms with difficult political circumstances. This same potential is more faintly traceable in Huck's transference with Jim.

Morrison's novel traces Denver's as well as Paul D's and Sethe's movement through a developing, healing, even politically effective series of such ghostly mediations with their "incredible political world," each ghostly mediation functioning partly as a turning away toward infancy, death, and the supernatural, but functioning also as a more or less understandable negotiation with the "gleaming, powerful world" beyond these temporary, "sometimes safe and other times risky" constructions of the self. Denver works negatively to reconsider Sethe's and her own mediations with a wider world but also more positively than Huck is finally able to do, to elaborate on those mediations and thus to "plot" new responses herself. She eventually offers an encouraging model for Paul D's developing response and their community's changing collective response to what is happening at 124.

The situation at 124 is one in which they are all variously more involved than they have been willing to recognize. As "everybody's child" (246), Denver offers them the chance to recognize their own unmet needs in her and to take responsibility for their own relationships with a wider world by offering Denver their support. This requires of Denver, as well as those who see themselves in her, both the negative freedom to mourn and redirect lost love and the positive freedom to "plot" love's expressions and substitutions in changed social relationships. As the narrator has earlier commented about "such plotting" on Denver's part, it "has changed Denver markedly" (121). She "is a strategist now," effectively "breaking through her own skin" to a "place beyond appetite" (118–19). The place where Denver's plots and stories intersect with theirs is a place where material drives and needs have more than one desperately self-protective, confining plot, where drives and needs can become both focused and resourceful enough to become a negotiable, sustainable relationship. This is not to say such relationships always survive, or that domination disappears, but that such breakthroughs are possible, and Twain's and Morrison's novels together call attention to this possibility.

As the community in Morrison's novel comes to see Denver and her mother not as outcasts but in terms of its own children and its own relations as parents, children, and friends, it is moved to act in ways that actually change the social context that contributed to Sethe's impossible choice. It is precisely the lack of such wider social recognition and support on the part of the more powerful whites that forced Sethe to choose between either not caring about her children enough to try to protect them or loving them enough to try to protect them in the only way her world seemed to offer. This repeatedly frustrated possibility of working together to create other available social options is how, where, and why Paul D wants to put his story next to Sethe's, in a way that suggests why Twain's might also, as Morrison says, be "begging for such attention" ("Unspeakable" 18).

Paul D learns from Denver and Sethe—better than Huck in his drifting and silence learns from Jim—the positive freedom and courage to care enough to commit himself and his previously unfocused love to Sethe and to "some kind of tomorrow" in a changing, more supportive community (273). And Sethe learns from Paul D the negative freedom to redirect the love she has so totally committed to Beloved in one desperately restricted expression of herself and of her own need and ability to live and love.

To return to Huck's ambiguous silence about Jim's separation from his family and his plans to bring them together again, any of Huck's lingering feelings remain unspoken in the next episodes, except as perhaps indirectly recognized by Huck in the grief of Mary Jane Wilks and her sisters at the separation of a mother from her two sons when the Wilkses sell their slaves. The enslaved mother's own grief gets less direct attention from Huck than Mary Jane's reaction, but it is Mary Jane's kindness toward Huck in his role as a servant and the example of her feeling toward her own family and the family of slaves that move Huck from his abject submission to the King and the Duke into critical, imaginative, and strategic action again on behalf of Mary Jane, her sisters, and the divided slave family.

Huck goes even further than Mary Jane in the way that he plans for Jim's safety by not revealing to her Jim's identity as a runaway slave. Huck is moved by Mary Jane's feeling for the divided slave family, but he also knows not to trust her to carry such feelings far enough to help an escaping slave. Like many sentimental heroines, she represents feelings largely contained by social orthodoxy. Twain gives her character just enough "sand" (244), however, so that she is not easily dismissed to a feminized realm of supposedly unrealistic and unrealizable sentimentality. Like Huck and Jim, she seems to live on beyond her role in the novel. As Lott writes, "The sentimentalist strategies for representing white women and blacks were often identical, each image lending the other emotional and political force. 'Blackness' was indeed a primary site of the religious appreciation of the emotions that came with the decline of Calvinism. . . . Like women, blacks were considered creatures of feeling at a time when feeling was paramount in the culture" (32). Mary Jane's character is thus another example of the potentially critical alternative to dominant values that is often sustained in nineteenth-century American literature but also relegated and sometimes isolated in that subordinated realm of the sentimental.[3]

Instead of elaborating such potentials in positively different plots, however, Twain shows Huck's transferences repeatedly overpowered—by the return of the King and the Duke to the raft, by their treachery in selling Jim back into captivity, and perhaps most seriously by the internalized dominant discourse of "shame" and "conscience" that threatens Huck again unless he writes to report Jim's whereabouts to Miss Watson, Jim's "rightful owner." Huck manages to avoid abject surrender to his internalized social conscience, however, by adopting a stance close to the other popular role he has internalized, that of the male hero defying social convention and all the odds.

Twain's readers have long applauded and identified with Huck's decision, partly because it seems to fit this popular American model of heroism, and partly because Huck's decision against his own antebellum southern society's conventions on slavery actually matches the social conventions of Twain's readers after the end of American slavery and Reconstruction. But Huck's climactic decision to tear up the letter he writes to Miss Watson is still a significant breakthrough, even if its more explicit potential is also eventually overpowered in Huck's capitulation to Tom.

The crucial breakthrough is neither Huck's defiant heroism nor his inner moral reform (the mea culpa) but his sense, at least temporarily, that neither of these is enough, that he also has to "set to thinking over how to get at it, and [so] turned over considerable many ways in my mind; and at last fixed up a plan" (271). Huck knows at some level that what he is trying to say and do, and what he is sometimes learning from Jim how to say and do, involves not only a moral but also a practical social problem, not only a negative freedom from society but also a positive freedom to articulate and address their overlapping social situations. His private declaration of independence from his slave-holding society also needs to face the more positive task of acting on his relationship with Jim, addressing their situation within that slave-holding society and addressing somehow even Jim's desire to "enter *into* the civilization that chafes Huck" (Holland 70).

Huck manages to plan what he will do and say not in the

language of defiant or moral heroism, nor certainly in nostalgia for infancy or death, but instead in those "unstable, open, undecidable spaces" (Kristeva, *Tales* 379–80) of his particular memories of Jim and in his reflective repetition of Jim's own articulations of their relationship. Huck remembers when Jim "said I was the best friend old Jim ever had in the world, and the *only* one he's got now" (270). He remembers Jim's voice not as Huck's infallible, authoritative father, nor as his archaic, undifferentiated mother, but as another subject who is also a reflection of himself, a singular partner in their particular circumstances and relationship with each other whose ability to listen to and respond to Huck also challenges him to take responsibility himself for acting on their relationship. That Huck can make such a breakthrough depends in part on his and Jim's floating space in the river, a delicate, unstable living space comparable to the space of reading, the particular natural, social, and psychic space where Huck and Jim's interaction manages intermittently to survive and grow. But Twain's novel calls attention to such a personal and interpersonal breakthrough on the raft and also insists on the power of larger surrounding social forces to overpower that potential.

The controversial last chapters of the novel offer neither moral triumph for Huck nor persuasive freedom or dignity for Jim. Despite his tearing up the letter and devising a plan, Huck is soon feeling betrayed by the King and the Duke, and he reverts again to "trusting to Providence," which comes to almost the same thing as his later trusting the middle-class example and guidance of Tom. Huck confuses Tom's show of independence and heroism in helping Jim to escape with his own more truly independent and more responsible decision (227). Huck slowly learns, however, as readers learn, that Huck and Jim's concerns are unlike everyone else's plans. What builds to a kind of climax in these last chapters is a frustrating sense of crisis in the language and behavior of their world, a sense of inadequate, false alternatives in the individualized heroics and generalized "brain fever" between which or aside from which there are only intermittent, delicate, unstable spaces for the articulation of other more promising possibilities. It is perhaps partly this frustration which has kept readers coming back to this unstable novel, at times turning its ongoing crisis into a work in progress.

One way this frustration can become part of a larger cultural project is by putting Twain's novel next to Morrison's. Twain's realism so overpowers its own socially unrealized possibilities that these possibilities can often seem like little more than sentimentalism or lies. Next to Morrison's work, however, these possibilities can begin to seem both critical and anticipatory, opening spaces that might be compared to the "quality of hunger and disturbance" Morrison appreciates in the spirituals and in jazz, which "always keeps you on the edge. There is no final chord. . . . A long chord, but no final chord" (quoted in McKay 429). Not only does Morrison's writing make its own jazzlike music out of such suspended possibilities; her writing also suggests how such suspended possibilities in work like Twain's might be recognized as real without necessarily being permanent or triumphant. Morrison helps readers reflect on what is different about Twain's work, and she expands on the possibilities of interpersonal and cross-cultural interaction attempted in Huck's dialogue with Jim.

One of the last long chords in Twain's novel, for example, is Jim's surprise announcement to Huck that Pap has been dead throughout most of the period covered in the novel. While Huck is almost silent about Pap's death and about the alternative possibility represented by the relationship he has developed with Jim, Denver in Morrison's *Beloved* has been able to imagine in more "detail" and with more "heartbeat" a similar encounter between her own mother and Amy. She can imagine and understand Sethe's helping Amy revise her genealogy by reassuring Amy that her former master was not her father. Denver can even understand Sethe's having decided to name her after Amy Denver—not as a patronymic debt to an idealized figure of power, nor as a matronymic fusion of identities, but as a living memory of a particular, delicate, unstable interaction more negotiable and sustainable than either.

The idea that people's identities are determined by just such particular, delicate interactions is recognized in a cultural tradition of nicknames described in Morrison's *Song of Solomon:* "The names they got from yearnings, gestures, flaws, events, mistakes, weaknesses. Names that bore witness" (333). Names like Denver, Amy (Aimée? her own mother's "Beloved"?), Sethe ("like the interior sounds a woman makes when she believes she is alone and unobserved at her work: a *sth* when she misses the needle's eye"? *Beloved* 172), Huckleberry, maybe Jim. Considering Huck and Jim in the light of this different tradition is a valuable way to think of what their names might mean to readers of American literature, not just names for who these characters were and what happened to them in Twain's novel, but names for their "yearnings, gestures, flaws, events, mistakes, weaknesses. Names that bore witness" to the often unrealized but important potential of their interactions with each other.

3

Learning from Invisibility and Blindness in Ellison's *Invisible Man*

LONG-STANDING CANONICAL READINGS of American romance, realism, and modernism have worked against the consideration of transformative encounters with other people and other traditions in American literature, while work like Ralph Ellison's and Toni Morrison's calls renewed attention to just this possibility. Not only do they call attention to this possibility in their own work and in African American cultural traditions, in which the self and the social are inextricably intertwined, they also challenge their readers to consider transformative encounters as an unappreciated potential in work like Twain's and Eliot's and in the call and response between different American works and traditions.

The narrator of Ellison's *Invisible Man* writes of "a peculiar disposition of the eyes of those with whom I come in contact. A matter of the construction of their *inner* eyes" (3). Ellison acknowledges the cultural power of American modernism's universalized irony, a sense of disillusionment with both the personal and the social in the widest possible sense, but Ellison's writing insists on a longer American history of personal and political challenges to such disillusionment, in "a subtle process of *negating* the world of things as given in favor of a complex of *man-made positives*" (xx). Instead of the devastation and *unmaking* of the world as such, Ellison suggests that the world "as given" is largely man-made and that it continues to be negated, made, and remade in human history, both on a personal scale and on a larger political scale as well.

This is perhaps the crucial generic difference between Eliot's poem and Ellison's novel. While the poem is focused on a mythic landscape in which "the world of things as given" has been devastated, the novel characterizes much the same wasteland instead as our only home, a cultural brier patch in which we must learn to live with others in a fragile, changing, and democratic "complex of man-made positives." Instead of surveying this cultural landscape as if from an ironic, disappointed distance above and apart from its inhabitants, recognizing but also avoiding the responsibilities and opportunities for learning implied by the "straight looks" of characters such as Twain's Jim and Eliot's Lil, Ellison's novel takes up what he later called "the sheer rhetorical challenge involved in communicating across our barriers of race and religion, class, color and region," by constructing "a plot that would bring [his main character and narrator] in contact with a variety of American types as they operated on various levels of society" (xxii). Whereas Eliot ironically contrasts the almost otherworldly river in *Huckleberry Finn* with the all-too-human world ashore, Ellison sees in Twain's river a flawed but challenging "raft of hope" for a larger national history, a deferred promise of American difference, democracy, and productive cross-cultural interaction.

Ellison's eventual acceptance of this rhetorical and social challenge as a writer is suggested by his descriptions in several essays of his first encounter in college with Eliot's poem. "*The Waste Land* seized my mind. I was intrigued by its power to move me while eluding my understanding. Somehow its rhythms were often closer to those of jazz than were those of the Negro poets, and even though I could not understand then, its range of allusion was as mixed and as varied as that of Louis Armstrong. Yet there were its discontinuities, its changes of pace and its hidden system of organization which escaped me. There was nothing to do but look up the references in the footnotes to the poem, and thus began my conscious education in literature" (*Shadow and Act* 159–60). Representing himself as a reader like so many others unable to account for the poem's power, understand its allusions, or discover its hidden system of organization, he might be expected to dismiss the poem altogether as *only* a heap of broken images, a wasteland, a universalized scene of cultural failure and incommunicability. Yet he responds especially to the poem's power to move someone who does not understand its own language. He even suggests that the poem's "own" language may not be its own at all, that it may owe much of its power to the rhythms, allusions, and discontinuities characteristic of jazz, a power which he suggests that neither Eliot, "the Negro poets," nor Ellison himself altogether understands or owns.

Instead of expressing dismay at a poem that advertises itself as a jarring disorganization of cultural voices, Ellison suggests in the discontinuities of jazz—and in his own reading of *The Waste Land* as a jazz poem—a model for an ongoing, promising dialogue among such different voices. He suggests a conscious, educational, democratic process of seeking out and learning more about the mixture of voices that he will continue to listen for both in Eliot's poem and in its footnoted sources in a variety of literatures and cultures. "I began to see my own possibilities with more objective, and in some ways, more hopeful eyes. . . . Reading had become a conscious process of growth and discovery, a method of reordering the world" (160–61). Although there are echoes here of Eliot's own fitful, ironic attempts to "set my lands in order," Ellison's emphasis on a hopeful, conscious process of growth and discovery that affects not just a private worldview but a larger world points distinctly away from Eliot's poem in the direction of Ellison's novel. Ellison returns to Twain's focus on the moral and social problems of American democracy even as he also acknowledges Eliot's sense that the American world and its myths have undergone dramatic change since the time in which Twain wrote.[1]

According to Ellison, race as a central question for American democracy had been driven largely underground in much of

Eliot, Hemingway, and Ellison's own century and literary milieu, as a result of a weakened cultural belief in the nation's "democratic dream": "And as always when the belief which nurtures a great social myth declines, large sections of society become prey to superstition" (*Shadow and Act* 41). What Ellison describes here as "superstition" may be compared to what Eliot describes in terms of modernism's "mythical method" as an aesthetic defense made necessary by the decline of an organizing social myth, "a way of controlling, of ordering, of giving a shape and a significance to the immense panorama of futility and anarchy which is contemporary history" ("Ulysses" 483).

A similar preoccupation in Hemingway's early writing with technique as a means of avoiding certain subjects reminds Ellison of a more modernist version of Huck Finn, one who would recognize his responsibility to Jim but would still send Miss Watson the letter turning Jim in and who would attempt to avoid his guilty memories thereafter: "Like a terrified child avoiding the cracks in the sidewalk, he [Hemingway] seeks protection through the compulsive minor rituals of his prose" (*Shadow and Act* 40). Ellison suggests here not only an individual, artistic, moral failing in Hemingway and other such twentieth-century writers but also broader cultural changes since the time of Melville and Twain.

The reason a writer like Hemingway seeks such protection is that he lacks a widely shared social myth like democracy that might better support him in addressing what he fears. It is modernism's preoccupation with the lack of any such widely shared social myth that prevents its functioning in the way that Ellison demands of his own writing, as the practice of an aesthetic and political myth that is thereby criticized, affirmed, and reinvigorated. "Writers like Eliot and Joyce made me conscious of the literary value of my folk inheritance" (*Shadow and Act* 58). This folk inheritance would be developed in Ellison's writing, however, not as the object of primitivist nostalgia for a lost consensus but as a living, changing cultural resource, valuable especially for its "sense of what it took to live in the world with others" (*Invisible Man* 574).[2]

"The American novel at its best has always been concerned," Ellison writes, with the contradiction between "the actualities of our conduct," especially with regard to African Americans, and the nation's "noble ideals" of justice, equality, democracy, as well as "the implicit pluralism of the country," and "the composite nature of the ideal character called 'the American'" (*Shadow and Act* 164, 165). Even if such moral ideals were inadequate to govern our social conduct in the nineteenth century, American fiction continued to address this as a crucial national problem. "During Melville's time and Twain's," this "basic moral predicament" was "an implicit aspect of their major themes." But "by the twentieth century and after the discouraging and traumatic effect of the Civil War and the Reconstruction it had gone underground, had become *understated*" (164). The attempt to manage that discouragement and trauma began to eclipse the abiding moral and social predicament, as in the ritualized "game" of mea culpa Laurence Holland reads in the ending of *Huckleberry Finn* and in the overriding concern with self-control, pathos, and dignity in the last section of Eliot's poem.

Although Ellison is pleased that such repressed subjects have returned "into explicit statement again in the works of Richard Wright and William Faulkner, writers who lived close to moral and political problems which would not stay put underground" (164, 165), even if that explicit statement is patently incomplete, Ellison repeatedly characterizes most of the American writing of his own century in terms of its avoidance of these most important questions of American democracy, especially the national "failure to resolve the problem symbolized by the Negro" (36). Such questions have been avoided either by understating the subject of race, by understating subject matter in general in favor of form, or by not living as "close" as Faulkner, Wright, or Ellison himself did "to moral and political problems which would not stay put underground." American artists of this century, according to Ellison, have focused too narrowly instead on "artistic individualism" and a "questionable personal freedom for the artist, which too often served to enforce the 'unfreedom' of the reader" (37, 38). The pathos and dignity salvaged for the ironic speaker in Eliot's *Waste Land*, for example, obscure the responsibilities, questions, and opportunities raised by the poem's general suggestion that its own organizing myths are powerless in the larger culture and especially in the larger world.

Eliot and Ellison both tend to see this absence or loss of myth as a modern historical development, even when Eliot dates that development in a seventeenth-century "dissociation of sensibility," which makes it seem almost less historical than mythical, the origin of postlapsarian history.[3] Ellison, however, makes another distinction more specific both historically and culturally to the United States. Although the restricted moral and social scope of much twentieth-century writing is "usually spoken of as a product of World War I disillusionment," Ellison writes, "yet it was as much the product of a tradition which arose even before the Civil War—that tradition of intellectual evasion for which Thoreau criticized Emerson in regard to the Fugitive Slave Law, and which had been growing swiftly since the failure of the ideals in whose name the Civil War was fought" (*Shadow and Act* 36). That is, the "intellectual evasion" of modernist writing may be the product not only of recent world-historical events, but also the latest phase of one specific tradition, one among others in an ongoing debate about questions of American domination and democracy. As C. W. E. Bigsby writes,

> The idea that America had lost its innocence in the nineteenth century, as Henry May suggests in his book *The End of American Innocence,* or with World War I must have struck the Negro as somewhat bizarre, since he had not encountered that innocence except in the sense of a brutally simplistic

vision. . . . Lacking such illusions, they lacked also the consequent despair, which so suffused the work of white writers.
There is no real equivalent in black writing to that lament over
the decline of liberal individualism which one finds in Fitzgerald or Nathanael West, and none of that desperate creation of
discrete linguistic and psychical enterprises in which alone
the solitary figure can snatch meaning from chaos. (*Second
Black Renaissance* 16)

Ellison's novel, however, neither could nor would ignore the
cultural power and influence of Eliot's poem, Eliot's criticism,
and the traditions they came to represent. Ellison's introduction
to the thirtieth anniversary edition of *Invisible Man* even describes the novel's composition in terms that recall his nonfiction
criticisms of twentieth-century American writing and its preoccupation with "World War I disillusionment." His abortive war
novel begins to sound like a pointed fictional critique of that
tradition. He describes *Invisible Man's* "unexpected" announcement of itself and its seven-year "challenge" to Ellison's imagination "at a time when I was struggling with a quite different
narrative": "it erupted out of what had been conceived as a
war novel" (vii). In that projected but displaced war novel, a
captured black American pilot faces again what Ellison saw as
the long-standing, classic American contradiction between the
"noble ideals" of his countrymen and their actual conduct toward him as a black American, or between democracy and
domination. But like the (white) modernist artists criticized in
Ellison's essays, this black pilot also faces this contradiction quite
alone, with neither social support from those around him nor
even conceptual support from the dominant American culture
that has long betrayed and cheapened its national promises and
myths. Although he is the "designated spokesman for his fellow
prisoners," he is also the only black prisoner, and neither the
Nazis nor his American adversaries support or even recognize
his isolated "inner struggle" (xii).

His paradoxical resemblance to and difference from Ellison's nonfiction portrait of the modernist artist deepens as Ellison suggests that this peculiarly hybrid character has evolved from that of another downed black pilot in an earlier short story ("Flying Home"), "who saw mastering the highly technical skills of a pilot as a dignified way of serving his country while improving his economic status" (xiii). However, while technical skill might uneasily protect a white American pilot or artist (the story's title is also that of a jazz song) from the "basic moral predicament" of his country's treatment of African Americans, it did not protect Ellison's black pilot. With neither social nor cultural support for even this technical role in his society, the captured pilot of Ellison's stalled war novel faced the "capricious event" of his own situation as a perhaps impossible dilemma, "hopelessly devoid of meaning" (*Shadow and Act* 41). "Much to his surprise he found his only justification for attempting to deal with his countrymen as comrades-in-arms lay precisely in those old betrayed promises proclaimed in such national slogans and turns-of-phrase as those the hero of Hemingway's *A Farewell to Arms* had found so obscene during the chaotic retreat from Caporetto. But while Hemingway's hero managed to put the war behind him and opt for love, for my pilot there was neither escape nor a loved one waiting" (*Invisible Man* xii).

Ellison can understand the Hemingway hero's bitter rejection of the "old betrayed promises," but he cannot afford that character's personal escape into romantic love—like Hemingway's and Eliot's aesthetic escapes into the pathos and dignity of irony. Such an escape appears to Ellison to rely on a racial privilege to avoid a larger social problem that Ellison's black protagonist simply could not avoid, even aside from the disillusioning shocks of the war. Ellison's pilot knew "that once the peace was signed, the German camp commander could immigrate to the United States and immediately take advantage of freedoms that were denied the most heroic of Negro servicemen" (xiii).

Ellison's projected war novel, then, was struggling with this most recent, modernist construction of a much longer American (and especially European American) tradition—"that tradition of intellectual evasion for which Thoreau criticized Emerson in regard to the Fugitive Slave Law" (*Shadow and Act* 36). Ellison can criticize that tradition of evasion as inadequate to the issues he wants to confront, but that tradition is also an unavoidable part of his own cultural condition, a national past that is "a part of the living present" (xvi), still depriving him and his pilot of the cultural and technical means to address these issues unless he also addresses that dominant tradition's power. That dominant tradition of "the pure American self divorced from specific social circumstances" (Baym 131) depends on and often assumes a certain social and economic power to sustain that self's sense of "solitude" and "separate confinement." It is a tradition that leaves his pilot's own experience out of focus, even psychologically: "I came to realize that my pilot was also experiencing difficulty in seeing *himself*" (xiii). This dominant cultural blindness toward his own therefore invisible self is partly the blindness of another culture but also an almost unavoidably internalized blindness, what Alfred Arteaga has described as autocolonialism, in which "the Other assimilates both [the hegemonic] discourse and the relationships it systematizes, so to the degree the discourse suppresses, the autocolonist effaces or denigrates him/ herself from within" (*An Other Tongue* 17).

"After such knowledge," Ellison asks in Eliot's phrase, "and given the persistence of racial violence and the unavailability of legal protection, I asked myself, what else *was* there to sustain our will to persevere but laughter?" (xv). Faced with an apparently impossible dilemma, Ellison's pilot sees no way out either through a sentimental trust in Providence (and the society organized to protect others' social positions more than his own) nor through the lonely pathos and dignity of modernist irony. What saves Ellison's novel from being immobilized by that dilemma, however, is a different tradition, "an ironic, down-home voice" in which Ellison detects "a subtle triumph" and a "secret, hard-earned wisdom that might, perhaps, offer a more effective strategy through which a floundering Afro-American novelist could convey his vision" (xv–xvi). It is a jazz voice whose "echoes of blues-toned laughter" invoke for Ellison's otherwise socially and culturally isolated protagonist the hard-earned social and cultural resources of African American culture, as a tradition long familiar with the sort of thorny dilemma this pilot discovers "much to his surprise" (xii)—in a common modernist aesthetics of shock.

The saving importance of African American culture to Ellison's novel and his protagonist is stressed in most readings of the novel, notably those of Robert O'Meally, Houston Baker Jr., and Henry Louis Gates Jr. (*Signifying Monkey*), but it is perhaps worth emphasizing that Ellison's version of African American culture is less nationalist or separatist than rhetorical and dialogic, closer to what Arteaga describes as hybridization. In a more purely nationalist response to colonialism, Arteaga explains, "the articulation of difference would seem to dehegemonize colonial authority by its presence alone," combining "native elements into a privileged discourse, *deaf* [*gluxoj*], as Bakhtin would say, to a deaf colonial discourse" (18). Even that purer nationalism, however, includes a significant dialogic dimension: "The move to *select* one discourse over another is dialogic," even if "the content of that selection, the nationalist monologue, is monologic" (18).

For Ellison's pilot and other black Americans, however, given American history, even such a qualified escape into a pure nationalism or romance seems impossible: "There was neither escape," as Ras might have hoped, "nor a loved one waiting" (*Invisible Man* xii), as Hemingway's hero hoped. Hybridized discourse like Ellison's, on the other hand, rejects the purer nationalisms of both Ras and Hemingway's romantic hero. It "rejects the principle of monologue and composes itself by selecting from competing discourses. Further, there is no detritus of difference; distinct elements remain so, relating in a dialogue of dissimilarity" (Arteaga 18).

What remains as inassimilable, incommensurable, unusable detritus in Eliot's *Waste Land* becomes in Ellison's novel the stuff of ongoing dialogue and learning. Although Ellison was certainly interested in making a largely invisible tradition in American culture visible, he seems to have conceived of this project—as he also seems to have conceived of that invisible tradition—less in an expressive sense than a rhetorical one, less as a cultural essence to be expressed than as an ongoing history of moral and political interaction.[4] Ellison is most inspired by "the sheer rhetorical challenge involved in communicating across our barriers of race and religion, class, color and region" (xxii).

Thus Ellison's novel encounters and challenges *The Waste Land*'s contemporary status as a universal aesthetic statement, a statement taken by many to be comprehensive in the pathos and dignity of its irony toward the unmet challenges posed by the world outside the poem. Ellison's novel also challenges certain social organicist and aesthetic organicist traditions of African American culture and criticism, as exemplified within the novel in Ras's social separatism and the signifyin' trickster Rinehart's formal shape shifting. The character of Ras serves as a crucial reproach to the protagonist's autocolonial tendency to adopt the dominant culture's (including the Brotherhood's) selectively blind and deaf effacement and denigration of himself and his race. Like pluralist multiculturalism, however, Ras's discourse on race is also portrayed as blind and deaf itself to that dominant culture's material power, its ability to define and limit the effectiveness of Ras's (and Garvey's) nationalism. Thus the protagonist comes to appreciate Ras's criticisms of the Brotherhood but also then to suspect that the riot is engineered and manipulated not only by Ras's nationalism, or by Dupre and Scofield's grassroots political action, but more powerfully by the white-dominated Brotherhood.

As for the more aesthetic separatist tradition represented in the novel by Rinehart (perhaps an allusion to the jazz musician Django Reinhardt), the invisible man comes to understand that

Rinehart's formal and economic success is achieved at the expense of any feeling or responsibility toward anyone but Rinehart himself. The invisible man realizes that his own temporarily similar plan to exploit his invisibility "rine and heart" and "agree them to death and destruction" threatens to destroy not only his enemies but those he cares about as well.

Writing his novel in the context of a modernist literary culture powerfully dominated by Eliot's poem, Eliot's criticism, and Eliot's literary audience, Ellison's novel stages its own parallel, explicitly comparable series of disillusionments with weakened and negated cultural ideals. Ellison can expect and directly address his readers' conditioned tendency to read his own novel's series of disillusionments and failing cultural ideals in terms of a mounting cynicism and self-confirming retreat from a cultural "wasteland" of apparently unresolvable contradictions into asocial, apolitical, ironic individualism, aestheticism, and isolation. Or, given the dominant culture's power over African American culture as well, he can expect and address tendencies even within African American culture toward another cynicism and self-confirming retreat into a comparably monologic, separatist social or aesthetic underground.

But Ellison's novel negates these various modernist and separatist options as the latest "world of things as given," insisting in a way that Eliot's poem does not insist on the inescapable, necessary, and even valuable hybridity of American cultures and on the inescapable necessity and value of somehow negotiating the disillusionments, contradictions, and surrounding chaos that threaten the end of Ellison's novel as they do Eliot's poem. This hybridity and negotiation are represented as necessary for those who are socially and aesthetically invisible, especially African Americans, but also for those like Eliot's Tiresias or Ellison's Norton or Brother Jack, who are socially and aesthetically blind in their different ways. Ellison insists on the necessity of his narrator's emerging from the hole of his own isolation and cynicism, despite his equally important cultural disillusionments and denunciations, in order to assume responsibility for his own socially negotiated complex of man-made positives, to reshape his social identity, and to enact his love—not only romantically or aesthetically but also socially and politically (580–81).[5] The novel enacts that same promised exit from isolation and cynicism in its self-conscious engagement with its reader, either by directly addressing the reader in the second person or by otherwise shaping its readers' responses to the novel.

Invisible Man's pointed difference from works like Twain's and Eliot's is emphasized from the beginning in the novel's two epigraphs. The first epigraph, from Melville, quotes Captain Delano's question to Benito Cereno, "more and more astonished and pained; 'you are saved: what has cast such a shadow upon you?'" (xxv). Without quoting Cereno's famous answer ("The Negro!"), Ellison calls attention to what we have seen in Twain's novel and what Morrison would elaborate further in *Playing in the Dark,* both the white desire for moral salvation and escape from issues of race, and the recognition that such an escape is not only impossible but also misguided in American culture. The second epigraph, from Eliot's *Family Reunion,* depends on its juxtaposition with the Melville epigraph to suggest the still haunting presence of race even in writing like Eliot's. Although Eliot's writing makes almost no explicit reference to race, it still strains to refuse any such racial or other social responsibility as might be suggested by a "straight look" like that of Twain's Jim or Eliot's Lil:

> HARRY: I tell you, it is not me you are looking at,
> Not me you are grinning at, not me your confidential looks
> Incriminate, but that other person, if person,
> You thought I was: let your necrophily
> Feed upon that carcase. . . .

As in "The Burial of the Dead" section of *The Waste Land,* the challenge suggested by these "confidential looks" is assumed to be coming from and addressed to the already dead, but it is also recognized as still unburied, still unaddressed in the surviving language and culture. Ellison's epigraphs thus call attention to openings in the dominant culture that his novel will take the measure of and elaborate. Like the yokel in Ellison's prologue who knocked out the "scientific" prizefighter despite his "violent flow of rapid rhythmic action," this is where Ellison promises to have "simply stepped inside of his opponent's sense of time" (8). Ellison's novel will analyze both the sentimentalized blindness characteristic of canonical nineteenth-century American fiction and the more aestheticist, alienated blindness characteristic of American modernism.

Ellison's prologue begins by attempting to address that same dominant language and culture in relatively direct but self-consciously unsuccessful ways, through self-expression and a kind of prose music or poetry, before he turns to a more rhetorical, more pedagogical strategy in the narrative that follows. His narrator opens with an expressive statement, "I am an invisible man," but this is followed immediately by an implicitly second-person correction of what he assumes readers accustomed to Melville, Eliot, Twain, or Poe are likely to think he means: "No, I am not a spook like those who haunted Edgar Allan Poe" (3). He then proceeds with a kind of ironic shrug to explain why such direct approaches (including this very explanation) will not succeed.

Although he is not a ghost but a "man of substance, of flesh and bone, fiber and liquids," he also knows he is still another kind of "spook" in the racialized vernacular and culture that have driven him underground. He knows, therefore, that a realist's plain self-expression (in the manner of Twain's Huck Finn) would not express or address that invisibility that is his particular identity and subject, since that invisibility is a socially, cross-culturally constructed condition. It is inextricable from encounters with a racialized culture upon whose blindness his invisibility depends. "I am invisible, understand, simply because people refuse to see me. . . . That invisibility to which I refer occurs because of a peculiar disposition of the eyes of those with whom I come in contact" (3). Furthermore, that social contact between invisibility and blindness is itself indescribable without addressing the "peculiar disposition" of a certain cultural blindness and invisibility. It is a blindness that is not exactly aesthetic and universal (as may be suggested by work like Eliot's), but traceably aestheticized and universalized (as in Ellison's juxtaposition of the epigraphs from Melville and Eliot). It is a blindness ironic about the failures of its ideals but innocent about the power that its irony leaves in place. Nor is the invisibility created by this blindness only particular, marginal, and social: it is, however, traceably particularized, marginalized, and sociologized (as in the racialized sense of "spook"), as if it were unrelated to that more powerful cultural blindness.

The narrator compares the temptation of directly "complaining" about or "protesting" the particular conditions of this existence with the futile "resentment" he feels when, "constantly being bumped against by those of poor vision, . . . you begin to bump people back" (3, 4). Neither self-expression nor physical force, he suggests, successfully addresses the more political, rhetorical problem of his invisibility, since he feels invisible even to himself. "You ache with the need to convince yourself that you do exist in the real world, that you're a part of all the sound and anguish, and you strike out with your fists, you curse and you swear to make them recognize you. And, alas, it's seldom successful" (4). The prologue will proceed with a kind of self-destructive modernist irony to prove this point about its own failure to communicate; however, this failure also opens the way to a different rhetorical strategy in the narrative to follow.

The prologue's third paragraph, where the narrator remembers his violent encounter with the blond "blind" man one night in the street, begins what he expects will be taken as a kind of violent, rhetorical bumping of his readers, as he acknowledges near the end of the prologue: "I can hear you say, 'What a horrible, irresponsible bastard!'" (14). He attempts a physical image of his invisibility in the description of his brightly lit, underground "home—or a hole in the ground, as you will" (6), then turns to a more phantasmagoric series of images in his reefer-induced dream-vision of Louis Armstrong's music. But if the invisible man appreciates Armstrong's music "because he's made poetry out of being invisible," there is also the suggestion that the popularity and "poetry" of Armstrong's music, his ability to bend "that military instrument into a beam of lyrical sound," may not capture and communicate that invisibility any more effectively than either self-expression or physical violence. Armstrong's "poetry" may depend, in fact, on *not* understanding that invisibility in the way that the narrator says he does himself, even though the narrator apparently cannot communicate that understanding either: "I think it must be because he's unaware that he *is* invisible. And my own grasp of invisibility aids me to understand his music" (8).

What "you hear vaguely in Louis' music" is what Ellison's narrator tries and fails to explain in his prologue and what he will turn to his narrative to explain differently and at greater length instead. It is what he discovers as "a new analytical way of listening to music. The unheard sounds came through, and each melodic line existed of itself, stood out clearly from all the rest, said its piece, and waited patiently for the other voices to speak" (8–9). But as he tries to record and communicate those unheard voices (less patiently) all at once in the prologue, we hear a barrage of contradictory statements on blackness, freedom, loving, and hating, until the narrator and also (as he suspects) his readers are thoroughly *"confused"* and *"dazed"* by so many contradictory voices speaking almost all at once in the *"music beating hysterically in my ears"* (11, 12).

The narrator can well understand the modernist longing for romantic or aesthetic escape from such hysteria—such as in the search for water in *The Waste Land* or the opting for love in *A Farewell to Arms*. But, again, his own situation rules this out as a viable option: "*I was sore, and into my being had come a profound craving for tranquillity, for peace and quiet, a state I felt I could never achieve. For one thing, the trumpet was blaring and the rhythm was too hectic. A tom-tom beating like heart-thuds began drowning out the trumpet, filling my ears. I longed for water and I heard it rushing through the cold mains my fingers touched as I felt my way, but I couldn't stop to search because of the footsteps behind me*" (12). He acknowledges the difficulty of sustaining that almost overwhelming sense of incommensurable differences: "to *see* around corners is enough. . . . But to hear around them is too much; it inhibits action." Unlike these poets, however, he does not therefore swear off action; instead, he swears off the drug that intensifies this vision because "I believe in nothing if not in action" (13).[6]

The lack of an accessible poetic or cultural form situated apart from, above, or even beneath these different voices' encounters, along with the lack of a social position he can entrust to Providence (as in Twain) or to "The Peace which passeth understanding" (as in Eliot), makes it impossible for the narrator to stop and contemplate the generalized scene either aesthetically or socially. "Besides," he adds, "the drug destroys one's sense of time completely," and the action to be undertaken by Ellison's novel, again, since it is rhetorical and historical, will depend on keen timing, like that of the "long shot" yokel who "stepped inside of his opponent's sense of time" (8).

Almost at the end of his prologue, the narrator acknowledges his irresponsibility and failure to engage more effectively with the blond "blind man" (though that might have meant using his knife, he suggests, bumping the reader again): "I became too snarled in the incompatible notions that buzzed within my brain" (14). Instead of continuing to bump his reader, however, he ends his prologue with a question followed by a request for the reader's patience and attention as he turns to a different rhetorical tack in the narrative to follow: "But what did *I* do to be so blue? Bear with me" (14). What we are guided toward as readers, in other words, is not necessarily an answer to our question so much as essential practice in listening to his response. What he will not offer is a moral explanation, as an implied reader of Twain's might expect, focused on what *he* did to be so blue, independent of larger social forces. Nor will he offer what Eliot's implied reader might expect, an ironic, generalized vision of the futility of anything that the invisible man or the "hypocrite lecteur" did or might have done to be so blue. He offers his readers instead—on the model of jazz improvisation, as Ellison has often argued, or perhaps on the model of pedagogy, as I might add here—a challenge and invitation to "bear with me," and a series of graduated exercises in doing so. He will match this patience and attention on the reader's part by starting his narrative in the position presumably (and historically) most easily approved by his most hostile readers. That is, he starts with himself as a young man in the southern black rhetorical position popularized by Booker T. Washington, accepting at face value the qualified promise of Emancipation and Reconstruction given to his grandparents, "that they were free, united with others of our country in everything pertaining to the common good, and, in everything social, separate like the fingers of the hand" (15).

That he will come to question this particular promise for reasons similar to those articulated by Du Bois in *Souls of Black Folk* is less important here than the rhetorical, pedagogical, and narrative process of cross-cultural learning that this initial position inaugurates. When the narrator does question this promise, for example, the image he uses also raises more general issues of blindness and invisibility that will recur in other contexts throughout the novel. From his days at the college modeled on Washington's Tuskegee Institute, he remembers the statue of the Founder, "his hands outstretched in the breathtaking gesture of lifting a veil that flutters in hard, metallic folds above the face of a kneeling slave" (36). The contrast between the word *flutters* and the "hard, metallic folds" it describes, along with the "rustle of wings" from the flock of starlings that soil the statue as the protagonist looks on, emphasizes the stationary, monumental nature of this figure for revelation and unobstructed vision, making the narrator think twice about the statue's immobility and its "empty eyes": "I am standing puzzled, unable to decide whether the veil is really being lifted, or lowered more firmly in place; whether I am witnessing a revelation or a more efficient blinding" (36). Whatever vision this lifting of the kneeling slave's veil is expected to reveal, it is the expectation of unobstructed, permanent revelation itself that effectively blinds both Founder and slave to the limitations of any one such newly revealed vision or truth, and to the necessity and value of ongoing democratic negotiations of each such vision with others that it obscures.

Any particular vision here, in other words, is less valuable than an ongoing dialogue. It is this rhetorical, pedagogical, and narrative dynamic that will be reinforced in the almost endless *series* of revelations and dialogues for both characters and readers in the course of Ellison's novel. None of these revelations or unpredictable dialogues is nearly so final in its effects as the widespread devastation represented in *The Waste Land,* for example. Both characters and readers of *Invisible Man* learn that becoming disillusioned does not result in seeing either the absolute truth or an absolute lack of truth. Nor does the lack of an absolute truth prevent anyone from acting by his or her best lights, though some learn to take more responsibility for their visions than others. Both characters and readers are disabused of a long series of different illusions, each tending to replace the one before as they learn from their experience and from each other. For example, the college with its Washingtonian promises of assimilation yields in the protagonist's view to another version of racial progress in Harlem closer to Du Bois's position, which yields again to the familiar taste of yams and its mildly pluralistic promise of respect for differences of background and taste, then to the Brotherhood's oppositional promise of a less vulnerable economic and political equality, then to Rinehart's ability to manipulate appearances, then to the riot with its promise of grassroots initiative and revenge, not to mention hundreds of other reversals on the smaller scales of episodes, dialogues, and thoughts. The novel challenges its characters and readers to learn gradually and irregularly to seek and expect in each new vision not a final unveiling but useful insights and transformations, along with their corresponding blindnesses, lessons learned and others not yet learned, reluctant negations and man-made affirmations.

It is a "hard-earned wisdom" about the limitations, divisions, and necessary negotiability of any one vision or truth, as summarized in the narrator's reminder in the epilogue that "the mind that has conceived a plan of living must never lose sight of the chaos against which that pattern was conceived. That goes for societies as well as for individuals" (580). Even when Ellison sounds as if he is most attached to an ideal of unassailable vision and knowledge, as in his remarks on creating African American characters who can "snatch the victory of consciousness from the forces that overwhelmed them" (xxi), that knowledge and consciousness tend to feature a knowledge of their own invisibility in relation to others' blindnesses.[7] That is, their consciousness is a social, rhetorical, political knowledge, not a moral or aesthetic escape from or transcendence of their social and rhetorical situations.

Nor can this rhetorical dynamic be trusted to a larger, predetermined historical scheme, which might afford a narrator or reader either a more confident or a more ironic view of the protagonist's blind struggle. The narrator has spoken in the prologue of a larger scheme of history that is in his experience not grandly dialectical (moving in a self-correcting series of American literary or historical periods, for example) but conflictual and contradictory—not an elegant spiral but a dangerous boomerang. The narrator says he has been "boomeranged across my head so much that I now can see the darkness of lightness" (6). That is, he can see now how that universalized, "larger" scheme has obscured a much more mixed and contradictory social vision. His narrative begins with the nation's promise to the narrator's emancipated grandparents, and it parallels several episodes of African American history—including Tuskegee, black veterans' return from World War I, the Great Migration, Harlem, Marcus Garvey, the Popular Front, zoot suits, and the Harlem riot of 1943.[8] Yet history here remains unpredictable, both personally and culturally challenging. It is not the effect of Providence or an "invisible hand," nor does it demonstrate those promises' inevitable unmasking or unmaking. It is instead the complex and changing result of a variety of social forces, including cultural and political action which may expand, limit, reinvigorate, or otherwise change the nation's original promises. The novel insists, therefore, not on a grand vision of history—as in Norton's idealized capitalist plans or the Brotherhood's teleological Marxism—but on the challenge, the experience, and the "hard-earned wisdom" of living with these persistent, boomeranging contradictions, learning to expect "the darkness of lightness" in a more radical democracy. The novel suggests that the nation's dominant tradition might have to learn such wisdom from an invisible tradition that has developed its own sense of "what it took to live in the world with others" (574), just as that invisible tradition has itself had to learn about the "peculiar disposition of the eyes" that has made it largely invisible. The novel also insists that the necessity for such learning across differences will never cease: "Now I know men are different and that all life is divided and that only in division is there true health" (576).

Thus even at the novel's end, readers who might have expected these differences and divisions to be resolved, or who might assume these differences are about to be resolved by the narrative's approaching end, are reminded that this kind of expectation can only lead to the same old paradox, the apparent formal resolution in ritual, superstition, and blindness that leaves the social contradiction intact: "Having tried to give pattern to the chaos which lives within the pattern of your certainties, I must come out, I must emerge" (580–81). This "disembodied voice" of the narrator is hereby "shaking off the old skin" of his role in this particular cultural blindness, "and I'll leave it here in the hole. I'm coming out, no less invisible without it, but coming out nevertheless" (581). That is, the conventionally aesthetic, novelistic, narrative resolution has not resolved his social invisibility in any final way. Yet his narrative has developed the recognition that his invisibility can never be resolved or escaped. This is part of the liability of interacting with other people, who are always prone to the patterns of their own certainties, but who can also come to recognize different patterns within those same certainties. Taking responsibility for his part in this ongoing process may give him "a socially responsible role to play" (581). But given the nature of his invisibility, his playing this socially responsible role will depend at least to some degree and in different ways on his readers, whether we be white, black, blind, invisible, or—more likely—hybrid combinations of these in complex ways. The novel thus ends not with the calm of an achieved social or aesthetic resolution but with a challenge to further aesthetic as well as social encounters of the unpredictable kind he has tried to teach his readers to expect.

He invites such ongoing, unpredictable, transformative encounters with his final, challenging question: "And it is this which frightens me: Who knows but that, on the lower frequencies, I speak for you?" (581). The question acknowledges what the narrator fears and what he cannot know for sure about his own and others' "lower frequencies," emphasizing the unpredictable nature of such encounters with the strangers within himself and the strangers within all of our divided, hybrid selves: Any possible resolution or vision is to be achieved not as an end in novelistic time but in particular encounters within this democratic and therefore unpredictable "complex of man-made positives," encounters with the chaos against which any pattern is conceived. It is out of this kind of encounter with others and out of the chaos within our certainties that the invisible man or woman will always emerge with his or her own plans, blind-nesses, ideals, and loves.

The process of learning about such blindness and invisibil-ity on one's own and others' parts is figured early in two impor-tant scenes in the novel's "Battle Royal" chapter, first when the protagonist and the other nine black boys are brought to the front of the mirrored ballroom to watch the white stripper, with the town's white "big shots" eagerly watching them watch her, and again when all ten blacks are paid to fight blindfolded in the battle royal, here too with the white men eagerly looking on. Both scenes show transference working on a relatively large so-cial scale. Encounters with those who emerge and speak from out of the otherwise unconscious and invisible chaos within and beyond our own certainties become occasions for dramatizing and potentially working through various social blindnesses. The protagonist is learning from others about the temptation to dis-place his own divisions onto someone else and the impossibility of doing so, as long as others can intervene in our psychic divi-sions. The protagonist comes to see in the white men's violent blindness toward the stripper what he otherwise tends not to see in their blindness toward him or in his own blindness toward her. He also manages to see in the woman's invisibility to them what he otherwise tends not to see in her invisibility to him or in his own invisibility to them.

Confronted at once with the stripper's nakedness and with his society's taboo against any suggested intimacy between him and a white woman, he notices first the contradictions being violently displaced by the white men onto him and the other black boys. It appears that the white men have brought the boys up front to watch this stripper as an attempt to deal with their own divided feelings about her dance, with its suggestions of sexual intimacy contradicted by its public, ritualized perfor-mance, her "abstract mask," "impersonal eyes," and "detached expression," such that even the white men might well feel unsure "whether the veil is really being lifted, or lowered more firmly in place" (19, 20, 36). By watching the boys watch the stripper, the men attempt to displace this bar to their own intimate knowledge of the stripper onto the much more violent bar to the black boys' sexual intimacy with any white woman, a bar these men are conventionally entitled to enforce—through Jim Crow laws and especially through the practice and threat of lynching. That is, they attempt to simplify the split they sense within their own position, as both all-seeing and barred from seeing, or as seeing and seen, by shifting this internal difference onto the difference between themselves as unrestricted seers and these more spectacularly restricted boys. The boys' knowledge and vision is supposedly well within their white surveillance and control, either to give within strict limits or to take away. "Some threatened us if we looked and others if we did not." One of the boys wears fighting trunks "much too small to conceal the erection" he tries to hide with his boxing gloves (19–20). In the language of feminist film criticism, these white men attempt to displace their own specularity and castration anxiety onto these boys in order to claim complete control of the gaze.

Like minstrel figures, however, these boys also more openly and clearly display their spectators' own contradictory feelings. Whether or not the white men recognize this dynamic ("some of the more sober ones" do help the stripper escape, 21), the narrator seems at least partly to recognize in their behavior his own temptation to resolve his contradictory feelings through a certain willful blindness toward his own divided feelings and toward her, as if his own unreturned look is all he wants or cares about: "Had the price of looking been blindness, I would have looked" (19). However, his own publicly staged position as both seer and seen, looking and exposed, reminds him repeatedly of the impossibility of securing either the white man's or his own position as only the seer or only the seen, only subject or object and not one subject among other subjects. He wavers, though, between the two split psychic positions this transference has both polarized and dramatized for more critical and creative consideration.

He wants to hide from this dominating gaze—both hide himself from the violence of the white men's gaze and hide her from the violence of theirs and his. On the other hand, he wants to enforce that willful blindness toward her through violence, attempting to turn against her the violence threatened against himself. Insofar as he also recognizes her as another subject, however, not just as a psychic figure for either the dominator or the dominated, he also wants to hide from the perspective of hers that helps him see his own divided position and the violence of his efforts to escape that same division: "I wanted at one and the same time to run from the room, to sink through the floor, or go to her and cover her from my eyes and the eyes of the others with my body; to feel the soft thighs, to caress her and destroy her, to love her and murder her, to hide from her, and yet to stroke where below the small American flag tattooed upon her belly her thighs form a capital V. I had a notion that of all in the room she saw only me with her impersonal eyes" (19).

When the white men seize and toss the stripper into the air, Ellison's protagonist is still caught in the middle: "and above her red, fixed-smiling lips I saw the terror and disgust in her eyes, almost like my own terror and that which I saw in some of the other boys" (20). What he sees beyond his own blindness is not her, exactly, but the possibility of his own invisibility "developed otherwise" as terror and disgust (Deleuze 310), an attempt to look back at and resist the white men's blindness rather than trying to escape, attract, or imitate that blind gaze. He learns from her not how to see clearly but how to see his own and others' blindnesses toward her, and to recognize the terror and disgust he feels about his own and others' invisibility to those he assumed could or would see him better than they actually do. In short, he learns more about his own blindness by seeing it mirrored in that of the white men, and he learns more about his own invisibility by seeing it mirrored in that of the other black boys and the white woman.

As he has announced in the chapter's first paragraph, "I had to discover that I am an invisible man" (15), and it is in scenes like this one that he makes that necessarily repeated discovery and models that process of repeated discovery for his readers. It is not a single unveiling resulting in a revelation of a static truth, but an ethical, social, rhetorical, and political lesson, such that he has to learn that lesson again and again in particular ways in his encounters with "a variety of American types as they operated on various levels of society" (xxii). He will learn that he is invisible in different ways depending on the particular blindnesses of, for example, Norton, Bledsoe, Brockway, Brother Jack, Ras, Mary, and Sybil. His series of lessons in invisibility argue not for his own or even everyone's pluralistic self-expression, but for the necessity of all such parties' learning continually from each other, not by trusting the higher justice of Providence or the pathos and dignity of *Shantih*, but by taking responsibility for what it takes "to live in the world with others" (574). It is Ellison's insistence on such interactive, transformative encounters that makes his vision of American democracy more demanding than pluralist multiculturalism, since he expects not just self-expression but listening and negotiation, and a more hopeful vision than that of oppositional multiculturalism, since he expects such interaction to result in significant transformations. Again, as Chantal Mouffe writes of this more radical sense of democracy, "it is not a matter of establishing a mere alliance between given interests but of actually modifying the very identity of these forces" (235).

The other conspicuous figure in the novel's first chapter for the conditions that Ellison's narrator suggests he shares with readers, comparably endangered, implicated, and challenged by our persistent blindnesses and invisibilities, is the protagonist's experience fighting blindfolded and anonymous in the battle royal. In this case the white men stage another spectacle that displaces onto the black boys both the willful, violent blindness of their own white supremacist society and the threat of violent retaliation against that white supremacy, a threat their own willful blindness attempts to render nearly invisible by representing it in this demeaning way. The blindfolding of their hired actors is designed to blind not only the boys but indirectly the men themselves, blinding them to what they might otherwise see in the looks of those they taunt, both the source of this staged violence in themselves (so that they will not have to see the black boys seeing them) and the threats of retaliation against themselves by the objects of their violence. Thus their violence and their racism become invisible to the blindfolded boys but also verbally more explicit once the blindfolds are in place: "Let me at that big nigger!" (21). They can also watch the violence of their own threats be carried out not by them but by the terrified boys themselves, and watch the return of that violence be directed not at the white men goading the black boys on but at the other boys.

Again, however, the men's attempt to simplify and displace onto others their own blindness also clarifies for the narrator and his readers both the white men's position in their society and the protagonist's own related position. The episode becomes another potential lesson for the narrator and his readers in how his own blindness is implicated in that of the white men and how his own invisibility compares with that of the other black boys in the ring. The narrator has come to understand that he became involved in the battle royal because "in those pre-invisible days," that is, before he realized he was invisible, "I visualized myself as a potential Booker T. Washington," determined to "lead his people in the proper paths," as defined and applauded by the white men in supposedly unthreatened and benevolent control of his society (18, 32). Blindfolded in the ring, however, he strains to distinguish the supposedly benevolent school superintendent's voice from the blind racism and violence dramatized by the white men's taunts. Their attempt to project their blindness and violence visually onto him has prevented him from seeing but has helped him *hear* both the racism and the violence that have become more explicit and less distinct from the white men's pretended benevolence. The protagonist's ritualized humiliation of himself in the battle royal and in the indignities of his speech—"What powers of endurance I had during those days! What enthusiasm! What a belief in the rightness of things!" (30)—begins to represent more dramatically the normally invisible price he has been blindly willing to pay for the white men's approval.

The battle royal dramatizes for the protagonist the otherwise unseen social humiliation and his participation in the humiliation of his peers: "I felt superior to them in my way, and I didn't like the manner in which we were all crowded together into the servants' elevator" (18). Although he manages to watch them through a loosened blindfold, thinking again (like the white men) that he sees while the others are blind, he still discovers too late what they have arranged among themselves for the final fight, invisibly to him in his assumptions about their suitability for their assigned roles. Thus he also discovers too late that Tatlock, whom he has seen as only a "stupid clown," wants to win that fight not just for the white men in his assigned role but for his own reasons (25, 24).

This opening chapter makes the white men's blindness and the black boys' invisibility spectacular, offering for the narrator's and his readers' transference these opportunities to begin reflecting on our own blindnesses and invisibilities. Before the narrator can do much reflecting, however, the surprise scholarship in the briefcase sets him blindly running again. Perhaps like Eliot, Ellison recognizes how such a rapid, potentially overwhelming succession of spectacles often inhibits the learning Ellison seems to hope these spectacles will model and provoke, at least in the more variable pace of reading.[9] But the protagonist's growing suspicions about what has happened to him throughout this chapter do at least resurface in his dream, and the chapter ends by stressing that these suspicions will not be easily dispelled. They will function instead as a premonition and as fertile ground for the elaboration and analysis of more such suspicions and lessons: "It was a dream I was to remember and dream again for many years after," although "at that time I had no insight into its meaning. First I had to attend college" (33).

In this potentially meaningful dream, then, set at a circus, the narrator's grandfather refused "to laugh at the clowns no matter what they did" (33). The narrator's battle royal experience is framed by the chapter's final return to its opening reflections on the puzzling example of this grandfather and the alternative tradition of "blues-toned laughter" (xvi) he represents. It is a tradition that the narrator has suggested he would only gradually learn to appreciate in the narrative to follow: "I am not ashamed of my grandparents for having been slaves. I am only ashamed of myself for having at one time been ashamed" (15). Instead of being ashamed of being a slave himself, and instead of laughing at the "clowns" in the narrator's dream in the way that the white men and the narrator have laughed at Tatlock and the other boys in the battle royal, this grandfather only laughs later, when the narrator recognizes the engraved document in his briefcase as a ploy to "Keep This Nigger-Boy Running" (33). And the grandfather laughs in a way that the narrator does not yet know how to laugh.

The grandfather's "blues-toned laughter" does not deny or escape the blindness or the invisibility he and his grandson share, their self-blinding implication in just such empty promises as well as the invisibility and suffering that such self-blinding attempts to ignore. His laughter does not attempt to displace that blindness and invisibility altogether onto someone else, but recognizes and learns enough from that dramatized reminder of his own blindness and invisibility to respond to his grandson's story both sympathetically and supportively, negatively and affirmatively, critically and yet also lyrically or idealistically, not in the privileged innocence of Huck's private moral decision, nor in the pathos and dignity of *The Waste Land*'s generalized irony, but in a blues-toned laughter or song. Ellison explains elsewhere that the blues "provide no solution, offer no scapegoat but the self" (*Shadow and Act* 94). "The blues is an impulse to keep the painful details and episodes of a brutal experience alive in one's aching consciousness, to finger its jagged grain, and to transcend it, not by the consolation of philosophy but by squeezing from it a near-tragic, near-comic lyricism" (78).

What the narrator suggests he will learn from his experience at college, then, is the importance and potential support of this alternative tradition of blues-toned laughter as he encounters the blindnesses and invisibilities of various American types. The end of the first chapter has introduced his experience at college as the first step in learning something from his grandfather's inscrutable laughter in his recurring dream. Ellison's allusions and imagery in the following chapter will also insist that his readers consider the lessons of this college in relation to blindnesses associated specifically with Eliot's *Waste Land*. These pages are dense with allusions to Eliot's title and phrases, and they are full of a similar imagery of memory, springtime, aridity, madness, a bell in a chapel tower, loneliness, a stagnant river, war veterans, sordid sexuality, castration, music, ironic disillusionment, and blindness.

Eliot's poem is alluded to most explicitly as Ellison's narrator closes his eyes to remember his own and others' blindnesses at the college (35). What he recognizes now but did not see then was how much the college's green and "flower-studded" promise obscured a barren and arid wasteland. Here again, where Eliot stresses especially historical and cultural change, Ellison stresses a difference in cultural perspective between the view of the college promoted by its administration and philanthropist trustees, and another view of the college that he has learned about since. What gives this wasteland its false bloom is not the cultural or educational revelation promised by Washington's figure of casting your buckets down wherever you are. Its bloom depends instead on the unreliable, condescending powers of philanthropic (white) northern multimillionaires (34–37),[10] along with their unacknowledged southern allies in white supremacy, "the kind of white man I feared," "those others," "stronger," who speak to the students "through blood and violence and ridicule and condescension" as if they are "themselves our thunder and lightning" (41, 112). In the blindness of his days at the college, as in the battle royal scene, the protagonist strained to distinguish the multimillionaires' benevolence from the violence of these unacknowledged allies, yet he looks back now as if the effect of both was the same, keeping him and the other black students running invisibly in place.

This Eliot-like juxtaposition of a once naively accepted ideal with an ironically disillusioned economic and social memory has been reiterated in all the novel's opening frames, as if this sense of a generalized cultural contradiction and dead end is the rhetorical and cultural common ground that the narrator assumes he shares with his readers and therefore the starting point of his own narrative, perhaps a starting point he is having trouble moving beyond ("I came to realize that my pilot was also experiencing difficulty in seeing *himself*" xiii). Coming just after the prologue and chapter 1, this opening section of chapter 2 is the last of these at least three opening frames for the novel. Counting the epigraphs from Melville and Eliot would make five frames, the thirtieth anniversary introduction would make six, and the aborted war novel would make seven. This multiplication of frames suggests the importance and difficulty of negotiating a space for a different (mostly invisible) vision within this more powerful (Eliotic) cultural context. Along with these other frames, this last, in which he remembers his blindness at the college, insists on the distance between himself now and "that other life that's dead," now that "neither that time nor that 'I' are any more" (37). Yet the novel is not ending here but still beginning, in a generalized modernist irony at the apparent obsolescence or failure of these naive cultural visions. To end in irony toward those naive cultural visions would mean pretending that he could escape as his pilot could not from the continuing social and economic power of those same visions.

Instead, the novel takes a dramatic turn in method away from Eliot's ironic juxtapositions of past and present to its own more rhetorically oriented narrative. That is, after the last in this series of explicitly double-voiced, then-and-now, ironic opening frames, the narrator will effectively close his eyes again and take up as a character a series of cultural blindnesses he is likely to share with at least some of his readers, modeling for them and for other characters his learning about his own particular blindnesses in his encounters with those of others. He will take up a series of blindnesses that correspond with various levels of society and also various periods in American cultural history. But instead of stressing the chronology of these cultural periods in any nostalgic, ironic, or teleological way, Ellison will emphasize the potential for cross-cultural learning between these various social levels and cultural periods as they continue to interact. He will demonstrate how such interaction and transference help cultures and individuals reflect on themselves and learn from each other, transforming themselves in their encounters with each other. "So why do I write, torturing myself to put it down? Because in spite of myself I've learned some things. Without the possibility of action, all knowledge comes to one labeled 'file and forget,' and I can neither file nor forget" (579). These experiences lead to learning and acting on what he learns.

Given the protagonist's initial "belief in the rightness of things," it is appropriate that he begins his narrative of his time at the college with his encounter with Mr. Norton, described as "a bearer of the white man's burden" and "a symbol of the Great Traditions," a man with "a face pink like Saint Nicholas'," who first speaks and acts from within American cultural traditions of idealism and romance (37). Norton exemplifies particular blindnesses of a romantic idealism that the protagonist at this time largely shares, except that their conversation allows the protagonist to look back at that vision from the perspective of one of its invisible objects and not just as one of its blind subjects. From this different angle, that idealizing vision looks as mystifying as it is inspiring.

Norton has supported the Founder's "vision" to turn what was once "barren ground" into this beautiful campus, and his voice seems "loaded with more meaning than I could fathom" as the narrator puzzles over how anyone's "fate" could "be *pleasant*" (38–40), which seems counter to his own harder experience and to what he has learned from his study of Greek plays. The man alludes to a likely literary source of such American idealism (and such ideas about fate) when he identifies himself as "a New Englander, like Emerson" (41) and thus as a member of what Ellison earlier called "that tradition of intellectual evasion for which Thoreau criticized Emerson in regard to the Fugitive Slave Law" (*Shadow and Act* 36).

Seeming to speak "to himself alone," Norton begins to attribute his own fate, as well as the protagonist's, to the almost otherworldly influence of his daughter, "a being more rare, more beautiful, purer, more perfect and more delicate than the wildest dream of a poet. . . . Her beauty was a well-spring of purest water-of-life, and to look upon her was to drink and drink and drink again" (42). Norton here speaks the language of escapist American romance in its idealization of the feminine, especially in landscape, as "compliant and supportive," with "the attributes simultaneously of a virginal bride and a non-threatening mother" (Baym 135). This language echoes the narrator's fondest memories of the college campus as he remembers how he identified himself "with the rich man reminiscing on the rear seat" (39). Yet he also remembers noticing the difference in power that leaves his own idealizations and identifications less protected than Norton's. He remembers wondering even then "what in the world had made him open his heart to me. That was something I never did; it was dangerous" (39, 43). Like the characters in

Morrison's *Beloved* who have learned to love "small," the narrator is reminded here of other social histories and other cultural traditions that urge a less idealized confidence than Norton has in the fates meted out in the larger world.

The blindnesses and invisibilities concealed in Norton's and the narrator's own romantic idealism become even clearer to the invisible man and his readers as he listens to Norton move from the rhetoric of romance to that of American realism and large-scale industrial and economic power. Although the language of realism is set off from the "dreamy," personalized purity of a younger American past, much as *Huckleberry Finn*'s realism and cynicism about post-Reconstruction America contrast with its nostalgia for a simpler national boyhood and private moral decisions, Ellison makes the historical shift from romance to realism seem less important than its cultural continuity in a "tradition of intellectual evasion," an evasion dependent on social and economic power to guard its personal space (*Shadow and Act* 36).

Norton's daughter is almost transparently a romantic cliché, and Norton begins to sound almost like Emmeline Grangerford mourning her death: "She was too pure for life, . . . too pure and too good and too beautiful," and she was already dying as she and her father crossed the Alps on their world tour (43). The narrator has noticed the contrast between the "soft, flimsy" fashions in her photo and the more contemporary, "smart, well-tailored, angular, sterile, streamlined, engine-turned, air-conditioned modern outfits you see in the women's magazines," in which "she would appear as ordinary as an expensive piece of machine-tooled jewelry and just as lifeless" (43). But in the conversation that follows, Norton's idealism and the narrator's come to seem less opposed to—and more dependent upon—that social and economic power that Norton already has and that the protagonist more blindly hopes to have sometime in the future.

Norton's monument to his daughter's memory is his "firsthand organizing of human life" (42). According to Norton's organizational plan, "Through you and your fellow students, I become, let us say, three hundred teachers, seven hundred trained mechanics, eight hundred skilled farmers, and so on." The protagonist is important, Norton explains, "because if you fail *I* have failed by one individual, one defective cog" (45).

There are plenty of hints for the protagonist and his readers here as to his own (and his readers') invisibility in Norton's larger plans: "You don't even know my name, I thought, wondering what it was all about" (45). But the protagonist distrusts such hints, since "in those pre-invisible days" (before he learned of his own invisibility), he identifies despite himself with Norton's project. He hopes to benefit from these "big shots'" position in that larger organization of society, and he is almost as blind as they are to the invisibility this social organization imposes on him and most others. For example, he denies the invisibility that the college imposes on those like Trueblood living just beyond its boundaries, those the students virtually blame for their own social exclusion: "How all of us at the college hated the black-belt people, the 'peasants,' during those days! We were trying to lift them up and they, like Trueblood, did everything it seemed to pull us down" (47). The narrator reenacts Norton's, his own, and other students' condescension and blindness toward Trueblood, but the narrator will also suggest an incipient awareness that he might also learn from Trueblood and others to recognize and return these blind looks "developed otherwise" (Deleuze 310).

The protagonist himself will later be called a "mechanical man" by the veteran and ex-surgeon at the Golden Day (94), who better understands from his own experience how this social and economic machine renders invisible not only the peasants but even the educated black professionals and middle class. Still later, when the protagonist tries to deny Peter Wheatstraw on the street in New York, Wheatstraw will also try to explain that "folks is always making plans and changing 'em," suggesting that Norton's machine is not the only possible blueprint for social organization. But the protagonist is still almost completely attached to his original plan, currently the most widely approved national plan for African Americans, as if they are not in fact largely invisible but only need to cast down their buckets where they are. While the protagonist thinks that changing plans is "a mistake. You have to stick to the plan," Wheatstraw will suggest living in a more negotiable and improvisational complex of man-made positives. "You kinda young, daddy-o," he says. "Damn if I'm-a let 'em run *me* into my grave" (175). Wheatstraw tries to explain that instead of accepting "the man's" organizing of human life as given and monolithic, immune to challenge and difference, "all it takes to get along in this here man's town is a little shit, grit and mother-wit" (176).

Instead of Norton's faith in the dominant social and economic machine, Wheatstraw urges a more democratic and flexible response to their social fate, one that is also more supportive and practical. Wheatstraw tries to remind the protagonist of a ready and useful source for that "shit, grit and mother-wit" in the African American folklore he now remembers learning as a child "back of school" (176). Wheatstraw also warns the protagonist against denying him on the street and thus denying what the protagonist might learn personally from him and from the traditions he represents: "I'll teach you some good bad habits" (176). And the blues song Wheatstraw sings suggests the humorous personal difference his own idealizations can make, even in a racist society:

> She's got feet like a monkey
> Legs like a frog—Lawd, Lawd!
> But when she starts to loving me
> I holler Whoooo, God-dog!
> Cause I loves my baabay,
> Better than I do myself.

(173)

Intervening as if to prevent the protagonist from becoming completely a "mechanical man," Wheatstraw speaks to Ellison's protagonist as Jim might have spoken to Huck if Twain's realism had not so overpowered the interpersonal potential of Huck and Jim's interaction. But Ellison's protagonist is still less interested in respecting and learning from people's varied perspectives and experiences than he is in pursuing his own grand, assimilationist, autocolonial plan to shape reality as much as he can in the image of his internalized ideal. This grand, inflexible plan is both a reflection on Norton's particular plan for African Americans and also a figure for any such blindness to the apparent "chaos against which [any] pattern [is] conceived" (580). One "realist" factor that works repeatedly and instructively to undermine the protagonist's dedication to Norton's plan, however, is his own lack of democratic power to help shape and carry out that plan except as a virtually blind and invisible "mechanical man."

Norton's "firsthand organizing of human life" (42) may effectively support Norton's own freedom to idealize his daughter's memory, but this support depends on power that the protagonist simply does not possess. Without that economic power, the protagonist can only focus vaguely on his own function within a larger machine that is distantly devoted to the mystified ideals of someone else. And he begins to notice the effects of this distance and detachment on his own relationships: "Perhaps everyone loved someone; I didn't know, I couldn't give much thought to love; in order to travel far you had to be detached, and I had the long road back to the campus before me" (177).

He is still dedicated anonymously to what he understands to be his society's dominant hierarchy of ideals. His inability to form his own idealizations or to love particular people is reflected in his socially sanctioned difficulty in giving sustained attention to any of the novel's women characters or even to African American characters such as Tod Clifton, Tarp, or others in his Harlem district. As a mechanical cog in Norton's monumental machine, he is in a sense already dedicated to the memory of Norton's daughter without understanding why. His continuing inability to love particular people, however, does show incipient signs of critical consciousness and change as he witnesses others' feelings and actions toward Tod Clifton and reconsiders his own during the funeral march, as well as his feelings and actions toward Sybil and Mary. These relationships, he is slowly coming to learn, demand particular, personal idealizations, as well as their careful extrapolation into political principles. Thus the protagonist will later realize he cannot just denounce the society that has hurt him so "because in spite of all I find that I love" (580). Even here at the novel's end, he still may not be ready to love anyone in particular, but he does at least affirm the personal and political principles based on such a democratic variety of loves and idealizations in "a complex of man-made positives."[11]

The protagonist is by no means the only one to assume a blind and invisible coglike place in a larger plan, and it is especially his instructive encounters with others' comparable blindnesses and invisibilities that help him learn gradually about his own. Bledsoe is one such "mechanical man," as Brockway is as well in his different sphere. Brother Jack enlists the protagonist in another such grand plan ("The organization had given the world a new shape, and me a vital role. . . . Life was all pattern and discipline; and the beauty of discipline is when it works" 382). Eventually, though, the protagonist learns from his encounters with Jack and the Brotherhood about the blindness of this plan toward Tod Clifton and the rest of the Harlem district, as he also learns from his encounters with Tod and others in Harlem about his own invisibility in the Brotherhood's plan.

The protagonist also considers the tempting blindnesses and dramatized invisibilities of Ras's plan and the plans of Dupre and others who participate in the riot. In his last waking dream, however, the narrator has begun to learn the danger of either creating or becoming such an inflexibly mechanical man. He has also begun to learn the difficulty of stopping such a mechanical man except by the "good bad habits" that Wheatstraw calls "shit, grit and mother-wit," including such habits as democratic negotiation and improvisation. In this last dream the "history" made by all those who have variously "run" the protagonist takes the form of an armored bridge dripping the blood and seed of his own blinding and castration; the bridge is *striding like a robot, an iron man. . . . And then I struggled up, full of sorrow and pain, shouting*"—to Jack, Emerson, Bledsoe, Norton, Tobitt, and others—" *'No, no, we must stop him!'* " (570). He has been tempted to seek revenge by adopting an ironic version of their realism, planning and watching with a sense of his own invisible power as others' plans assumed an iron life of their own or "exploded in their faces" (511). He might thus earn a certain pathos and dignity similar to that of the speaker of Eliot's *Waste Land*. But he has also learned how much he and people he does care about are all involved in the intricate mechanisms of all these plans—how Clifton, Sybil, Dupre, Lottie, Scofield, and others can get invisibly caught up in these explosions—and how they are all therefore responsible for their parts in either watching helplessly or intervening in their overlapping histories.

Thus the invisible man's plans in the epilogue to emerge from his hibernation are conceived not independently of these other plans nor as a triumph over these other plans with an unassailable plan of his own. Instead he has learned from each of them, having "finger[ed] its jagged grain." He has both acknowledged and challenged the historical, cultural, and personal power of each of these other plans. He has learned from Bledsoe, for example, about the power of white supremacy despite the college's rhetoric of faith in American promises, but he comes to reject Bledsoe's self-serving cynicism. He also learns from the Brotherhood about the power of economic structures as well as the power of organization, but he has seen their organization overlook or refuse racial and personal questions. In the series of lessons he learns from each of these visions, he reminds his readers and himself of the more general idea that "the mind that has conceived a plan of living must never lose sight of the chaos against which that pattern was conceived" (580). This does not mean that he will end with only a generalized modernist irony at the chaos that underlies and undermines any and every such plan. It means that even his own final word has to reopen itself somehow to what he cannot see or predict from others but what he invites in our response.[12]

He ends, then, with a question to his unpredictable readers: "Who knows but that, on the lower frequencies, I speak for you?" (581). This ending of Ellison's novel in a "hole in the ground," able only to promise and invite ongoing engagements with his readers, does come dangerously close to endorsing the culturally powerful position of ironic modernist detachment that I am arguing his novel attempts to challenge. But his final question suggests that he still depends on interacting with and being recognized by others. He has not achieved a final detachment or escape; instead, he is trapped until his question gains a response.

The scene at Trueblood's cabin may serve as one final instance of what can be learned from cross-cultural encounters generally and from the more specific encounter between the "shit, grit and mother-wit" of Ellison's novel and the modernist irony exemplified by Eliot's poem. The language of the second chapter changes again here from the romantic idealism of Norton's memories of his daughter and the realism of his powerful "organizing of human life" to the modernist irony of Eliot's poem.

As the invisible man drives Norton beyond the boundaries of the campus toward Trueblood's cabin, they are "swept by a wave of scorching air and it was as though we were approaching a desert" (46). As in the chapter's opening memories, the image here of a wasteland and "heart of darkness" (579) just beyond the college's most idealized facade is reinforced by Norton's "horror" as he hears about and meets Trueblood: "You have looked upon chaos and are not destroyed!" (50, 51). Trueblood's story invites an irony toward both Norton's romantic ideals "too pure for life" and his attempt to organize society in the image of those ideals. That is, it invites, then veers away from, a much more generalized irony at the apparent corruption of any and all idealization or love beyond human repair—though implicitly not beyond contemplation from a modernist position of relative safety, pathos, and dignity. Like the other white male audiences who have asked Trueblood to repeat his story again and again, Norton is obviously fascinated. Norton considers Trueblood's story from the relatively detached perspective of horror, but his fascination invites suspicion about the supposed purity of his own idealization of his daughter in his memory and in his "first-hand organizing of human life."

The wider social echo of that idealization of Norton's blond daughter is recognizable in Trueblood's own fantasies and fears of sex with a white woman dressed in white as he sleeps beside his daughter, Matty Lou. Norton's own possessiveness toward his daughter is also recognizable in the mirror of Trueblood's own jealousy of Matty Lou and his half-dreaming, half-waking act of incest. Norton's blindness toward his daughter and everyone else who is made invisible by his "machine" becomes most clearly dramatized in Trueblood's wife's and Matty Lou's own horror at what he has done to them in his sleep. Trueblood's story drama- tizes much that was only implicit in Norton's own account of his love for his daughter. The effect is not only the realist sense of a personal ideal overpowered or overtaken by larger social forces but an ideal corrupt to its very core, its heart of chaos and darkness.

But Trueblood recounts his story after having learned some- thing from a night of singing the blues, and it is here that the difference between Eliot's poem and Ellison's novel perhaps be- comes clear. Trueblood has been tempted to leave, but "I made up my mind that I was goin' back home and face Kate; yeah, and face Matty Lou too" (66). "I wanted to go off by myself agin, but it don't do no good tryin' to run off from somethin' like that. It follows you wherever you go. Besides, to git right down to the facts, there wasn't nowhere I could go. I didn't have a cryin' dime!" (67). Again, what Ellison seems to appreciate in the "near-tragic, near-comic lyricism" of the blues (*Shadow and Act* 78) and the "blues-toned laughter" of Trueblood's storytelling (xvi) is the tendency to refuse, or at least to make do without, escape, scapegoats, or other escapist solutions—solutions such as trusting to private morality or to Providence, as in Twain's novel, or to "a loved one waiting," as in Hemingway's novel, or trusting to *Shantih* or the pathos and dignity of irony, as in Eliot's poem.

Trueblood invites and challenges his immediate audience, both the relatively "blind" Norton and the relatively "invisible" protagonist—as well as the narrator's blind and invisible, varied and hybrid readers—to supply an explanation for two things he says he does not understand about his own story. First, when he tells about flinching under Kate's ax like Gawain under the Green Knight's ax, when "Anybody but Jesus Christ hisself woulda moved," he says that "the part I don't understand" is that, "more'n the pain and numbness I feels relief" (64). Readers are likely to wonder, why would he *not* feel relief at having escaped the ax? But as far as Trueblood is concerned, any such ending in relief would make no more than momentary sense. What might be a Providential, comic solution were this the magical ending of his story, as it virtually is in Gawain's romance or in the myth of the Fisher King that Eliot makes so much use of in his poem, cannot be a viable solution in Trueblood's situation: he has still committed incest, and both Kate and Matty Lou are still deeply offended, shamed, and pregnant. They are not merely the American romance plot's feminine "entrappers and domesticators" (Baym 133). Trueblood knows that his own story cannot end in the relief of comedy or idealism. Nor can it end for Trueblood in an ironic sense of tragedy, though many like Norton have listened intently to his story and paid him off as if he functions for them as a scapegoat and a catharsis. His question about why he would feel relief, then, implies a more challenging question about why his listeners might also mistakenly feel relief.

This is directly related to the second thing he challenges his audience to try to understand: "That's what I don't understand. I done the worse thing a man could ever do in his family and instead of chasin' me out of the country, they gimme more help than they ever give any other colored man, no matter how good a nigguh he was" (67). What Trueblood does not understand—any more than Louis Armstrong is said to understand his invisibility in the novel's prologue, despite his proficiency in the blues—is how his audience could so mistake the "near-tragic, near-comic lyricism" of his experience as to interpret it either as comic idealism or tragic irony. Ellison invites his readers instead to recognize how Trueblood serves as a necessary scapegoat for both those traditions of blind idealism and blind escape, serving both to distance and to dramatize what is otherwise invisible and denied in those traditions. Trueblood's story dramatizes these traditions' implication in Trueblood's own idealization of white women and his correspondingly possessive, incestuous idealization of his daughter. His story also dramatizes how these traditions project onto people like Trueblood the motivations and consequences of those same idealizations. But Trueblood's story also proposes for his listeners' consideration his own response to his own story, the near-comic, near-tragic lyricism of the blues, thereby inviting his listeners to take responsibility for their own response.

Ellison recognizes and demonstrates how a relative lack of social and material power ("there wasn't nowhere I could go. I didn't have a cryin' dime!") can powerfully encourage a sense of inescapable responsibility like Trueblood's. He also recognizes how that inescapable responsibility has been creatively shaped into valuable traditions of "shit, grit and mother-wit" in confronting shared problems without ready solutions or escapes, but with courage, loyalty, and creativity. These traditions in

American culture have often been learned "back of school," for example, in African American folklore, in the blues, or in jazz. They emerge out of the invisibility and "chaos" against which more powerful traditions have been conceived: that of American romance, with its often idealized sense of Providential freedom and escape from the confinements of the Old World, or American realism, with its frequent sense that such escapes are inevitably overpowered by larger social or natural forces, or American modernism, with its often generalized irony toward all idealization and its tendency to offer no alternatives to the idealizations it undercuts, effectively leaving those unchallenged ideals in place. These dominant traditions have much to learn from the countertraditions taught and learned "back of school," and much of American literature models this fitful, sometimes eager, sometimes anxious attempt to learn from what it has also often tried to deny and forget, learning about its own most familiar stories as well as about others that show its own in different lights. The democratic, cross-cultural encounters in which this learning sometimes occurs are among this nation's most promising resources.

4

The Challenges of
Responsibility in
T. S. Eliot's *The Waste Land*

THE WASTE LAND (1922) MAY SEEM STRANGE COMPANY for Morrison's, Twain's, and Ellison's novels to keep in this study of domination, democracy, and cross-cultural learning in American literature. It does not address political questions of class, gender, and race as explicitly as these three novels do, or at least it is not often read as if it does. But both the form and content of Eliot's poem posed for Ellison and others important cross-cultural and interpersonal issues in American modernism, especially in terms of the accelerated, cosmopolitan clash of genres and cultures associated with both high modernism and the jazz age, and in terms of modernism's dramatized sense of its own hermetic isolation. Ellison's novel insists on the repeated process of surviving the clash of cultures and emerging from isolation and disillusionment, the process of recognizing each other and taking responsibility both for our various certainties and for what those certainties might conceal. *Invisible Man* models a necessary, healthy, ongoing dialectic of negation and repair as we recognize and negotiate our differences.

One reason for reversing chronology in my treatment of Ellison and Eliot is the hope that Ellison's emphasis on this possibility of repair in the wake of negation can help readers appreciate the different focus on negation in Eliot's poem, represented by Eliot as a near-total breakdown of personal and cultural abilities to recognize differences. As Jessica Benjamin writes in more psychoanalytic terms, "The experience of repair can retroactively light up destruction's creative, differentiating side, which has the effect of placing the other in a space outside coercive reconciliation" (*Shadow* 97). Next to Ellison's novel, it is easier to see how Eliot's poem does dismantle and differentiate false unities and reconciliations in dominant American cultural traditions. Eliot's poem both recognizes a challenging responsibility toward cultural and personal difference and explores a personal and cultural inability to meet that challenge.

The Waste Land thus becomes a dramatic reflection on what Morrison calls the "solitude" and "separate confinement" of canonical American literature, considered not just as a symptom but as the poem's focus and struggle. I will attempt to demonstrate, largely through a close reading of the poem, that the explicit problem in *The Waste Land* is not that there is too much difference for any one cultural center to hold within its orbit, as the poem is often read, but that there is far too little difference within the poem's world, or rather that there is too little difference that the poem and its most familiar cultural traditions quite know how to address.

The poem invokes a fearful sense of potentially transforming differences and encounters, but it focuses on the personal and cultural indifference and fear of difference that prevent such necessary metamorphoses, as suggested by the "arid plain" named in the poem's title and by the figure of Tiresias, "the most important personage in the poem, uniting all the rest" (424, 218n).[1] In Tiresias, all characters "melt" into one (218n); as for events, Tiresias has "foresuffered all" (243) and "foretold the rest" (229).

Eliot suggests a more positive cross-cultural potential in his 1950 introduction to *Huckleberry Finn,* explaining how "Huck in fact would be incomplete without Jim." Citing Jim's redefinition of "trash" as "what people is dat puts dirt on de head er dey fren's en makes 'em ashamed," along with Huck's reluctant apology, Eliot's comments suggest something about his own characteristic focus as a reader and writer of such encounters with other people and other cultures. While Jim's own pathos and

dignity are "moving enough . . . what I find still more disturbing, and still more unusual in literature, is the pathos and dignity of the boy, when reminded so humbly and humiliatingly,
that his position in the world is not that of other boys, entitled
from time to time to a practical joke; but that he must bear, and
bear alone, the responsibility of a man" (324). What Huck learns
here from his own humiliation and from Jim's humble reminder
of their cross-cultural friendship is described in terms of Huck's
unshared, masculine, and adult "responsibility" to Jim. He is
expected to bear that responsibility alone and not to shift it onto
"other boys."

Because of their higher class status (and racial status), "other
boys" like Tom would feel entitled to an occasional practical
joke at Jim's expense, they would condone such practical jokes
by others like Huck, and they would even demand that Jim condone such practical jokes at his own expense. Huck's difference
from Tom appears not merely in Huck's lack of, or skepticism
toward, the conventional habits of reading and imagination on
which Tom and his society depend, but in this second, more
challenging sense of responsibility or responsiveness toward another person speaking a different idiom from his own. But this
possibility is precisely where Eliot stops, describing Huck only
in vague, negative terms: "his position is not that of other boys,"
he is not Tom, he is not in control in this situation. When Eliot
attempts to give this responsibility and relationship a less ambiguous form and a name, he can only call it a "style" (as perhaps Ellison and his character Peter Wheatstraw would as well),
something not quite spoken but which would appeal nonetheless to shared recognitions, conventions, rituals. And it is precisely the style of *The Waste Land* that has proven most useful
to other writers, perhaps because its style allows for and calls
attention to the challenge of negotiating and evaluating the
meaning and value of its "heap of broken images" in a recognizably modern variety of cultural and cross-cultural contexts.

But Eliot's essay characteristically shifts its focus at this point from the encounter between Huck and Jim to their encounter with the River, which he describes less in interpersonal or cross-cultural terms than in terms of the natural and the supernatural compared to Huck's own "unconsciousness": "It is Huck who gives the book style. The River gives the book its form." Social and racial questions do not quite disappear, but they seem impossible to address. In the ensuing description of the Mississippi River as "a treacherous and capricious dictator" which sometimes "runs with a speed such that no man or beast can survive in it," and which then "carries down human bodies, cattle and houses" (324, 325), there are obvious traces of the history of slavery and race which Eliot's abstraction here almost covers over. The traces of that largely unspoken history and the traces of Jim's ability to respond to Huck tend to be reframed as the unspoken and perhaps metaphysically unspeakable, in a limit-case of silence, death, and absolute submission to the natural force of the River. Eliot has written about such traces in less muted terms in his "Dry Salvages" (1941), published nine years before this introduction:

> . . . the torment of others remains an experience
> Unqualified, unworn by subsequent attrition.
> People change, and smile: but the agony abides.
> Time the destroyer is time the preserver,
> Like the river with its cargo of dead Negroes, cows and
>   chicken coops.
>
> *(Collected Poems* 195)

But this "agony of others, nearly experienced, / Involving ourselves" (195), when it cannot quite be articulated and mourned in terms of Eliot's sense of the surrounding and surviving world, when it remains as apparently unspeakable as the "dead Negroes" floating unnamed and unburied throughout Eliot's poem, as sometimes also in Twain's and Morrison's novels, becomes for Eliot not a question Huck and Jim could attempt to negotiate in their relationship with each other, but a figure for the forever unspeakable, the eternal, "Time" itself. The interpersonal, cross-cultural challenge shifts to the metaphysical, though the river's description as a "strong brown god" (192) still shows the marks of race.

Less dramatically than he would in *The Waste Land* itself, Eliot writes in his early essays of a modern civilization of such "great variety and complexity" that "the poet must become more and more comprehensive, more allusive, more indirect, in order to force, to dislocate if necessary, language into his meaning." The language available to the poet needs such forcing and dislocating because it cannot otherwise accommodate either the variety and complexity of modern life or the meaning of modernity's effects on the poet's "refined sensibility" (*Selected Essays* 248). In the "mythical method" that he admires in Joyce's *Ulysses*, that he has used himself in *The Waste Land*, and that he here indirectly attempts to explain, Eliot suggests a similar dislocation of myths into unaccustomed encounters across centuries and cultures. But he makes the whole procedure sound like a forced unity, a false reconciliation of the variety and complexity of modern life. It is an aesthetic that seems to reflect on a failing colonialism, a failing social hierarchy, and a failing religious discourse. Modern life presents a challenge he feels almost alone in addressing, unsupported by his own most familiar culture's history, order, or systems of belief.

The Waste Land's title, epigraph, and opening section title, "The Burial of the Dead," suggest the aftermath of a disaster. That disaster has often been read in natural terms, but it is also a disaster that has overwhelmed personal and cultural means of renewal, recovery, and renegotiation, prompting a vague fear of interpersonal and cross-cultural encounters and the responsibilities attendant on those encounters. The poem begins with a nod to Chaucer and to the quasi-mythic, epic tone of culturally shared epigrams and seasonal catalogs, but the epic beginning is undercut by a contrast with present feelings and circumstances.

The poem's opening dramatizes the repeated failure of any such higher vision and soon retreats into unconnected private nostalgias ("And when we were children, staying at the arch-duke's, / My cousin's" 13–14). As the poem attempts to begin again in its second stanza, as if with a new decorum, the tone is less that of epic than a parodic, whining, unheeded jeremiad, recalling the epigraph's image of the weary, mocked, and imprisoned sybil. Like the sybil's, this prophecy sounds less outraged than exasperated about any possibilities of renewal or transformation: "What are the roots that clutch, what branches grow / Out of this stony rubbish?" (19–20). And in the reply to this question, we hear not what God says to his prophet, as in the source identified by Eliot's note, but another parodic reminder *as if* from God of the limitations of the prophet's own culture and religious language: "Son of man, / You cannot say, or guess, for you know only / A heap of broken images" (20–22).

The only exception here to the general uselessness, opacity, and infertility of our heaped and broken images is the "shadow under this red rock" (25). Even this supposedly promising difference, though, is described as if we cannot see past our own shadows and fears, our own projections and our feelings toward those projections: "And I will show you something different from either / Your shadow at morning striding behind you / Or your shadow at evening rising to meet you; / I will show you fear in a handful of dust" (27–30). Although in Isaiah 32:2 "the shadow of a great rock in a weary land" serves as a focusing image of the Messiah's reign, in Eliot's poem the addressed poet, speaker, or reader knows only that this shadow is supposed to represent something other than his or her own personal shadow, though it might be only one's own incoherent "fear in a handful of dust." The 1915 manuscript drafts of "The Death of St. Narcissus," from which these lines of *The Waste Land* are taken, elaborate this sense of isolation with one's own illusions and the consequent turn to God not as an answer but as a kind of religious madness and death: "So because he was struck down mad by the knowledge of his own beauty / He could not live men's ways, but became a dancer to God" (*Facsimile* 91).

The rest of *The Waste Land*'s second stanza offers other gestures toward some phrase or idiom that would address this isolation in images of human love or encounter, but the images further suggest the prevention of love's contact by absence, impotence, speechlessness, blindness, ignorance, innocence, or death. When these romantic images seem to turn again to the spiritual—"looking into the heart of light, the silence" (41)—they also evoke the title of Conrad's novel of colonialism, *Heart of Darkness*. Conrad's novel is the source of Eliot's original epigraph, with its own explicitly failing image for an unnamed and barely articulated fear: "He cried in a whisper at some image, at some vision,—he cried out twice, a cry that was no more than a breath—'The horror! the horror!'" (*Facsimile* 3). But even Conrad's vague rendering of Kurtz's final and "supreme moment of complete knowledge" was perhaps too confident of what it could see and communicate to fit Eliot's purpose here. Eliot himself would write in 1950 that Conrad "remains always the European observer of the tropics, the white man's eye contemplating the Congo and its black gods" ("Introduction to *Huckleberry Finn*" 326), and *The Waste Land* likewise focuses not on anything Kurtz or Marlowe learns about the Congo or its black gods, but on the "white man's eye" in its moments of failure and blindness. Eliot's poem invokes both colonial and religious judgments, but it repeatedly demonstrates those colonial and religious judgments' failures to provide a viable idiom for moving beyond the self into interpersonal or cross-cultural encounters. Ralph Ellison, at least, would appreciate and elaborate the poem's unanswered appeals and questions as parts of a challenging cultural work in progress.

First in Madame Sosostris's tarot reading, then in a haunted dream vision of London suggested by Baudelaire, the last two stanzas of "The Burial of the Dead" continue the guarded search for a usable language or set of images for the fearful differences between cultures and a fearful loss of identity. As if the poem's opening ambitions for an epic tone have been dismissed, and even the lesser prophetic tone has been trivialized, Eliot's note to this stanza lightly remarks that he has "quite arbitrarily" adapted the tarot cards "to his own convenience." Although an impressive number of the poem's recurring images are collected in this one stanza, the tarot reading hardly pretends to govern or organize the poem from any higher or more comprehensive plane that might make contact or communication with others possible.

The reading by Madame Sosostris (the name alludes to a male Aldous Huxley character dressed as a female fortune-teller) is an obvious dislocation and forced manipulation of an exotic myth. She plays her role, and her audience (customer, poet, and reader) plays along, but we do not play along in order to be re-made in any epic sense or to see in any prophetic sense so much as to confirm our own blindness and limitation. The scene calls attention to the blindness and limitations of both this prophet and the silent audience she addresses: "Here, said she, / Is your card, the drowned Phoenician Sailor, / (Those are pearls that were his eyes. Look!)" (46–48). We are told to look, but her reading, as though professionally sensitive to our own solitary concerns, points like Eliot's poem not *through* but *to* our eyes (or the eyes on the card she selects as ours), hard, opaque, thereby stressing not what we see so much as our very inability to see. The allusions to a drowned Phoenician sailor, Shakespeare's *Tempest,* and to "crowds of people, walking round in a ring" (56) suggest the failure of other rites for the burial of the dead, especially in the context of encounters with alien cultures.

Madame Sosostris even provides an image for the proscribed limits of her own vision, along with that of the one-eyed merchant: "this card, / Which is blank, is something he carries on his back, / Which I am forbidden to see" (52–54). Nor does she see what might have served as an ethnological or religious trump card—"I do not find / The Hanged Man"—the card that

Eliot's note says is "associated in my mind" with both Frazer's Hanged God and "the hooded figure in the passage of the disciples to Emmaus in Part V" (54–55). Throughout this stanza, such hooded, veiled suggestions of a miraculous resurrection or "sea change" all focus instead just short of that transformation, insisting on a personal blindness and fear of the unknown. Neither Madame Sosostris nor her customer can see or even begin to travel beyond his or her own life or land without what seems like a risk of absolute loss: "Fear death by water" (55). This fear of one's own shadow and the fear of change perpetuate each other, locking the self in a struggle with its own demons and preventing encounters with other people or with difference of almost any kind. As in Tournier's novel, "when Others are missing from the structure of the world . . . there reigns alone the brutal opposition of the sun and earth, of an unbearable light and an obscure abyss: the 'summary law of all or nothing'" (Deleuze 306). Our fortune-teller's breezy tone as she takes her money introduces an even more blinded defense against that fear of the unknown in the wider cultural blindness to be explored in the following stanza.

The haunted dream-vision from Baudelaire in this first section's final stanza widens the poem's focus again from the personal to a more cultural problem, from the fortune-teller's client, warned by the cards to fear death by water, to an immense crowd of the already virtually dead. For this crowd flowing over London Bridge and into the "Unreal City" one smoggy winter morning as if to their day's work (particularly in London's financial district), it is a question less of personal blindness and fear than of a cultural blindness to fear, a cultural state of institutionalized torpor and ennui that seems to overrule and silence any particular encounter. Individual isolation and limited vision are ensured by the cultural isolation and blindness of the entire civilization, with the possible exception only of odd, unaccountable phenomena like a church bell's "dead sound on the final stroke of nine" (68).

An allusion to the "ships at Mylae" suggests a colonial context for the burial of the dead through a comparison of World War I and Rome's commercial war against Carthage, as if the millions of World War I dead died to as little purpose, fighting for control over colonial trade. The speaker accosts one passerby (as the specter does in the Baudelaire poem) as if to waken him from this domestication of imperialism and war, this daily death march of a nation of bankers and gardeners with no renewal or transformation in sight: " 'That corpse you planted last year in your garden, / Has it begun to sprout?' " (71–72). The speaker hastens to warn the passerby, however, against the misguided or misleading intentions even of his conventionally most loyal friends or most auspicious adopted omens. Apparently, no such conventions familiar or foreign will serve for the kind of encounter represented by this culture's hastily buried fears: " 'O keep the Dog far hence, that's friend to men, / Or with his nails he'll dig it up again!' " (73–74). Neither our own nor other cultures seem to be of any help in confronting our fears.

At the end of this entire "Burial" section, the speaker turns suddenly to accost and surprise the reader, as if the reader were another or perhaps the same trudging member of the deathly funeral crowd. He accosts the reader directly with the line with which Baudelaire has already accosted Eliot himself as a reader of Baudelaire: " 'You! hypocrite lecteur!—mon semblable,—mon frère!' " (76). Even our relationship with the poem, the line reminds us, is based on shared, deadening conventions that the speaker both invokes and mocks. Barring the miraculous sprouting of a corpse, we are likely to wake from the blindness and dull isolation of our lives and cultures only when we are accosted on the street with the incongruous language of such a question put directly into our faces (as dramatized again in the prologue to Ellison's *Invisible Man*) or perhaps in our dreams. But Eliot limits such an encounter here to one of shock, as if there were no available means for renegotiating the loss of what conventions we already have.

The potential, fearful significance for Eliot of such an unassimilated, a-signifying phenomenon as the church bell's "dead sound" is suggested by James Longenbach's description of Eliot's Diltheyan "existentialist historicism." According to Longenbach, Eliot acknowledges in his dissertation and elsewhere a certain relativity of interpretation which he attempts to counter with the necessity of a constantly expanding but coherent *system* of interpretations. A single phenomenon may thus demand a dauntingly complete reorganization of the current system. This movement is most familiar from Eliot's "Tradition and the Individual Talent": "The existing order is complete before the new work arrives; for order to persist after the supervention of novelty, the *whole* existing order must be, if ever so slightly, altered" (*Selected Essays* 5). Cleo McNelly Kearns stresses in Eliot's encounters with others' words, ideas, and traditions in his reading and criticism (4–5) a similarly persistent movement from surrender to recovery, as if the negotiation of new material were often seen by Eliot not as an expected, necessary, ongoing process of negotiation or interaction, but as a wholesale, fearful surrender of one system or form in order to give oneself utterly to another, a risk that may well seem too great to take. *The Waste Land* focuses on that fearful surrender and the tendency to shrink from such surrender in favor of deadening defenses of the same.

The culturally defensive posture of this sense of whole, coherent systems at stake is part of what Mitchell Robert Breitwieser notes in early white appropriations of jazz, when culturally inflected musical tendencies toward the symphonic and scored encountered the more improvisational, interactively negotiated forms and riffs of African American jazz.[2] This improvisational, interactive quality in jazz is also related to what Ellison's Peter Wheatstraw calls the "shit, grit and mother-wit" that the invisible man will need "to get along in this here man's town," that is, in a town dominated unpredictably by a "man" who cannot even see the invisible man (176). Such riffing in jazz and in Wheatstraw's "mother-wit" are characterized by provisional, partial forms improvised in clashes and negotiations with other unpredictable systems, phenomena, human movements, and in appeals for potential social support, in contrast to an apparently existing, coherent order temporarily threatened and then restored.

Such a contrast in cultural styles of encounter with an unorganized physical and cultural circumstance might be reasonably attributed to a difference in a person's relative power to organize one's circumstances or, rather, to the relative power of a person's social affiliations (family, race, gender, nation, etc.) to organize those circumstances even without marked effort or will—so that the existing order may come to seem not forced, manipulated, or negotiated, but natural, even perhaps eternal. Unexpected challenges to such an accepted order may therefore seem less natural, personal, or cultural than supernatural. In other words, the more stable and coherent a system of circumstances one apparently stands to lose, the more threatening and even supernatural any reorganization or renegotiation is likely to seem. "The Burial of the Dead" shows such natural, personal, and cultural challenges being translated repeatedly into the shadowy terms of the supernatural and "buried" there, even though those supernatural terms do not finally seem to work any better than any others, except to shift the issue vaguely somewhere else.

This suggestion about cultural styles is fairly explicit in Eliot's *Family Reunion* (1939) in an observation about Harry, Lord Monchensey, by Downing, his servant and chauffeur:

> We most of us seem to live according to circumstance,
> But with people like him, there's something inside them
> That accounts for what happens to them. You get a feeling of it.
> So I seem to know beforehand, when something's going to
>   happen,
> And it seems quite natural, being his Lordship.
>
> (289)

Not only does Downing assert Harry's independence of the unknown "circumstance" that others (like Huck or Jim, for example) expect to have to negotiate, Downing's language in the last line also equates the somewhat mystified and naturalized "something inside" people like Harry with the social power of his title ("being his Lordship"). In Downing's view, at least, what happens to people like Harry hardly "happens" at all in the sense of unpredictable events. What happens is not unexpected but a function of the world that his Lordship (that is, his Lordship in the social position to which he is as entitled as Tom Sawyer to play occasional practical jokes) organizes and naturalizes, such that it all comes to seem "quite natural" both to Downing and to Harry himself. When something actually does happen to someone like Harry, when he encounters phenomena, language, or circumstances beyond the limits of his familiar forms and systems, it is likely to seem not "natural" at all. Nor is the unexpected event likely to seem only *unnatural* or even *cultural,* since neither of these categories would sufficiently account for the unexpected affront to his own accustomed knowledge and control. Such an event is more likely to seem *supernatural,* an effect of a power unaccountably higher than his, though even that supernatural power may be named and institutionalized in relatively familiar ways.

One such encounter of Harry's in *The Family Reunion* with an unexpected (perhaps moral or ethical) affront to his (Lordship's) power is cast as his encounter with the apparently supernatural Furies, and it would later be adopted as one of two epigraphs to Ellison's *Invisible Man.* In Ellison's novel it is followed almost immediately by the novel's central, invisible narrator's insistence that he is not a supernatural "spook" like Poe's, like Harry's Furies, or like Benito Cereno's haunting "Negro!" (in the novel's other epigraph), but rather "a man of substance," invisible not for natural or supernatural reasons but for cultural reasons, "because of a peculiar disposition of the eyes of those with whom I come in contact. A matter of the construction of their *inner* eyes" (3). Eliot does focus on such a cultural blindness, but he also demonstrates the powerful cultural and perhaps personal tendency to construct that blindness in supernatural terms. We may see and hear no farther, *The Waste Land* will suggest, than Saint Mary Woolnoth's church bell's ominous but unexplored "dead sound on the final stroke of nine." This focus on cultural blindness and on the blindness of religious faith allows for both religious readings of the poem like Calvin Bedient's and deconstructive readings like Harriet Davidson's and Eloise Knapp Hay's. The present reading considers the religious as one discourse privileged over others in the poem but not necessarily any less a dramatic failure than others still traceable throughout the poem—notably those associated with culture, class, gender, ethics, and love. Whereas in Morrison and less explicitly in Twain one purpose of the supernatural "is to keep the reader preoccupied with the nature of the incredible spirit world while being supplied a controlled diet of the incredible political world" (Morrison "Unspeakable" 32), in Eliot the supernatural remains a privileged discourse for staging and almost dignifying the failures of other discourses, failures which are thereby kept more strictly and defensively under control. Again, this would become a point of contention for Ralph Ellison, whose novel would elaborate the aftermath of those same failures in terms of both their irresponsibility and their possible renegotiation.

The Waste Land's second section, "A Game of Chess," tends to focus less on burials or personal repressions or repudiations than on culturally reinforced blindnesses and distractions from the sometimes fearful failures of world, language, vision, and transformative encounter stressed in the poem's first section. The section title, "A Game of Chess," along with Eliot's note to line 137, alludes to a game of chess in a Thomas Middleton play that distracts a woman while her daughter-in-law is seduced on a balcony onstage. Eliot's own "Game of Chess" is similarly divided between two scenes, each of which features a similar distraction from an "agony of others" that is left unspoken, if not unspeakable. The two scenes also play against each other, as in the Middleton play, but the juxtaposition here calls special attention to an extreme difference in class. One scene features the aristocracy and the other the working class; each portrays a different, characteristic kind of distraction from the "agony of others."

The importance of class differences in Eliot's thinking about responsibility to and distractions from challenging cultural circumstances is suggested in an essay published one year after *The Waste Land* on the death of popular music hall performer Marie Lloyd, whom Eliot praises as "the expressive figure of the lower classes" (*Selected Essays* 407). Eliot here contrasts these lower classes with the middle class and the aristocracy: "The middle classes have no such idol: the middle classes are morally corrupt. That is to say, their own life fails to find a Marie Lloyd to express it; nor have they any independent virtues which might give them as a conscious class any dignity. The middle classes, in England as elsewhere, under democracy, are morally dependent upon the aristocracy, and the aristocracy are subordinate to the middle class, which is gradually absorbing and destroying them. The lower class still exists; but perhaps it will not exist for long" (407).

Lacking its own expressive figures and independent virtues, the middle class shifts its moral responsibility onto the aristocracy. Eliot makes an analogous argument about the unacknowledged dependence of humanism on older religious traditions (in "The Humanism of Irving Babbitt," *Selected Essays* 419–28). Thus, too, commercial interests in the British Empire had long shifted responsibility onto the aristocracy's idealized role as a civilizing influence throughout the world. Eliot suggests that the aristocracy, at the same time, shifts its own responsibility onto the middle class and its increasing financial and social power. And "with the decay of the music-hall, with the en-croachment of the cheap and rapid-breeding cinema, the lower classes will tend to drop into the same state of protoplasm as the bourgeoisie" (407). Without sustaining their own different idiom (and without the difference that their existence and their idiom pose for an aristocratic or middle-class fan of their art like Eliot), they will disappear as the one remaining class figure for the "independent virtues" and "responsibility" that Eliot de-scribes here in terms of "that collaboration of the audience with the artist which is necessary in all art and most obviously in dramatic art" (407).

As in Eliot's introduction to *Huckleberry Finn,* here again the figure for that necessary, challenging difference and its corre-sponding responsibility is marked by colonialism and race as well as class. The British lower classes' absorption and disap-pearance is finally compared to that of the vanishing "natives" of Melanesia, an island whose name, according to the *OED,* "modeled after Polynesia, was intended to mean 'the region of islands inhabited by blacks.'" [3] The middle class absorbs the lower and upper classes in much the same way it has colonized other cultures. As David Chinitz has suggested, the relationship of popular culture with its audience (including Eliot himself) offered Eliot at least the possibility of a less colonialist sort of "collaboration" between artists and audiences that would allow for the interactive renegotiation of conventions, both within and between cultures. But Eliot is inclined to pronounce this pos-sibility to be either impossible or vanishing fast in the cultures he knows best.

"A Game of Chess" juxtaposes two such scenes of failed en-counter and responsibility, one set in an aristocracy already largely absorbed into the distracted "protoplasm" and "listless apathy" of the middle class, and the other set in a working class possibly disappearing into the same state of irresponsibility. The potentially vital differences of these two classes from that middle class and from each other may be traced in the poem's contrast between the two class settings, a contrast that suggests again the importance of interpersonal and cross-cultural encounters, even if those encounters remain here unappreciated, unheeded, perhaps unspeakable.

Instead of what Eliot calls "that collaboration of the audience with the artist which is necessary in all art," a dramatic call and response, the aristocratic section of "A Game of Chess" represents art as a collection of colonial trophies on the wall. Instead of waking a sense of "responsibility" to "the torment of others" or to the difference, friendship, or love of others, these works of art overwhelm, drown, and "hush" any such sense in the stifling press of leaning, "staring forms" that effectively enclose the room rather than open it toward other rooms and other stories.

"A Game of Chess" begins with an allusion to Antony's first encounter with Shakespeare's Queen of the Nile, but Eliot's own Cleopatra is a worn, weary, overdone convention of exoticism. Instead of the human marvel from another world, she has become a self-absorbed figure framed in an ornate "glass" among a collection of all too many "other withered stumps of time" whose unheeded stories are "told upon the walls" (104–5). The only painting focused on in the verse ("As though a window gave upon the sylvan scene" 98) both portrays this indifference and meets with the same indifference itself. The nightingale and the painting itself both tell of "The change of Philomel, by the barbarous king / So rudely forced," but the story falls then and "still" falls now, unhelped by art, on "dirty ears" (102, 103).

The deadening sensory overload in this entire scene anticipates the effects of the work of art in an age of mechanical and mass cultural reproduction, as Eliot contrasts these effects with the effect of Marie Lloyd's performances on her more responsive audiences. Eliot thus describes the effects of the cinema on its typical spectator: "His mind is lulled by continuous senseless music and continuous action too rapid for the brain to act upon, and will receive, without giving, in that same listless apathy with which the middle and upper classes regard any entertainment of the nature of art" (407). In Eliot's poem, when the woman in the mirror begins to speak, she speaks as if addicted to just such mechanical, superficial, unthinking stimulation, "too rapid for the brain to act upon": in an almost cartoonish image, her words appear almost to result not from thought but from a kind of static electricity generated by her brush: "Under the firelight, under the brush, her hair / Spread out in fiery points / Glowed into words, then would be savagely still" (108– 10). Her lines of dialogue are correspondingly jerky, repetitive, flickering, as if to cover the silence of her own thinking and that of her silent interlocutor. She pleads listlessly with him to say something, anything, but what her partner in this quasi-dialogue seems to be thinking is that any spoken response is futile. His thoughts are recorded in lines that require Eliot's note to a later section of the poem even for Eliot's readers to under-stand. They refer to lost bones that have been forgotten by the living, "Rattled by the rat's foot only, year to year" (195), in another figure for the disturbing failures of responsibility and encounter incompletely buried in "The Burial of the Dead," fail-ures to which these distracted characters of "A Game of Chess" seem almost more oblivious than these scurrying rats.

   The woman in the glass concludes apathetically that her partner knows, sees, and remembers nothing, that he might as well be dead himself; her partner remembers only a fragment, a rag from Shakespeare ("Those are pearls that were his eyes"). This figure of ambiguous blindness repeated from the Sosostris reading leads almost automatically into three lines from the cur-rently popular *Ziegfeld's Follies:* "O O O O that Shakespeherian Rag— / It's so elegant / So intelligent" (128–30). This "Shake-speherian Rag" with its built-in self-advertisement demonstrates (like Eliot's poem) the distracting commodification not only of the encounters that might have been traced once in Shake-speare's plays and songs but also those encounters that might have been traced in the more currently popular tunes of the mu-sic halls. The line demonstrates the commodification of both a (now) "high" aristocratic culture and a "lower class" culture, both of which might otherwise address their vital differences to the reigning indifference of the middle class. The uncharted movements of Eliot's own poem from one allusion to the next, highbrow and low, suggest that culture in all its forms in the modern wasteland threatens to become an undifferentiated, commercialized mix, "too rapid for the brain to act upon."

Though the couple wait listlessly "for a knock upon the door," their attention will be tuned to their daily routines, including "a game of chess, / Pressing lidless eyes." They have themselves become two more of the "staring forms" surrounding and closing them in. Yet by calling attention to their deadening routine, the poem keeps its focus on the differences and challenges they fail to meet.

The next stanza thus moves abruptly outside this lavish room to a working-class monologue in a pub, where the "continuous senseless music" of modern life prevents not only an adequate appreciation of the encounter and responsibility represented by art but even the responsibilities of encounters face to face. The more direct experience that might have helped the aristocratic couple appreciate what was happening in the art they viewed so abstractedly ("As though a window gave upon the sylvan scene" 98) is no longer missing in the scene in the pub. Yet the pub scene's directness is itself hampered by a lack of even the most provisional "independent virtues" of the kind that Eliot hoped might be supported and sustained by a popular art like Marie Lloyd's, as against the encroaching cultural and economic irresponsibility and "general equivalent" of self-interest represented by the middle class. The juxtaposition of these two scenes suggests again that both the idealism of the aristocracy and the hard-earned experience of the working class have become almost completely commodified. Their cultural differences are valuable but disappearing.

The first sentence of the latter scene emphasizes its directness—"I didn't mince my words, I said to her myself"—but the speaker's narration of her meeting with Lil seems motivated mostly by an effort to evade the responsibility suggested by Lil's having given her a "straight look" (151). The speaker's own advice is apparently limited to the internalized middle-class admonition that her friend Lil should "make yourself a bit smart. / He'll want to know what you done with that money he gave you / To get yourself some teeth" (140–42). When the speaker warns Lil that "others" would give Lil's husband a good time if Lil does not look "smart" enough to do it herself, Lil's reply and "straight look" ask for more responsibility from her friend than that. The speaker shifts again, however, to the evasive language of market consumerism: "If you don't like it you can get on with it, I said. / Others can pick and choose if you can't" (153–54). In the present narration, she speaks in a nonstop monologue. Her present audience is silent throughout the story of her encounter with Lil, never challenging her in the way Lil did or not allowed to do so.

The speaker is allowed to reduce even the most difficult questions of responsibility to undeveloped asides in oral parentheses. She has tried to blame Lil herself for looking "antique / (And her only thirty-one)," but Lil has reminded her why she is in bad health and why she took "them pills": "She's had five already, and nearly died of young George" (156–57, 159–60). The speaker remains unchallenged even when she appeals to contradictory clichés, trying first to shrug the responsibility for Lil's problem from herself onto Albert—"Well, if Albert won't leave you alone, there it is, I said"—then trying to shift responsibility again from Albert to the very nature of marriage—"What you get married for if you don't want children?" (163–64). She does not dwell on the support she might have offered or the questions she might have raised for Lil, for herself, or for her present audience in the pub (and for Eliot's readers). Instead, in its "continuous senseless music and continuous action," her speech shifts abruptly to the middle-class ritual of the hot Sunday dinner, but it is soon broken off in the midst of more distractions: "HURRY UP PLEASE IT'S TIME."

As the scene and "A Game of Chess" end, both the bartender's official farewells and the patrons' more informal farewells are made to seem themselves like formulaic distractions from the more challenging responsibilities faintly traceable both in "high art" and in interpersonal encounters such as the one just overheard. The pub scene speaker's and perhaps Albert's evaded responsibilities to Lil are just traceable in the reminders of Lil's potentially imminent death by childbirth in the bartender's accelerated echo of Marvell's death-laced seduction poem ("To His Coy Mistress") and in the patrons' echoes of Ophelia's song before drowning herself. These evaded responsibilities to Lil are traceable by readers, perhaps, but they remain unrecognizable by the characters involved, who are easily distracted from Lil and from each other. Only the poem's readers can see perhaps what these aristocrats might learn from Lil's "straight look" in the pub, or what Lil's friend might learn from the story of Philomel framed on Cleopatra's wall. The more popular "Good Night, Ladies" might be more recognizable to the characters involved; it might elicit, like one of Marie Lloyd's music hall songs, that "collaboration of the audience with the artist which is necessary in all art," but it appears more likely here to fall, just as the nightingale's song did in another class setting, on "dirty ears."

These movements of the poem's first two sections set the direction for the third, "The Fire Sermon," in an increasingly portentous evasion of encounters like the one described by Eliot between Huck and Jim. If the emotional keynote of "The Burial of the Dead" is a defensive fear of interpersonal and cross-cultural encounters and their attendant responsibilities, and if the keynote of "A Game of Chess" is a concerted cultural and personal distraction from such encounters and responsibilities, the cultural and emotional state of mind portrayed in "The Fire

Sermon" represents another step in the same direction, an almost complete indifference to interpersonal or cross-cultural encounters or responsibilities. The lack of fear, attention, or response to personal or cultural difference here, in an economic and cultural climate of widespread commodification, effectively reduces the world to (and reifies, naturalizes it as) an almost protoplasmic nondifference, an actual absence of difference. This is most explicit in Eliot's note explaining the role of Tiresias as a spectator among characters who "melt" into other characters in the poem, so that "all the women are one woman, and the two sexes meet in Tiresias" (218n). Tiresias describes himself within the poem as an "old man with wrinkled female breasts" (228). The asceticism suggested by the title "The Fire Sermon" and named in Eliot's note implies a wider-ranging, more thoroughly unrelieved, hopeless representation of life in the modern wasteland. It is futile for poets or prophets to call for courage as against fear or for focus as against distraction. Almost everything one touches here is destructive, "burning" with the corrupting flames of lust. Worse still, everyone here, like Shakespeare's Ophelia in her madness, is "incapable of her own distress, / Or like a creature native and indued / Unto that element" (*Hamlet* 4.7.177–79). Even the poet and reader's possible difference outside the scene is partly undercut by the note identifying Tiresias as himself a spectator not different from but exemplary of all the other characters' indifference to each other.

The opening lines of "The Fire Sermon" mark these changes from the previous section with another faint echo of Ophelia's death and another reference to the wind heard under the door in the Cleopatra scene. The wind that was a nagging enigma before is now unheard, and Ophelia is now past singing "snatches of old lauds" as she did for Shakespeare before sinking to her "muddy death" (4.7.174–82). Not even rubbish is left behind to recall or distinguish the loves and lusts of summer nights. Allusions to Spenser's *Prothalamian,* Psalm 137, and Marvell's "To His Coy Mistress" are displaced and distorted in this context almost beyond recognition as love songs, the last parodic allusion turning the expected echo of "Time's wingèd chariot" into "The rattle of the bones, and chuckle spread from ear to ear" (186). Like a morbid practical joke, the allusion dismisses all these losses of loves and lives: these no longer even have names in the way that Philomel and Lil did in "A Game of Chess."

The effective disappearance in "The Fire Sermon" of the challenging but potentially instructive differences that still lingered precariously in "A Game of Chess" between classes, genders, persons, and genres, as well as the differences between love and lust, life and death, past and future, is even more spectacular in another long opening to "The Fire Sermon" that Eliot eventually cut on Pound's advice. That opening, in a parody of Pope's "Rape of the Lock" and with echoes of a Swiftian disgust, mixes "dreams of love" with "pleasant rapes," "soothing chocolate" with the "needful stool," perfumes with the "hearty female stench," in effect reducing "all the women" to "one woman," as in Eliot's note about Tiresias, but with a misogynistic vengeance, or maybe a panic at a loss of distinctions that seems bound to spread from all women to men as well: "The same eternal and consuming itch / Can make a martyr, or plain simple bitch"; "For varying forms, one definition's right: / Unreal emotions, and real appetite." What the woman character reads is called a "chaotic misch-masch potpourri" and is mimicked in this phrase's own redundant mix of Greek, German, and French (*Facsimile* 23, 27).[4]

This undifferentiated misch-masch suggests a lack of significant difference and discernment that seems unheeded by the culture at large but that frightens the poet even more than the unmet challenges of addressing difference. It is as if the threat to identity posed by an encounter with difference has assumed the nightmarish dimensions of a loss of absolutely all mental and physical boundaries and distinctions, a process of increasing and irreversible disorder similar to Henry Adams's idea of a cultural and historical entropy. Any possibility of mourning, love, or other transformative encounter is submerged in this idea of misch-masch, drowned out by the broken sounds of horns and motors in the spring (287–88). These relatively undifferentiated street sounds have been mentioned prominently before in Eliot's writing, in a review of Stravinsky's *Rite of Spring* in the first of Eliot's "London Letters" to the *Dial*, dated a few months before he submitted *The Waste Land* draft to Pound. Eliot's review suggests that the way to make music of modern life is to bring it into transforming encounters with something strikingly different from itself, the primitive, for example, since "In art there should be interpenetration and metamorphosis" (453). Recognizably similar to his later description of the "mythical method" in Joyce's *Ulysses*, his comments on Stravinsky's music stress the importance for modernity of such transforming encounters with radical difference: "Whether Stravinsky's music be permanent or ephemeral I do not know; but it did seem to transform the rhythm of the steppes into the scream of the motor horn, the rattle of machinery, the grind of wheels, the beating of iron and steel, the roar of the underground railway, and the other barbaric cries of modern life; and to transform these despairing noises into music" (453).

This is a fair description of the kind of music Eliot's own poem makes of the "barbaric cries of modern life," a music that dramatizes Eliot's and others' uncertainty about whether these encounters represent only ephemeral possibilities, bewildering wake-up calls likely to fall on dirty ears, or a more sustainable music, a cultural method like that of jazz that might be able to thrive on just such discontinuities. Stravinsky did incorporate some jazz elements in his music, notably in his *Soldier's Tale, Rag-Time,* and *Piano Rag-Music* of 1918 and 1919, and others like Ellison have appreciated the jazzlike music made by Eliot's poem without accepting its skepticism about the value or future of this kind of music. Again, Michael North has traced the importance to many modernist writers of differences variously and ambivalently attributed to the primitive, the artistic, and other nonstandard "dialects" of modernism. The modernist ambivalence with regard to these differences most often concerns whether the nonstandard nostalgically represents a lost and irrecoverable "native" truth or whether it signals the "conventional nature of all art" (63), conventions that in a modern, multicultural world are not supernatural or given but changing, cultural, and negotiable.

Eliot's poem suggests an alternately fearful and ironic distrust of this entire process of "interpenetration and metamorphosis" in modern art, despite Eliot's overriding sense of its necessity, importance, and timeliness. As many have noted, *The Waste Land*'s sudden juxtapositions of the modern with the mythical, the familiar with the exotic, and the aristocratic with the working class conspicuously omit the conventional transitions that might too easily falsify, control, or mediate those fearful, challenging, potentially transforming differences. More ironically, however, the poem also suggests an advanced state of cultural irresponsibility and even indifference toward these same differences, as if they have all already collapsed into one indiscernible heap, all reduced irresponsibly and indifferently to the one-dimensional "general equivalent" of colonialist and bourgeois conventions and concerns. The poem seems almost unable to discern and respond to such differences itself, though it does confront those differences, but it seems convinced that the wider culture offers no terms responsible or appropriate to the task. Faced with such a "crisis of undifferentiation" (as René Girard has called it in other contexts, 49–51), Eliot's poem is both tempted by and wary of another more transcendent, sacrificial response, the search for the one overriding difference that would dwarf the minor differences of the chaos he surveys. Eliot suggests in another passage excised from this section of the poem that such a search for the one such (usually religious or imperialist) key to all mythologies may avoid the normal indifference and ruin only at the risk of madness and cryptographic paranoia:

> Some minds, aberrant from the normal equipoise
> (London, your people is bound upon the wheel!)
> Record the motions of these pavement toys
> And trace the cryptogram that may be curled
> Within these faint perceptions of the noise
> Of the movement, and the lights!
>
> (*Facsimile* 43)

After a pause, the line following these invokes Plato to rule out this kind of "higher" vision, at least in this world: "Not here, O Ademantus, but in another world." This would seem to return attention and responsibility to the possibility of transforming encounters with differences more cultural and personal than metaphysical.

The following "Metropole" stanza of the published poem pretends to settle, at least temporarily, for this more mundane, indifferent music of modernity, an "interpenetration and metamorphosis" that does not transform utterly or even sufficiently, but at least calls needed, arresting attention to the problem. This stanza focuses on such indifference as if for lack of any more promising alternative, but not without a sense of ironic alarm at this same indifference, exaggerated in luridly xenophobic and homophobic images of nondifferentiation. Though heavy on alliterations, assonances, rhymes, and off-rhymes, the stanza recounts in businesslike, matter-of-fact, narrative language another encounter in the "Unreal City," echoing that of the stanza that begins with this same line in the poem's opening section. This encounter, however, has none of the fearful expectation and strangeness of the earlier section's representations of encounters with another world and another time. "Mr. Eugenides, the Smyrna merchant" is thus identified as Turkish, but the definite article also suggests he is someone known to the speaker as an agent of the British commercial empire. In his pocket he has a legal receipt for the imported currants for sale, and his comparable proposition of "a weekend at the Metropole" is at once lurid and businesslike. It is an ironic instance of the potentially untransforming "interpenetration and metamorphosis" suggested by a personal encounter reduced to money or an art reduced to the "one consuming itch" of "appetite." The misogynistic images of previous stanzas imagining the elimination of differences among women become here a xenophobic and homophobic image of cultural and sexual nondifferentiation as well.

Only four lines later comes Eliot's note explaining the role of the twice transsexual, bisexed, and implicitly bisexual Tiresias, a note which almost completely displaces any remaining hopes for a modern music or idiom adequate to the potentially transforming encounters associated thus far with the personally or culturally different. These hopes are displaced by a sense of alarm at a generalized human "crisis of nondifferentiation," a commodification without responsibility to specific differences. "Just as the one-eyed merchant, seller of currants, melts into the Phoenician Sailor, and the latter is not wholly distinct from Ferdinand Prince of Naples, so all the women are one woman, and the two sexes meet in Tiresias" (218n).

Eliot's note quotes "the whole passage" on Tiresias from Ovid's *Metamorphoses* for its "great anthropological interest" in this regard. The passage suggests that Tiresias's blindness and his powers of prophecy may be more closely related to each other than they appear: his powers of prophecy may function not only as compensation for his blindness, as conventionally understood, but also as an ironic metaphor for that same blindness. Tiresias knows "love from both points of view," which may mean here that he knows love not from his own close encounter with another subjectivity in love, but from his own direct, unmediated, but still individual experience of both his own and another's point of view in what therefore may hardly be love at all, but the lust, appetite, and self-absorbed indifference characteristic of the encounters portrayed throughout this section of Eliot's poem. More likely here than a dialogue with the other is either no "interpenetration" at all or a complete "metamorphosis," an indifferent melting into the other altogether.[5]

Tiresias's two transsexual experiences have resulted, in fact, not from love or sex but from his meddling interruption of sex between "two huge snakes who were copulating in the forest." His blindness is likewise the result of his interference in a "sportive quarrel" between Jove and Juno over whether women have greater pleasure in love than men. Juno blinds him, perhaps, for presuming as "arbitrator" to litigate the differences (what Jean-François Lyotard might call the differend) of partners' emotions in love, or for presuming to eliminate the necessary strangeness or otherness of one's partner's emotions in love. Jove's gift of prophecy to Tiresias may appear to be an "honor compensating him for the loss of sight," but it is also a more honorable euphemism for his particular blindness to difference and change—his having "foresuffered all" and "foretold the rest"—a blindness that Eliot might well consider the "great anthropological interest" of Ovid's story for the modern world. It is a blindness or indifference to difference that has come to seem as much an ironic curse as a prophetic gift.

Eliot's Tiresias is a mirror of both the man and woman whose encounter he observes so indifferently. He is "throbbing between two lives," just as "the human engine waits" in general at a certain evening hour, like clockwork or machine work, "like a taxi throbbing waiting" or like the typist here, waiting not to experience "fear in a handful of dust" or to look into "the heart of light, the silence," or even to be accosted on the street by an oddly familiar stranger, but waiting only for "the expected guest." The indifference of Tiresias and of the typist to the impending encounter is matched by the indifference of her middle-class guest with his "one bold stare," much like that of the unheeded "staring forms" in "A Game of Chess," or like this guest's caresses, "unreproved, if undesired." The sense of an opportunity for transforming encounter and responsibility awakened in Huck by Jim, for example, is missing here, but no one misses it within the scene. The typist's guest acts less like Huck than Tom, as if entitled to a practical joke: "His vanity requires no response, / And makes a welcome of indifference" (241–42). "Hardly aware of her departed lover," the typist "smoothes her hair with automatic hand, / And puts a record on the gramophone" (250, 255–56).

The poem's needle jumps again, however, reviving or at least recalling hopes of a sea change: " 'This music crept by me upon the waters' " (257). Linking the typist's recorded music to Ariel's unaccountable song in *The Tempest*, Eliot attempts again to discern in the differences of such popular music rising and falling throughout *The Waste Land*, as in the music his own poem creates from the "barbaric cries of modern life," the conditions for that "sea change" he still expects and hopes to provoke in art: "that collaboration of the audience with the artist" which results in "interpenetration and metamorphosis" (*Selected Essays* 407, "London Letter" 453). At a point in his poem when such sea changes seem least likely, when the poem verges like Tiresias on its own ironic or cynical dismissals of all such possibilities, the speaker bears witness as well to occasional, unexpected, and "inexplicable splendour" in the clatter of different sounds and styles, perhaps but not necessarily subordinated to the religious:

> O City city, I can sometimes hear
> Beside a public bar in Lower Thames Street,
> The pleasant whining of a mandoline,
> And a clatter and a chatter from within
> Where fishmen lounge at noon: where the walls
> Of Magnus Martyr hold
> Inexplicable splendour of Ionian white and gold.
>
> (259–65)

The music that follows this scene, however, in what Eliot's note calls "The Song of the (three) Thames Daughters," drifts choppily through another three indifferent seductions, one without explanation, one without comment or resentment, and one without connection or expectation. Even Lil with her "straight look" expected something from her friend. One male partner here has wept, but his responsibility and promise seem directed toward his own guilt, not toward her: his promise of "a new start" suggests a renunciation of her along with his sin (298). Only a musical wail unformed into words, taken from Wagner, attempts to mourn the love that is missing here, and that refrain trails off to a feeble "la la" (306). The section ends with references to "representatives of eastern and western asceticism" (307–9n). Reflecting their example, the verse turns from the unrelieved "Burning burning burning burning" of this world of lust and appetite to completely otherworldly help, "O Lord Thou pluckest me out" (309), as if to conclude again with Plato, "Not here, O Ademantus, but in another world" (*Facsimile* 43). But Tiresias, at least, "throbbing between two lives," seems to have ruled out even other worlds. The section thus ends characteristically not with that otherworldly hope, but with only the one-line, one-word stanza, "burning" (311).

"Death by Water," the poem's fourth section, represents another more extremely ascetic, "negative way," like the rich man's or the camel's way through the eye of the needle, in order to move beyond the hopelessly familiar world of accountable but irresponsible "profit and loss" (314). This briefest section has been cut from ninety-three lines in the original draft to ten in the final copy, as if most of Eliot's writing here has gone the way of Phlebas the Phoenician's dead flesh: "A current under sea / Picked his bones in whispers" (315–16). This last word, however, anticipates the faintly promising, strange "whisper music" left to eddy and float throughout the poem's final section. As if to shed at once all these layers of cultural indifference and distraction, the poem addresses its readers directly as in "The

Burial of the Dead," challenging us to consider Phlebas "entering the whirlpool" (318) without the least sense of where this current is likely to lead. And Pound's and Eliot's cuts to "Death by Water" have in effect put readers in a similarly "inexplicable" position. What clues remain from the original draft stress the same ambiguous qualities of unconsciousness, unpredictability, yet daunting responsibility that Eliot later notes in Twain's representations of Huck's encounters with the unfamiliar and uncontrollable. This surrender of the stable and familiar evokes seductive but also terrifying fantasies of oceanic fusion. On the other hand, such encounters demand a culture's utmost creativity and skill to address responsibly its unknown others and unburied dead, much more creativity and skill than Eliot thinks his culture can manage or even support.

The draft that elaborates these ambiguities in "Death by Water" also helps explain Eliot's admiration for Twain's raftsmen, for the fishmen lounging in the public bar in Lower Thames Street, and for the sailor represented earlier on "your card, the drowned Phoenician Sailor":

> The Sailor, attentive to the chart or to the sheets,
> A concentrated will against the tempest and the tide,
> Retains, even ashore, in public bars or streets
> Something inhuman, clean and dignified.
> (*Facsimile* 55)

Throughout the "seaman's yarn" that follows in Eliot's draft, this "something" retained by the sailor from his experience is ambiguous, linked on the one hand to the sailor's humbling, transforming encounters with the unspecified, "inhuman" forces of nature and the supernatural, and linked on the other hand to his encounters with the sea's more anthropomorphic "many voices" that "Moaned all about us" until "No one dared / To look into another's face" (*Facsimile* 57, 59). But even the end of this story, after the eventual shipwreck, places less stress on these many voices or other faces, or on the inhuman forces of nature and the supernatural, than it does on the personal and cultural inarticulateness for which these voices and faces are two sets of characteristically inadequate figures, so much language just on the verge of collapsing into wordplay, noise, and indifference: "And if *Another* knows, I know I know not, / Who only know that there is no more noise now" (*Facsimile* 61).

Eliot would later compare his two main sources for this section of the original "Death by Water" in Dante's and Tennyson's versions of Ulysses: "Dante is telling a story. Tennyson is only stating an elegiac mood" (*Selected Essays* 289, qtd. by Valerie Eliot in *Facsimile* 128n1 to p. 55). For this section of *The Waste Land,* Eliot apparently decided with Pound to delete the "story" entirely (as well as the possibilities offered in stories and in the process of time for transforming events and encounters with other people) and preserve even less than the "elegiac mood," less even than the earlier admonition to "Fear death by water." Here we are warned only that upon "entering the whirlpool" we do not know what to expect (not even the simply stated "Nothing" of the third Thames-daughter): "Gentile or Jew / O you who turn the wheel and look to windward, / Consider Phlebas, who was once handsome and tall as you" (319–21). Neither religion nor skill can help us, nor can we help each other, this section seems to conclude, thereby salvaging and offering the reassurance only of this ironic knowledge of our own unconsciousness and inefficacy. It is perhaps the poem's most dramatic approximation of what Deleuze describes as "what happens when Others are missing from the structure of the world" (306). As in Tournier's novel, once Crusoe has lost his sense of a structure inhabited by other people, "The known and the unknown, the perceived and unperceived confront one another absolutely in a battle with nuances," almost all of which nuances have been eliminated from this section of Eliot's poem. As Tournier's character says, "My vision of the island is reduced to that of my own eyes, and what I do not see of it is to me a total unknown.

Everywhere I am not total darkness reigns" (306). As in Huck's experience of the fog, this total preoccupation with one's own isolation, blindness, and inefficacy also implies a concession of power to dominant cultural forces, as will become more obvious as the poem draws to a close.

The Waste Land's fifth and final section, "What the Thunder Said," settles into and elaborates this ironic position with regard to the poem's entire inquiry into cultural conditions for responsible, transforming encounters with the unfamiliar and unspoken. Such encounters are virtually declared here to be unspeakable. After the fearful sense of failed responsibility explored in "The Burial of the Dead," after the mass cultural distractions of "A Game of Chess," after the crisis of nondifferentiation in "The Fire Sermon" and the apocalyptic inarticulateness of "Death by Water," "What the Thunder Said" begins with its own anaphoric series of lines beginning with "After," signaling its own emotional tone of ironic aftermath. It is as though the poem hopes to emerge now on the far end or other side of the whirlpool in "Death by Water." But the chastened tone and the allusions to the journey to Emmaus in the immediate aftermath of Jesus's crucifixion suggest that even such climactic scenes of sacrifice and apocalypse have not yet led and are still unlikely to lead to salvation, resurrection, or transformation, nor even to a state of fear, distraction, ascesis, or melodrama. Such scenes seem to lead here instead only to a more stable and manageable condition of ironic patience: "He who was living is now dead / We who were living are now dying / With a little patience" (328–30). The possible loss of the familiar is offset by the knowledge of what to expect, a knowledge made possible by counting the loss as already lost, and by defining it vaguely enough as a generalized "dying" (as in much other modernist literature). Patience can thus displace any more specific sense of responsibility by shifting it vaguely somewhere else.

Eliot's religious imagery is itself relatively patient, not insisting on the privilege of Christian imagery, but effectively allowing responsibility to shift in that direction. His note to this section identifies three of its themes as "the journey to Emmaus, the approach to the Chapel Perilous (see Miss Weston's book) and the present decay of eastern Europe"; other notes refer to a bird handbook and the account of an Antarctic expedition (*Facsimile* 148n, 148n357, 148n360). As in the introduction to *Huckleberry Finn*, he has set religious and colonial imagery in the midst of the mythic, literary, historical, political, naturalistic, and scientific. He has placed both religious and colonial nostalgias in the midst of a series of terms for something that none of them seems to capture by itself. His tone of patience and irony thus appears to make no assertion on behalf of either religious or colonial nostalgias. Yet that apparently innocent lack of assertion also allows the naturalized cultural power of the religious and colonial imagery to reassert itself as if by its own inherent power.

The emotional stability he attempts here is suggested in a letter to Ford Madox Ford in 1923, where Eliot called the twenty-nine lines of the next two stanzas the "*good* lines in *The Waste Land*" as opposed to the rest as "ephemeral" (qtd. *Facsimile* 129n2 to p. 71). Whereas the poem often elsewhere simulates and attempts to ironize the effect of the cinema's "continuous senseless music and continuous action too rapid for the brain to act upon," the twenty-nine lines of this "water-dripping song," as Eliot called it, slow the poem's pace almost to a stop.[6]

It is not as simple here as only escaping modern bourgeois distractions, corruptions, and expectations, as if that would by itself allow the return to an unspoiled state of nature ("Here is no water but only rock / Rock and no water and the sandy road" 331–32). Nor does escape lead to silence, solitude, or primitivism ("But red sullen faces sneer and snarl / From doors of mud-cracked houses" 344–45). Still, these negations of prevailing conventions are among the most tempting tropes throughout modernist art for naming what is lost, absent, or unspeakable in a degraded modern culture. These are the tropes that are both ironically undercut as insufficient, conventional representations and yet used nevertheless to represent that unspeakable absence. In a recent reading of William Faulkner, for example, Philip Weinstein has highlighted in a single image the combination of the state of nature, silence, solitude, and the primitive, in Faulkner's modernist appeals to "the infinitely precious, socially inconsolable Benjy deep within us" (123), where "private (predication-free) identity is celebrated as a priceless though violated resource, as personal depth, speechlessly resonating" (160). Eliot's poem has criticized this kind of metaphysical idealism as a confinement of individuals and cultures, yet his poem will now allow this same idealism to reassert its cultural power.

This urge toward a sort of precultural minimalism is certainly one direction that modernism explores in its reactions against both outmoded colonialist and dominant modern, capitalist, imperialist ideologies. However, Ellison and others would find more challenge and promise in other modernist moves that have at least been raised as challenging possibilities in Eliot's poem, moves less universalist and metaphysical than cosmopolitan and transcultural.[7] Modernism in Eliot as well as Faulkner and others at least sometimes also attempts to look to other ideologies *as* ideologies, not only for the ironic effect of vertigo that demystifies all such ideologies in relation to each other, but also for potentially valuable, positive cultural help in the necessary reconstruction of less exclusive, more improvisational and democratically negotiable works of art and culture.[8] But at this point in Eliot's poem, that sense of responsibility to and collaboration with others' voices appears to be less viable or important than the achievement of a certain ironic patience at the loss of one's own most familiar sense of voice.

Thus, compared with the cinematic or jazzy jumpiness of much of the rest of the poem (a signal for what Eliot sees as the culture's distracted substitute for responsible interpersonal and cross-cultural encounter), the pace of this water-dripping song is easier and the focus of its voice and description is more sustained. It may not actually be a great deal easier to "stop or think" critically in reading these lines than it is said to be in their dry, mountainous setting or in the rest of Eliot's poem. But the pace of these lines and their barren setting do allow the poem to focus on a thirst for something that is at least negatively defined as not here, not present, not familiar: "Here one can neither stand nor lie nor sit" (336, 340). Even such vaguely negative statements are given a certain stylistic continuity and stability unusual in the poem, and even what is said to be missing begins to seem almost familiar, if only because it is imagined here first and last in terms of the same "water" that the poem began by both calling for and warning against. The water-dripping song concludes, though, "But there is no water" (358).[9] Eliot's irony here effectively admits that this conventionally naturalistic and religious image of water may not be the right image at all, but this ironic admission allows him to use it nevertheless. The irony seems to acknowledge that this water image is perhaps not a symbol already infused with meaning, not a transparent sign but a naturalized convention, a sign of signs, but its effect here relies on a certain religious privilege nevertheless.

Eliot's imagery for the encounter with the unspeakable continues to shift in the next stanza even more clearly from the naturalistic to the scriptural context of the journey to Emmaus. Even though Eliot's note directs attention to the psychological and dialogic context of an account of an Antarctic expedition, the scriptural context is not quite undercut by these secular reminders, only ironically qualified and excused. His note thus sets up the same effect in our reading that the stanza describes in the action, a kind of conscious blind spot in our directed, critical vision that grants authority instead to our innocently peripheral (and culturally overdetermined) vision: "When I count, there are only you and I together, / But when I look ahead up the white road / There is always another one walking beside you" (360–62). This unaccountable "third" might be only a hallucination, as suggested by the word *delusion* in Eliot's note on the Antarctic expedition, but we are also encouraged to distrust this same critical, observational ability to discern the phantom's identity either by movement, dress, or even gender: "Gliding wrapt in a brown mantle, hooded / I do not know whether a man or a woman" (363–64). In this peculiarly nondirective way, the stanza implies quite strongly, without directly asserting as much, that we might as well trust the peripheral vision provided us by the biblical story and its accumulated cultural power, even if that vision is also ironically acknowledged to be conventional and not equal to critical examination.

The cultural power of colonialism is similarly allowed to assert itself in the following stanza as Eliot takes up and expands this image of the hooded "third" in the wider cultural and political context of Eastern Europe's "hooded hordes swarming / Over endless plains" (368–69). Eliot's use of words like *hordes* and *swarming* evokes current American and Western European racist discourse directed against immigrants from Eastern and Southern Europe and the Middle East, Spengler's theories of the decline of Western culture, as well as political discourse directed against Bolshevism in the new Soviet Union, even though Eliot's note to this stanza seems to acknowledge that such fears may well result from middle-class insularity and blindness. In the passage Eliot cites from Hermann Hesse's *Blick ins Chaos* (1920), the offended Bürger—the bourgeois city-dweller—merely laughs at the Eastern Europeans' songs on their path toward Chaos along the edge of the precipice, songs described ambiguously as drunken but also hymnlike. The Bürger thus fails to discern either who these "hooded hordes" are or what their songs mean. He also fails to discern the threat to his own cultural position. The saint and the seer, on the other hand, hear the same songs with tears, suggesting faintly perhaps a regret at such failures of responsibility toward this "murmur of maternal lamentation" (368). But the tears and even the lamentation are finally associated more closely with the Bürger's own losses and separations in the vision of a city that "Cracks and reforms and bursts in the violet air" (373). The towers that might have been thought to defend the Bürger are falling, as are the cities themselves, "Jerusalem Athens Alexandria / Vienna London" (374–75). These cities are all perhaps as unreal as visions "in the violet air" (372), or so the irony suggests, but these cities are at least named, as the undifferentiated "hooded hordes swarming / Over endless plains" are not. Again, any sense of responsibility toward these other voices has been displaced by an effort at ironic patience at the loss of one's own cultural voice. Those other voices are allowed almost to disappear.

The next two stanzas challenge readers to hear or imagine what appears to be fairly settled now as simply unimaginable, unless by means of more conventional imagery that is qualified but also excused by Eliot's modernist irony. The poem offers another variation on the Cleopatra figure who earlier brushed her hair into frantically "fiery points" and the typist who smoothed her hair "with automatic hand." After being invited to judge both those failures of encounter and responsibility, readers are now challenged to hear and imagine in another such scene—or probably fail to hear and imagine—an almost inscrutable music: "A woman drew her long black hair out tight / And fiddled whisper music on those strings" (377–78). Can we hear more in this music than Hesse's Bürger did? Can we hear bats whistle and see "bats with baby faces in the violet light" as they crawl "head downward down a blackened wall" (379, 381)? Can we hear in such images from Bram Stoker's *Dracula* the current fear of Eastern Europe's "hordes" as a threat to the West, a fear that may be unasserted here but that also remains unchallenged? Dare we imagine in their strange image ("And upside down in air") what is vaguely assumed to be our own more familiar "towers / Tolling reminiscent bells, that kept the hours" (382–83)? Can we at least remember the now lost "voices singing out of empty cisterns and exhausted wells" (384)? The poem offers no answers to these cross-cultural challenges and questions and seems here to expect none, even though the questions are framed in the second person. In keeping with the tone of this final section, the poem offers and expects only "a little patience" for their articulation.

Eliot's next stanza invokes the Grail legend on which his poem is partly modeled. The stanza also thus suggests a reflection on the entire poem's practice. But the suggestion here is that the poem has made no such invocation, as if it has only allowed the Grail legend to speak for itself. "In this decayed hole among the mountains," somehow "the grass is singing" around this "empty chapel, only the wind's home" (385–88). The poem protests its innocence ("Dry bones can harm no one"), since it has attempted less either to act or speak than to relinquish action and speech in favor of patience: "It has no windows, and the door swings" (390, 389). The poem looks and listens for what is beyond its power to invoke, imagine, effect, or even interpret, although its religious imagery may suggest more than it claims:

> Only a cock stood on the rooftree
> Co co rico co co rico
> In a flash of lightning. Then a damp gust
> Bringing rain
>
> (391–94)

As if to disavow the most naturalized, most Christian associations of this conventional imagery, Eliot here again shifts his cultural context. When the thunder speaks, it is now the Indian jungle that is "crouched, humped in silence" (398). This setting suggests another specter of the empire under threat, yet Eliot will attempt to imagine a keener and more specific sense of responsibility in cross-cultural encounters than we have seen thus far in the poem's last section. In the Hindu fable cited in Eliot's note, three groups (gods, men, and demons) offer different interpretations of what the thunder said, and all three are deemed to have comprehended the thunder's meaning. Presumably, each interpretation is judged appropriate to that group's relative po-

sition. Though Eliot's poem does not make here a positive statement or reach the climax of a sustained narrative, it does attempt
in these passages a relatively positive, specific series of possibilities. It is important to note that these more positive possibilities
occur not in the event of the poem's ironically or innocently
shaking off ideology to return to a nonideological self, but in its
encounter with a fable from another cultural tradition than Eliot's and most of his readers' (though Eliot studied that other
tradition extensively),[10] and in his consideration of three interpretations of the same phenomenon, each of which suggests
something different to learn from what the thunder said, depending on each interpreter's position relative to the others.

Eliot considers first what the most familiar discourse, that of
men, might learn from the thunder's speech. The discourse of
men may easily be compared to the poem's consistent representation of the dominant discourse of the middle class. "The awful
daring of a moment's surrender / Which an age of prudence can
never retract," spoken of in candor to a "friend," suggests a
valuable counter to the bourgeois preoccupation with prudence,
obituaries, memories, and wills that the middle class would tend
to leave behind "in our empty rooms" (402–9). One might think
here of the second Thames-daughter's sexual partner, who wept
and tried to withhold or retract his love and responsibility to
her in favor of clearing his own moral slate with a prudent promise of a new start, or the typist's sexual partner, whose "vanity
requires no response, / And makes a welcome of indifference"
(241–42). However, the challenge of uncharacteristic giving and
surrender here is worded in such extreme terms—"The awful
daring of a moment's surrender / Which an age of prudence can
never retract"—that the challenge seems less likely to be met
than litigated away. Members of a group or class represented to
be this bent on prudence and acquisition are likely to hear such
reminders to "give" only in sounds as insignificantly challenging to their own world as conventional Sunday and holiday admonitions or in sounds as foreign to their own world as speaking

thunder. As a reminder to "give" translated from Hindu legend into a British context, this admonition might also appeal to popular British ideas of magnanimity as a justification for colonialism. In other words, insofar as the thunder's message remains as vague and abstract as this quasi-religious allegory for unaccustomed and challenging encounters, the anticipated response also remains rather vague and abstract.

"Sympathize" is Eliot's translation of what is heard in the thunder's syllable by the demon, who might be compared with a member of the lower classes as represented in Eliot's poem. Hearing and thinking repeatedly and resentfully of the one key that imprisons him or her in the starvation of families and the opaque isolation of individuals alluded to in Eliot's note, each such demon prisoner thereby "confirms a prison" (414). This image also resembles a common view of the poor as selfishly resentful and unsympathetic in ways that are thought to confirm and even sometimes to justify their social position. This view of the poor has surfaced before in the first pub scene's discussion of Albert and Lil, where Lil's "straight look" evokes no loyalty or compassion from her embittered friend. Nor is there any alternative here of the kind heard from the fishermen's bar in Lower Thames Street, in "The pleasant whining of a mandoline / And a clatter and a chatter from within" (261–62), or in Eliot's descriptions of Marie Lloyd's performances. The only unlikely hope mentioned here for the demons is that "aethereal rumours" of sympathy might move even such a proverbial enemy of the people as Coriolanus: "Only at nightfall, aethereal rumours / Revive for a moment a broken Coriolanus" (415–16). It was Shakespeare's Coriolanus, after all, who understandably urged, "All bond and privilege of nature, break!" but whose eyes were made nevertheless "to sweat compassion" by the entreaties of his mother, wife, and son on behalf of the people of Rome (5.3.25, 197). But again, as in the case of the lesson supposedly learned by the "men" in the Hindu legend, this lesson for demons is represented as an almost unspeakable impossibility, even "for a moment" in the midst of impending general ruin; furthermore, it is represented as a possibility that may be out of their hands, since it seems to depend on the sympathy of others acting on their behalf.

The third group in the Hindu fable, the gods, hear "control" in the sound of the thunder, according to Eliot's translation of *damyata* in his note, or "control ourselves," according to the translation in the German source he cites. This ambiguity has been sustained throughout the poem, in what appears to be a profound anxiety as to whether there is any alternative to the strict defense of authoritarian control, other than the threat of its absolute loss. Although the poem seems to recommend for those concerned only with prudence (the middle class) "the awful daring of a moment's surrender," the poem has difficulty imagining for those accustomed to control (the aristocracy) any more surrender than to "control ourselves." While this stanza does make tentative motions in the direction of some ongoing dialectic of control and being controlled by someone else, the terms of this dialectic as control and self-control suggest a reluctance or inability to move beyond issues of control to questions of responsibility, commitment, friendship, love, interaction, or being made and remade by each other. The lines here oddly compare the heart's obedient response to "controlling hands" with a boat's response "to the hand expert with sail and oar" (422, 419). There is only the faintest suggestion here of a more conditional, interactive sort of control. That is, the boat is not altogether an inanimate object of control: it "responded gaily," both to the expert hand and to the lucky fact that "the sea was calm." And the second-person address is not imperative but conditional: "your heart would have responded / Gaily, when invited" (420–21). It is this willing animation in the response— with the sense of responsibility awakened by that animated response—which gives the "control" imagined here its potentially interactive character. And it is precisely the absence of any such lively response or responsibility that has made the forcing of Philomel "by the barbarous king" a rape; such an absence of response has also made the unheeded painting of the event one of the "withered stumps of time" (99, 104). It is worth noting again, however, that the responsiveness suggested for the first-person speaker here is closer to a certain restraint or tact on the part of "the hand expert with sail and oar," closer to self-control than being controlled or being made or remade by anyone else, even conditionally or tenderly. Like the men and the demons, the gods also have something to learn here but seem unlikely to learn it.

The poem's last lines review the "many voices" encountered throughout the poem, figured here not as a challenging, trans-forming series of "straight looks" but as an "arid plain behind" the speaker, who sits patiently "upon the shore," not listening, seeking, or hunting but rather more blindly and patiently "fish-ing" (423–24). He speaks in terms of preparing himself as if for death, hearing in a children's song an elegiac, straightforward reminder that London Bridge and the familiar civilization it rep-resents are "falling down" (426). He remembers from Dante's *Purgatorio* the example of the Provençal poet Arnaut Daniel, who accepted a similar loss and destruction with a pathos and dignity similar to Huck's, "then hid himself in the flames that refine them," as if that patience and dignity in death is now his only responsibility. This line from Dante begins an accelerated series of fragmentary citations from several languages and litera-tures, with the effect of resigning the poem's own voice to the cinematic purgatory of modern life, with only a trace of irony. The fragments suggest a somewhat faint and tragic-sounding fi-nal wish on the speaker's part that he could bear witness in the way that Dante's Daniel has and in the way that the swallow and nightingale's songs do; however, his choice of citations and the pace of their representation almost ensure that they will all re-main as unheard as his own voice is here. The next line's allusion to the prince in the ruined tower turns the focus again to the poet's own lonely pathos and dignity. This pathos and dignity is his irony's reward, the same lonely reward Eliot was willing to offer Huck with his "unconsciousness" and "grim precision," salvaged from the failure of his more challenging sense of responsibility to other people and cultures: "These fragments I have shored against my ruins" (430). What to do with those fragments now, Eliot's draft suggests, perhaps "*Another* knows," but "I know" only, with pathos and dignity, innocently and ironically at once, that "I know not" (*Facsimile* 61).

Eliot's next line, taken from Thomas Kyd's *Spanish Tragedy*, briefly raises the possibility of a more creative, strategic use of the means at hand to respond to the situation—"Why then Ile fit you"—only to imagine and warily dismiss that strategy at once as a revenge tragedy, bent toward disaster, a strategy apparently and perhaps actually mad (431). Having put such questions of response firmly behind him now in favor of salvaging his own pathos and dignity, his last two lines expand instead on that patient, formal dignity. First he repeats the three interpretations of the thunder, almost as if his poem had learned and responded to their lessons and not merely cited them in the form of nearly impossible admonitions. Then the last line effectively displaces all such questions of responsibility and learning altogether with a religious "formal ending" in "Shantih shantih shantih." Eliot's final note explains, " 'The Peace which passeth understanding' is a feeble translation of the content of this word," but this translation also suggests that a more attentive translation is beyond our powers anyway. Questions of cross-cultural and even interpersonal translation and responsibility raised throughout the poem have yielded the poem's ultimate place to an invocation of religious peace, even if the terms of that religious peace are culturally unfamiliar.

Ralph Ellison, however, for one, would not allow such questions of cross-cultural learning and responsibility to end there, or rather he did not believe that they did or could end there.

Eliot's poem has repeatedly raised but also repeatedly put to rest these challenges of necessary cross-cultural learning and responsibility. Eliot's poem displaces these personal and cultural challenges into contexts of religion and colonialism that his modernist irony has carefully qualified, denaturalized, but also effectively excused. Ellison's fiction and criticism, by contrast, would raise those challenges again by drawing on traditions more practiced in just such necessary cross-cultural learning and responsibility. Ellison would stress the movement of recovery, but he would also appreciate the importance of the moment of breakdown emphasized by Eliot, that necessary, repeated disruption of false unities and false reconciliations, including the universalization of dominant traditions and the rigid and exclusive complementarities of self and other, male and female, black and white. "They have picked poor Robin clean," Peter Wheatstraw sings almost tauntingly to Ellison's picked-over narrator, but Wheatstraw also thereby reminds that narrator of other changing bodies of cultural experience that are not brought up short by such cross-cultural encounters and challenges, not horrified, distracted, indifferent, resigned, but practiced and resourceful in "what it took to live in the world with others" (*Invisible Man* 574). Wheatstraw reminds Invisible Man of the cultural and personal resources of "shit, grit and mother-wit" available to and adaptable by him in order to try to make something else from such desolation, even to remake that apparent desolation into "a new jazz style," giving support and courage to himself and others as well (Ellison, *Shadow and Act* 231–32).

CONCLUSION

Learning from Difference

I HAVE ATTEMPTED TO DEMONSTRATE the value of reading four canonical works of American literature with a focus on transformative encounters with the world beyond the self. This is a world that is neither escapable through transcendence (as in the critical tradition of American romance), nor automatically hostile or nonnegotiable (as in traditions of realism and modernism), but a world of other people to whom we are responsible, from whom we can learn, and with whom we share the most significant dimensions of our lives. I have proposed that the reading and teaching of American literature be conceived in terms of the challenges and rewards of such interactions with other people, instead of tracing the fate of representative American individuals—or tracing the fates of groups conceived on the model of such representative, undivided, and separate selves.

The promise as well as the difficulty of these transformative, democratic interactions is perhaps less explicit in Twain's or Eliot's writing than it is in Morrison's and Ellison's writing—or in the writing of Benjamin and Kristeva, the two women analysts from whom I have drawn my model of transference. But I hope the preceding readings have suggested the value of putting these questions of interpersonal and cross-cultural relationships even to two of our most traditional canonical works.

I have placed Twain's and Eliot's works next to Morrison's and Ellison's to show how all four of these works, with all their differences, speak both directly and indirectly back and forth on crucial and persistent questions of individual freedom, ethical responsibility, and political democracy in American life. Twain and Eliot in many ways exemplify more established critical traditions of American romance, realism, and modernism, traditions into which Ellison's and Morrison's work have not easily fit. However, these African American writers do address the continuing historical and cultural power of these more established traditions—as powerful traditions, though not the only traditions, of American literature. And these more established traditions do address the questions of transformative, democratic interaction addressed more explicitly by Ellison and Morrison. All four of these writers, along with many others I could have chosen, participate in an ongoing national dialogue on questions of domination and democracy, ranging from the largest scale of politics, culture, and history to the more intimate scale of interpersonal relationships.

Teaching American literature always involves addressing not only the cultural and personal currents represented within the literature, but also the cultural and personal currents that inform our readings as teachers and students of that literature. We read *about* Americans and their various histories and cultures, but of course most of us also read *as* Americans *through* our own personal and cultural lenses, and teaching involves subtle and complex shifts between these possible focuses of our attention. The complexities of American cultures as represented *within* the literature are usually the more direct object of attention in our classes. American cultures as represented in *how we read* that literature are usually a more reflective and indirect focus, perhaps because this focus is even more variable and context-specific, changing in every classroom and every reader's experience.

Although this other dimension of our reading is perhaps harder to talk or write about, it is certainly no less important. Hoping perhaps to encourage critical reflection on some of our most fundamental and powerful cultural ideas without provoking an uncritical defensiveness about those same ideas, teachers of American literature usually focus more direct attention on the worlds represented within the work and the worlds surrounding the work, rather than the worlds informing our own reading and discussion. But teaching American literature does require at least indirect attention to how our histories and cultures affect *how we read* that literature.

Students and teachers bring to courses in American literature powerful cultural ideas about their reading that should be recognizable in the preceding chapters' discussions of cultural currents represented within these literary works. For example, students confronted with apparent cultural differences between these works, between characters within these works, or between their own and other students' responses to these works, may well be drawn to the still powerful cultural idea that every educated reader (or every American) could and should identify with the universalized (or nationalized) subject positions and truths of a canonical national literature. These universalized positions and truths are expected to be amenable to moral, national, religious, aesthetic, or philosophical adjudication, without significant regard to differences of history, culture, or circumstance.

The cultural power of this idea of a universal, usually moral resolution to cultural and social differences is addressed within both Twain's *Huckleberry Finn* and Morrison's *Beloved,* but it will be evident as well in student responses and classroom discussions of these novels. Either Huck becomes the American hero whose good-hearted individualism will transcend his social circumstances, as in the more escapist traditions of American romance, or he exemplifies how such individual good-heartedness is repeatedly overpowered by a social and natural reality that is defined in terms of competing self-interests, as in traditions of American realism and naturalism.

The power of these cultural tendencies in our reading may be usefully and indirectly addressed by devoting classroom attention to questions raised about these and other supposedly universal ideas, as suggested both within these works and in the relationships between these works. Both works suggest, for example, that a universalized moral resolution in terms of individual freedom is insufficient to either Huck's or Sethe's particular circumstances: neither can simply assert his or her own freedom without addressing hard questions about the freedom of someone else to whom he or she feels inescapably responsible. Both Huck and Sethe look to other cultural traditions and ideas to help them address their own emotional, ethical, and political situations. Focusing attention on how these characters differ and learn from other characters, and on how these works differ from and interact with each other, is one way to model and call at least indirect attention to how readers also differ from and interact with each other, instead of considering such differences as insignificant or unproductive. Instead of debating Huck's, Jim's, Amy's, or Sethe's heroism from supposedly universal positions, students can compare the different ideas and traditions according to which they see these characters trying to live, along with other ideas and traditions from which they might be trying to learn. Students can thus learn to recognize the ideas and traditions that are part of who they are, as well as other ideas that are part of who they have been or might become.

Students and teachers may also bring to courses in American literature popular ideas of multiculturalism, as a result of recent canon debates, progressive social movements, and economic globalization. Instead of thinking that every reader could and should identify with the same universalized subject positions and truths, without regard to differences of history, culture, or circumstance, students and teachers may regard these differences as simple, decisive, and nonnegotiable. In an extrapolation of the powerful American ideas of radical individualism and pluralism to the level of cultures, genders, and ethnicities, students of different backgrounds and affiliations may expect to recognize their own cultural or gender identities in this greater variety of literary texts, but they may be unable to account for the different identities being negotiated within the same reader, the effects that different identities have on each other, or the possibility or value of readers and cultures recognizing and interacting productively with each other. Such readers may be adept at finding signs of differences in culture, gender, or power, but may avoid signs of internal difference or of interactions across these various differences.

This sense of essentialized, nonnegotiable differences of gender or culture is addressed within both Eliot's *Waste Land* and Ellison's *Invisible Man,* along with another idea that is at least considered in both works—the idea that, somehow, this interaction does take place and these differences do get negotiated one way or another. Eliot's poem stresses the extreme necessity and importance of such interactions, if also their extreme difficulty, whereas Ellison's novel tends to model and provoke our own ability as readers to respond to the challenge of these interactions. This interaction and negotiation of differences also takes place, of course, in our readings and discussions, and teachers and students can productively call attention to these interactions. As Jay writes about his own experience teaching a multicultural American literature, "Students do make connections across the insulating boundaries we have taught them to respect, and they do find this adventure in dis-orientation challenging and exhilarating" (*American Literature* 132).

Even if one cultural or gender identity seems most recognizable and familiar in much of our reading, our imaginative involvement with other identities in the transferential experience of reading calls attention to the limits of our own most familiar identities. It reminds us of, and gives us valuable practice in, the process of self-recognition and even subtle self-transformation in our encounters with others' organizations of experience and the self. If such possibilities for meaningful interaction become a more explicit focus within the works we read, students and teachers will be more likely to acknowledge both their own differences and what they can learn from these differences. Minority students and teachers will not be expected to speak for all minority characters or readers. Teachers and students can acknowledge the limitations and complexities of their own positions, as well as what they have learned from other traditions and people.

The importance of individual or cultural self-recognition in reading and teaching was certainly underestimated before the canon debates of the last decades. Self-recognition in the canon's universalized subject positions and ideas was less an issue for the canon's most influential readers than it became for another generation of newly influential students and teachers. But in the course of these canon debates, the importance of individual or cultural self-recognition may have diverted necessary attention away from the negotiation of difference, even though such negotiations with difference are probably more often at issue in newer canons than in the old. The process of self-recognition in reading has perhaps been given most attention in feminist film criticism, but this is also where this process of identification has come to seem most complex, as critics have noticed the shifting, splitting, and varying of identifications and cross-identifications as various people watch the same films (see, e.g., Clover and Silverman).

A similar complexity is now receiving more attention in literary experience, as critics study, for example, how the quintessentially American colloquial speech of Huck Finn may have derived from Twain's listening to the speech of African Americans (Fishkin, *Was Huck Black?*), or how T. S. Eliot's poetic resistance to "standard language" may have depended on his preoccupation with his own "nigger drawl" (North), or how as Ellison and his brother as children learned of *Huckleberry Finn* and replayed some of its antics, they identified not only with the black Jim but also with the white Huck (Fishkin 107, 134).

People may well read to recognize themselves, but that self-recognition also involves the articulation and understanding of our various differences and of our connections, interactions, and identifications with other people. Moreover, we read to imagine and learn about experiences different from our own and about ways of making sense of dimensions of our own experience that have often gone unrecognized, unarticulated, or undeveloped. We learn about other people and thus also, in Kristeva's phrase, about the strangers within ourselves. In short, we read not only for self-recognition but also for interaction and transformation. The stories we read remind us repeatedly that our own most familiar ideas and stories are reflections of our histories as well as our choices. We can better take responsibility for these histories and choices with a knowledge of how they differ from others and how they are not our only possible choices or even our only possible histories.

In the act of reading, we participate in a dialectic of domination and democracy that also figures as a persistent challenge throughout our national literature, throughout our political and ethical lives as citizens, and throughout our imaginative experience as readers. We attempt to remake the works we read in our own image, and we allow ourselves to be remade wholly or partly in the image of others. Teaching a more culturally diverse American literature is likely to be a fragmented experience for teacher and student alike unless sustained attention is paid not just to the process of recognizing oneself and one's own position within a larger world but also to this challenging process of negotiating and learning from the differences within and between ourselves.

Certainly this process of encountering difference in the interactions among students and teachers deserves its own explicit attention in every classroom. But one effective way to approach this process of teaching and learning, as well as the process of reading, is by means of the indirection and transference made possible in literary experience, allowing for both participation in and reflection on American society and history. By paying more careful attention to the transformative encounters with difference to be found throughout American literature, we can also indirectly address the comparable encounters with difference so important in our reading and education. This is a large part of what I have tried to do here.

NOTES

Introduction

1. This model of transference is adapted from Jessica Benjamin's *Shadow of the Other: Intersubjectivity and Gender in Psychoanalysis*. Benjamin describes the classic Freudian, intrapsychic model of transference as an overly oedipalized "opposition between analyst as knowing subject and analysand as known object," a "subject-object complementarity, in which the subject who observes disavows his own participation" (xiv, xv). Benjamin's model draws on the Freudian and Lacanian attention to the experience of such intrapsychic splittings and repudiations, as well as on object-relations theory's attention to the experience of intersubjectivity as a negativity that repeatedly survives and challenges intrapsychic experience. The position of the analyst in Benjamin's model of transference derives not from the oedipal father as the first or only entry into symbolic speech and thinking, but from the maternal activity of "containment, holding, recognition, affect attunement . . . that is necessary to form the somatic sense of self and to perceive and think about the me and not-me environment; in other words, to become one's own container, able to own affects rather than be overwhelmed by them. The mother acts as an outside other who is able to help the subject to process and tolerate internal states of tension" (27). This developmental "evolution from a concrete to a metaphorical experience, . . . through which the body [of the mother and then of the child] metaphorically becomes the mental container" (27) is repeated at another level in the therapeutic relationship, "understood as the incremental transposition of the experience of retaliation and abandonment (often felt as literal repetition, for long stretches, by one or both participants) into metaphor. This metaphorical capacity allows us to hold onto the reality of thoughts and feelings and own them as part of the self without insisting that they be the whole story" (107). Benjamin suggests other ways such intrapsychic and culturally reinforced "oedipal complementarity" limits our experience, "insisting on polarity, mutual

exclusivity, black and white, male and female, have and have not" (70). She also calls attention to a "postoedipal" model of subjectivity that may sometimes better describe the experience of reading, in which "the formal elements of the complementarity, like taking in and putting out, [or, as above, black and white, male and female, have and have not, activity and passivity,] become less antithetical, more oscillating and alternating" (77).

2. For a fuller contrast between Morrison and Faulkner, see Philip Weinstein's *What Else but Love? The Ordeal of Race in Faulkner and Morrison.*

3. Gregory Jay traces this ideology to the American Revolution, which "saw itself as a revolt against feudalism's policy of rigidly assigning human beings to fixed places in the social hierarchy," an idea which he describes as "in context, a liberating move, even if the new freedom was initially intended largely for the rising bourgeoisie" (*American Literature* 76). He also traces some of its invocations and adaptations by members of other groups.

4. See Henry Wonham's collection for a useful sampling of such work, including Shelley Fisher Fishkin's bibliographic essay, "Interrogating 'Whiteness.'" Morrison's own nonfiction is an example of recent changes in American studies in general, including what Gates has called "a new black aesthetic movement," featuring close readings of the social text "to reveal cultural contradictions and the social aspects of literature, the larger dynamics of subjection and incorporation through which the subject is produced" ("African American Criticism" 309). Drawing on but avoiding "both the social organicism of the black arts movement and the formalist organicism of the 'reconstructionists,'" Gates writes, such readings problematize both the "black" and the "aesthetic": "No longer, for example, are the concepts of black and white thought to be preconstituted; rather, they are mutually constitutive and socially produced" (309). Thus in Morrison's fiction and nonfiction both, there is less stress on declaring her social or formal independence from an American cultural context that is itself largely characterized by just such declarations of independence than on changing, contextualized encounters and interactions between a racialized culture and the sometimes unspoken but irrepressible presence that she has called here "the ghost in the machine" ("Unspeakable" 11). A notable example of such work in African American literary criticism is Craig Werner's *Playing the Changes*. Other important recent studies of such intertextual, interracial, and intercultural dialogue in American literature would include Emily Miller Budick's *Engendering*

Romance: Women Writers and the Hawthorne Tradition 1850–1990, Ann Douglas's *Terrible Honesty: Mongrel Manhattan in the 1920s,* Shelley Fisher Fishkin's *Was Huck Black? Mark Twain and African American Voices,* Eric Lott's *Love and Theft: Blackface Minstrelsy and the American Working Class,* Michael North's *The Dialect of Modernism,* Eric Sundquist's *To Wake the Nations: Race in the Making of American Literature,* and Kenneth W. Warren's *Black and White Strangers: Race and American Literary Realism.*

5. See Weinstein's comparisons of legacies and paternities in Faulkner's and Morrison's work (*What Else but Love?* 87–132).

6. This other idea is elaborated most fully in Freud's *Beyond the Pleasure Principle,* especially in his theory of the death instincts—which "strive towards the reduction of tensions to zero-point . . . to bring the living being back to the inorganic state" (LaPlanche and Pontalis 97)—as well as in the radical genealogical critiques discussed by Steele, theories which help explain internalization but not resistance or agency. I have discussed the importance of this compulsive "clinging to misery" in Faulkner's work in *Faulkner and Modernism.*

7. William Simmons makes the useful generalization that the weaker party in almost any relationship knows the stronger party better than vice versa (68–69). The weaker party simply cannot as well afford to rely on comforting or simplistic stereotypes.

8. See Winfried Flück for a useful recent critical history of the idea of American romance.

9. A small group of us visited the school board attorney to ask that juniors be allowed to continue at Baton Rouge High for our senior year instead of being assigned to a newly drawn, almost all-white school district. We suggested we could help make desegregation work, despite dire predictions to the contrary. Although he finally agreed to our request, the school board attorney preferred the dire predictions, privately comparing desegregation to a war in which he was trying to limit his and our (white) losses to one school. Some years later, the school was made into a "magnet" school in a belated effort to counteract continuing white flight.

10. Benjamin Demott traces a recent surge in moralistic images of interracial friendship in American films, which he describes as a kind of alibi for a surge in political opposition to affirmative action and poverty programs. Michael Lind discusses how such moralistic issues distract public attention from the much more serious damage inflicted by the growing inequality between America's credentialed, global oligarchy and the rest of the nation and world.

11. Eric Lott makes a similar argument about the complex imaginative and social function of popular minstrel shows for white working-class audiences in the nineteenth century.

12. Ellison writes that the experience of reading *The Waste Land* in college was for him "the real transition to writing" from his initial college plans to study music (*Shadow and Act* 159).

Chapter 1

1. Eric Sundquist writes of "the hypocrisy, violence, and racial loathing that *Adventures of Huckleberry Finn* (1885) keeps barely in check by the constraining good conscience of Huck and his authorial double, Mark Twain" (*To Wake the Nations* 226). Sundquist suggests that the surrounding social context, the world of Tom Sawyer, would return to the foreground of Twain's work in *Pudd'nhead Wilson* (1894).

2. I have found Jessica Benjamin's and Kelly Oliver's work especially useful and promising in suggesting an ethics of difference modeled on maternity. Oliver writes in *Womanizing Nietzsche:* "Within the imaginary of Western culture, the first call or invitation from an other comes from the mother. Her call is an invitation to speak, to respond. Her body opens an invitation to both sexes without discrimination. It provides the first model of discourse as a call that cannot be reduced to either biology or culture. It provides a model for an economy of exchange that is not defined by a violent struggle to the death" (200–201).

3. See Goldfield for an incisive political history of this ideology.

4. Such transference seems a particular case of what Deleuze describes as the general value of a structure that includes others. "As for the objects behind my back, I sense them coming together and forming a world, precisely because they are visible to, and are seen by, Others. And what is *depth*, for me, in accordance with which objects encroach upon one another and hide behind one another, I also live through as being *possible width* for Others, a width upon which they are aligned and pacified (from the point of view of another depth). In short, the Other assures the margins and transitions in the world. . . . He prevents assaults from behind. He fills the world with a benevolent murmuring. . . . Others, from my point of view, introduce the sign of the unseen in what I do see, making me grasp what I do not perceive as what is perceptible to an Other" (305–6).

5. In Kristeva's terms, too, the mother-infant dyad needs a third party, someone else for the mother to love, in order for the infant's monologue to become not a mirror but a duet with another subjectivity. The mother is usually the infant's first connection with other stories (*Tales of Love* 22). Benjamin stresses, instead of the infant's recognition of the mother's relationship to another subject, the infant's own relationship to some third party. In either case, the resulting triangulation works against monologue, domination, and the loss of intersubjectivity.

6. Compare Kristeva's remarks on the relation of depression to language—and the other voices it may connect with one's own. "Language starts with a *negation* (*Verneinung*) of loss, along with the depression occasioned by mourning. 'I have lost an essential object that happens to be, in the final analysis, my mother,' is what the speaking being seems to be saying. 'But no, I have found her again in signs, or rather since I consent to lose her I have not lost her (that is the negation), I can recover her in language.' Depressed persons, on the contrary, *disavow the negation:* they cancel it out, suspend it, and nostalgically fall back on the real object (the Thing) of their loss, which is just what they do not manage to lose, to which they remain painfully riveted" (*Black Sun* 43–44).

7. Again, Sethe's withdrawal and depression function in the way Kristeva describes the mother-infant romance that threatens to collapse from two into an indistinguishable one, into abjection and devouring.

8. Shirley Stave's essay "Toni Morrison's *Beloved* and the Vindication of Lilith" explores the novel's implicit critique here of a powerful cultural model of mothering as complete sacrifice.

9. This is also Foucault's argument in "Two Lectures," and it is one implication of W. E. B. Du Bois's famous idea of "double consciousness." It is also assumed in James Berger's essay on *Beloved* as a reflection on African American intraracial violence.

Chapter 2

1. See Fishkin (*Was Huck Black?*) on the function of such ghost-chasing tales in African American culture (83–86), and David Smith, "Huck, Jim, and American Racial Discourse."

2. Kristeva speaks of transference giving the traumatic memory another more bearable sense, that is, both another meaning and another direction ("Mémoire").

3. See Tompkins; see also Porter 231–32.

Chapter 3

1. In terms of Craig Werner's comparison of African American literary and musical forms in *Playing the Changes*, Ellison's writing sustains what Eliot's early writing mostly does not of the jazz musician's gospel-derived sense that the music must address not only other musicians but also the larger community (268–69, 299).

2. Werner makes a similar argument about Melvin Tolson: "In *Harlem Gallery*, Tolson suggests that, if the artist can establish contact with the members of a particular audience through the use of techniques and themes already familiar to it, then he/she can use that contact to initiate the audience into new aesthetic and social experiences. In theory, Tolson's mastery of irony and Euro-American tradition should enable him to communicate something of the blues sensibility to an audience comfortable with the performances of Pound and Eliot. His familiarity with call and response and the details of Afro-American experience should enable him to communicate the value of the Euro-American tradition to an audience which associates it primarily with an oppressive social system" (471).

3. Writing later about U.S. history and his own family background, however, Eliot seems to date the fall of mankind in the mid to late nineteenth century (see Sigg 18–19 and the letter to Herbert Read quoted in chapter 4 below).

4. William Lyne argues that in Ellison's *Invisible Man* "the primary double-voiced tools" of African American expressive culture—spirituals, the blues, jazz, and folk narratives, which "are supposed to undermine and transform the official hierarchies"—are both rediscovered and also shown to "serve the hierarchical purpose of keeping the invisible man invisible" (328). However, African American expressive culture defined as such might well be expected to fail to subvert, transform, or achieve organic independence from dominant cultural hierarchies, precisely because the problem is not just expressive but historical, political, rhetorical, and cross-cultural.

5. Compare Robert Stepto's reading of Ellison's achievement in *From behind the Veil* 163–94.

6. Thomas Hill Schaub argues that Ellison's novel does effectively swear off action, especially oppositional political action, in accordance with much U.S. cold war criticism and politics. Partly because my own study measures Ellison's novel against Eliot's poem, I read Ellison's novel as an argument *for* political action, though not without an acute sense of its historical and cultural position.

7. Again, Schaub emphasizes this attachment on Ellison's part to a modernist, New Critical, cold war ethic of literary consciousness as a substitute for political action. I emphasize instead Ellison's effort to recognize, but also to resist and counter, the powerful cultural attraction of that very ethic of literary consciousness and political complacency. Jay cautions, "Ellison's championing of the blues and folklore can come to seem like other paeans to popular culture, that is, as an account that over-estimates the 'resistance' power of popular culture and mistakes the artistic expression of oppression for the practical undoing of its material and political causes." And yet, "in the current swing away from essentialism and identity politics, Ellison's . . . move away from Marxism and social determinism toward an existentialism of the blues emphasized the power of choice, or agency, in a way that resonates in the aftermath of the determinism spawned by structuralism and social constructionism" (*American Literature 93*).

8. See Eric Sundquist's *Cultural Contexts for Ralph Ellison's Invisible Man* for a useful collection of documents for the study of such historical connections.

9. Such a rapid succession of spectacles is what seems to overwhelm Ellison's narrator in the prologue and perhaps Eliot's narrator in *The Waste Land*. It is also the danger Eliot warned against in mass culture.

10. The source of the college's magic promise is suggested in the last paragraph of this allusion-studded passage:

> The grass did grow and the green leaves appeared on the trees and filled the avenues with shadow and shade as sure as the millionaires descended from the North on Founders' Day each spring . . . each leaving a sizeable check as he departed. I'm convinced it was the product of a subtle magic, the alchemy of moonlight; the school a flower-studded wasteland, the rocks sunken, the dry winds hidden, the lost crickets chirping to yellow butterflies.
> And oh, oh, oh, those multimillionaires! (*Invisible Man* 36–37)

11. Craig Werner's comment about the representation of women in Richard Wright's *Native Son* might also serve for comment on Ellison's *Invisible Man:* "As many feminist critics have demonstrated, a deep current of misogyny runs through Wright's work. Yet *Native Son* demonstrates at least a subliminal awareness of the nature of the problem" (209).

12. In Benjamin's psychoanalytic terms, "repeated experiences of breakdown [of recognition and intersubjectivity] and repair result in the

subject's confidence in the possibility of reinstituting tension after break-down. This confidence is what allows her/him to relinquish ossified forms of complementarity, to risk the negotiation of difference" (*Shadow* 97).

Chapter 4

1. Quotations from the poem will be cited by their line or line-note number in the text of the first edition as republished in the 1971 *Facsimile* edition; other quotations from the *Facsimile* edition will be cited by page. This first edition counts two lines as one at about line 346; line numbers thereafter are one number lower than in other editions.

2. Compare Terence Hawkes on the written, commercialized character of works like the *Ziegfeld's Follies'* "Shakespeherian Rag" as opposed to the oral, performative, African American traditions of the blues and jazz from which the "Shakespeherian Rag" derives. Eliot may not have been aware of jazz at the time of writing *The Waste Land*. As Mitchell Breitwieser informed me in November 1997, "By 1922, the only recorded jazz was for the most part by white bands and did not feature the sort of improvisations that came into recorded prominence with Armstrong's hot fives later in the decade. Eliot might have heard jazz live, or been familiar with African American dialogisms in Missouri."

On the performative nature of convention, see also Michael North, especially his discussion of performative African American traditions in the work of Zora Neale Hurston:

> Joe's is a ceremonial pretense that Missie May shares, while Slem-mons's pretense is his alone. His money is no good not because it lacks some intrinsic characteristic of value—all money is conventional and, therefore, to some extent misleading—but because it is not shared in a reciprocal system of exchange. All behavior, all speech, like all money, is conventional, imitative, and yet this does not undermine the distinction between truth and falsehood. The truth is any variety of language that works in a ceremony that affects people's daily lives. Joe's word is his bond, to take one of Austin's favorite locutions, because it is given as part of a performative ex-change with another person; Slemmons's word, like his money, is only valuable to himself. (184–85)

Eliot's poem is full of characters like Slemmons, with only the faintest hints of the possibility represented here by Joe's "performative exchange with another person."

3. As for more current usage and connotation, the *OED* also cites Andrew Lang's *The Making of Religion* (1898): "the Melanesians, Africans, and other savages" (vol. 8, 167). Michael North has traced the appeal of African American dialect for Eliot, Pound, and other modernists as an appropriated model for their own poetic resistance to the Standard Language Movement.

4. A similar fear of mixture and melting would flare up again in the University of Virginia lecture reprinted in *After Strange Gods* in 1934 and later suppressed by Eliot: "The population should be homogeneous; where two or more cultures exist in the same place they are likely either to be fiercely self-conscious or both to become adulterate" (19).

5. Jessica Benjamin suggests that the difference between selves is still a crucial factor even in erotic experience: "The shared confrontation with de-differentiation—that is, the dizzying loss of self in erotic experience—is what counteracts the element of one person's reducing the other to his (undifferentiated) thing" (*Like Subjects* 186).

6. In a different reading of this passage, Cleo McNelly Kearns suggests that Eliot's hermit-thrush in the pine trees, with its echo of Walt Whitman's elegy "When Lilacs Last in the Dooryard Bloomed," is one of many signals in *The Waste Land* for Eliot's movement both in this poem and in his poetic career toward the exoteric and sexual openness he would have associated with Whitman and Bertrand Russell. Kearns discusses Eliot's vexed and changing relationship with Whitman's poetry in what might be considered another cross-cultural encounter. I would suggest, however, that this exoteric and sexual openness is still a distant possibility in *The Waste Land*. The poem's last section settles more modestly on working toward a certain unattained emotional stability, at the acknowledged expense of any particular openness to transformative events or encounters with other people. Thus Gregory Jay argues that "poems like 'Gerontion' and *The Waste Land* that so lament the loss of the Center are more metaphysically idealistic," despite their radical formal experiments, "than the Heraclitean meditations of *Four Quartets*" (*T. S. Eliot* 25).

7. See David A. Hollinger, esp. 79–104, for an elaboration of this distinction in American cultural and intellectual history and for this sense of the word *cosmopolitan*.

8. This is how Gloria Anzaldúa describes her project in *Borderlands / La Frontera: The New Mestiza*: "Our role is to link people with each other—the Blacks with Jews with Indians with Asians with whites with

extraterrestrials. It is to transfer ideas and information from one culture to another" (84–85).

9. As noted above, the first edition of *The Waste Land* as republished in the *Facsimile* edition counts two lines as one at about line 346. Line numbers thereafter are one number below those in other editions.

10. See Kearns on Eliot's study of Indic traditions.

BIBLIOGRAPHY

Anzaldúa, Gloria. *Borderlands / La Frontera: The New Mestiza*. San Francisco: Aunt Lute Books, 1987.

Arteaga, Alfred. "An Other Tongue." *An Other Tongue: Nation and Ethnicity in the Linguistic Borderlands*. Ed. Alfred Arteaga. Durham: Duke UP, 1994. 53–92.

Baker, Houston, Jr. *Modernism and the Harlem Renaissance*. Chicago: U of Chicago P, 1987.

Baym, Nina. "Melodramas of Beset Manhood: How Theories of American Fiction Exclude Women Authors." *American Quarterly* 33.2 (Summer 1981): 123–39.

Bedient, Calvin. *He Do the Police in Different Voices: The Waste Land and Its Protagonist*. Chicago: U of Chicago P, 1986.

Beidler, Peter G. "The Raft Episode in *Huckleberry Finn*." *Modern Fiction Studies* 14 (Spring 1968): 11–20.

Benjamin, Jessica. *The Bonds of Love: Psychoanalysis, Feminism, and the Problem of Domination*. New York: Pantheon, 1988.

———. *Like Subjects, Love Objects: Essays on Recognition and Sexual Difference*. New Haven: Yale UP, 1995.

———. *Shadow of the Other: Intersubjectivity and Gender in Psychoanalysis*. New York: Routledge, 1998.

Berger, James. "Ghosts of Liberalism: Morrison's *Beloved* and the Moynihan Report." *PMLA* 111 (1996): 408–20.

Bersani, Leo. *A Future for Astyanax: Character and Desire in Literature*. Boston: Little Brown, 1976.

Bhabha, Homi. *The Location of Culture*. New York: Routledge, 1994.

Bigsby, C. W. E. *The Second Black Renaissance: Essays in Black Literature*. Contributions in Afro-American and African Studies 50. Westport, CT: Greenwood P, 1980.

Breitwieser, Mitchell Robert. "*The Great Gatsby:* Grief, Jazz, and the Eye-Witness." *Arizona Quarterly* 47.3 (1991): 17–70.

Brenkman, John. *Culture and Domination.* Ithaca: Cornell UP, 1987.

Brown, Sterling. *The Negro in American Fiction.* 1937. New York: Atheneum, 1969.

Budick, Emily Miller. *Engendering Romance: Women Writers and the Hawthorne Tradition 1850–1990.* New Haven: Yale UP, 1994.

Chase, Richard. *The American Novel and Its Tradition.* Garden City: Doubleday, 1957.

Chinitz, David. "T. S. Eliot and the Cultural Divide." *PMLA* 110 (1995): 236–47.

Clover, Carol. *Men, Women, and Chain Saws: Gender in the Modern Horror Film.* Princeton: Princeton UP, 1992.

Davidson, Harriet. *T. S. Eliot and Hermeneutics: Absence and Interpretation in "The Waste Land."* Baton Rouge: Louisiana State UP, 1985.

Deleuze, Gilles. *The Logic of Sense.* Ed. Constantin V. Boundas. Trans. Mark Lester with Charles Stivale. New York: Columbia UP, 1990.

Demott, Benjamin. "Put on a Happy Face: Masking the Differences between Blacks and Whites." *Harper's Magazine* 291.1744 (September 1995): 31–38.

Donaldson, Susan. "Welty, Faulkner, and Southern Gothic." American Literature Association Symposium. Hotel Grande. Cancun, Mexico, 14 December 1996.

Douglas, Ann. *Terrible Honesty: Mongrel Manhattan in the 1920s.* New York: Farrar, 1995.

Douglass, Frederick. *Narrative of the Life of Frederick Douglass, an American Slave.* Ed. Houston A. Baker Jr. New York: Penguin, 1982.

Du Bois, W. E. B. *The Souls of Black Folk.* 1903. New York: Penguin, 1989.

Eliot, T. S. *After Strange Gods: A Primer of Modern Heresy.* The Page-Barbour Lectures at the University of Virginia, 1933. London: Faber, 1934.

———. *Collected Poems, 1909–1962.* New York: Harcourt, 1963.

———. "An Introduction to *Huckleberry Finn.*" *Adventures of Huckleberry Finn: An Annotated Text, Backgrounds and Sources, Essays in Criticism.* Ed. Sculley Bradley, Richmond Croom Beatty, E. Hudson Long. Norton Critical Editions. New York: Norton, 1962. 320–27. Rpt. *The Adventures of Huckleberry Finn.* London: Cresset, 1950. vii–xvi.

———. *The Family Reunion. The Complete Poems and Plays 1909–1950.* New York: Harcourt, 1971. 223–93.

―――. "London Letter" to the New York *Dial* 71 (1921): 452–55. Qtd. in Longenbach 523.

―――. *Selected Essays: New Edition*. New York: Harcourt, 1960.

―――. "Ulysses, Order, and Myth." *Dial* 75 (1923): 480–83.

―――. *The Waste Land: A Facsimile and Transcript of the Original Drafts Including the Annotations of Ezra Pound*. Ed. Valerie Eliot. New York: Harcourt, 1971.

Ellison, Ralph. *Invisible Man*. 1952. New York: Random House/Vintage, 1989.

―――. *Shadow and Act*. 1964. New York: Random House/Vintage, 1972.

Faulkner, William. *Go Down, Moses*. New York: Vintage, 1990.

Fishkin, Shelley Fisher. "Interrogating 'Whiteness,' Complicating 'Blackness': Remapping American Culture." *Criticism and the Color Line: Desegregating American Literary Studies*. Ed. Henry B. Wonham. New Brunswick: Rutgers UP, 1996. 251–90.

―――. *Was Huck Black? Mark Twain and African American Voices*. New York: Oxford UP, 1993.

FitzGerald, Jennifer. "Selfhood and Community: Psychoanalysis and Discourse in *Beloved*." *Modern Fiction Studies* 39.3–4 (Fall/Winter 1993): 669–87.

Flück, Winfried. "The American Romance and the Changing Functions of the Imagination." *New Literary History* 27 (1996): 415–57.

Foucault, Michel. "Two Lectures." *Power/Knowledge: Selected Interviews and Other Writings, 1972–77*. Ed. Colin Gordon. Trans. Colin Gordon, Leo Marshall, John Mepham, Kate Soper. New York: Pantheon, 1980. 78–108.

Gates, Henry Louis, Jr. "African American Criticism." *Redrawing the Boundaries: The Transformation of English and American Literary Studies*. Ed. Stephen Greenblatt and Giles Gunn. New York: MLA, 1992. 303–19.

―――. *The Signifying Monkey: A Theory of Afro-American Literary Criticism*. New York: Oxford UP, 1988.

Gillman, Susan. *Dark Twins: Imposture and Identity in Mark Twain's America*. Chicago: U of Chicago P, 1989.

Gillman, Susan, and Forrest G. Robinson. "Introduction." *Mark Twain's Pudd'nhead Wilson: Race, Conflict, and Culture*. Eds. Susan Gillman and Forrest G. Robinson. Durham: Duke UP, 1990.

Girard, René. *Violence and the Sacred*. Trans. Patrick Gregory. Baltimore: Johns Hopkins UP, 1977.

Goldfield, Michael. "The Color of Politics in the United States: White Supremacy as the Main Explanation for the Peculiarities of American Politics from Colonial Times to the Present." *The Bounds of Race: Perspectives on Hegemony and Resistance.* Ed. Dominick LaCapra. Ithaca: Cornell UP, 1991. 104–33.

Guattari, Felix. "The Three Ecologies." Paper delivered to Dept. of French and Francophone Studies, LSU, Baton Rouge, 6 March 1990.

Hartz, Louis. *The Liberal Tradition in America.* New York: Harcourt, 1955.

Hawkes, Terence. "That Shakespeherean Rag." *Shakespeare's "More Than Words Can Witness": Essays on Visual and Nonverbal Enactment in the Plays.* Ed. Sidney Homan. Lewisburg: Bucknell UP, 1980.

Hay, Eloise Knapp. *T. S. Eliot's Negative Way.* Cambridge: Harvard UP, 1982.

Hirsch, Marianne. *The Mother/Daughter Plot: Narrative, Psychoanalysis, Feminism.* Bloomington: Indiana UP, 1989.

Holland, Laurence B. "A 'Raft of Trouble': Word and Deed in *Huckleberry Finn.*" In *American Realism: New Essays.* Ed. Eric J. Sundquist. Baltimore: Johns Hopkins UP, 1982. 66–81. Rpt. from *Glyph 5: Johns Hopkins Textual Studies* (Baltimore, 1979).

Hollinger, David A. *Postethnic America: Beyond Multiculturalism.* New York: Basic Books/HarperCollins, 1995.

Jameson, Fredric. "Modernism and Imperialism." *Nationalism, Colonialism, and Literature.* Ed. Terry Eagleton, Fredric Jameson, and Edward W. Said. Minneapolis: U of Minnesota P, 1990. 43–66.

Jay, Gregory S. *American Literature and the Culture Wars.* Ithaca: Cornell UP, 1997.

———. *T. S. Eliot and the Poetics of Literary History.* Baton Rouge: Louisiana State UP, 1983.

Jehlen, Myra. "Gender." *Critical Terms for Literary Study.* Ed. Frank Lentricchia and Thomas McLaughlin. Chicago: U of Chicago P, 1990. 263–73.

Kearns, Cleo McNelly. *T. S. Eliot and Indic Traditions.* Cambridge: Cambridge UP, 1987.

Kristeva, Julia. *Black Sun: Depression and Melancholia.* Trans. Leon S. Roudiez. New York: Columbia UP, 1989.

———. "Mémoire et santé mentale." Académie universelle des cultures conférence à l'Unesco. Paris. April 1998.

———. *Tales of Love.* Trans. Leon S. Roudiez. New York: Columbia UP, 1987.

LaPlanche, J., and J.-B. Pontalis. *The Language of Psycho-Analysis.* Trans. Donald Nicholson-Smith. New York: Norton, 1973.

Leonard, James S., Thomas A. Tenney, and Thadious Davis, eds. *Satire or Evasion? Black Perspectives on "Huckleberry Finn."* Durham, N.C.: Duke UP, 1992.

Lind, Michael. "To Have and Have Not: Notes on the Progress of the American Class War." *Harper's Magazine* 290.1741 (June 1995): 35–39, 42–48.

Longenbach, James. "Guarding the Horned Gates: History and Interpretation in the Early Poetry of T. S. Eliot." *ELH* 52.2 (1985): 503–27.

Lott, Eric. *Love and Theft: Blackface Minstrelsy and the American Working Class.* New York: Oxford UP, 1993.

Lyne, William. "The Signifying Modernist: Ralph Ellison and the Limits of the Double Consciousness." *PMLA* 107.2 (March 1992): 319–30.

Lyotard, Jean-François. *The Differend: Phrases in Dispute.* Trans. Georges Van Den Abbeele. Theory and History of Literature 46. Minneapolis: U of Minnesota P, 1988.

McKay, Nellie. "An Interview with Toni Morrison." *Contemporary Literature* 24 (Winter 1983): 413–29.

Marx, Leo. "Mr. Eliot, Mr. Trilling, and *Huckleberry Finn.*" *Adventures of Huckleberry Finn: A Case Study in Critical Controversy.* Ed. Gerald Graff and James Phelan. Boston: St. Martin's/Bedford, 1995. 290–305. Rpt. *The American Scholar* 22 (1953): 432–40.

Moreland, Richard C. *Faulkner and Modernism.* Madison: U of Wisconsin P, 1990.

Morrison, Toni. *Beloved.* New York: Knopf, 1987.

———. *Jazz.* New York: Knopf, 1992.

———. *Playing in the Dark: Whiteness and the Literary Imagination.* Cambridge: Harvard UP, 1992.

———. "The Site of Memory." *Out There: Marginalization and Contemporary Cultures.* Ed. Russell Ferguson et al. Cambridge: MIT P, 1990. 299–305.

———. *Song of Solomon.* New York: Knopf, 1977.

———. "Unspeakable Things Unspoken: The Afro-American Presence in American Literature." *Michigan Quarterly Review* 28 (Winter 1989): 1–34.

Mouffe, Chantal. "Democratic Citizenship and the Political Community." *Dimensions of Radical Democracy: Pluralism, Citizenship, Community (Phronesis).* Ed. Chantal Mouffe. London: Verso, 1992. 225–39.

North, Michael. *The Dialect of Modernism: Race, Language, and Twentieth-Century Literature*. New York: Oxford UP, 1994.

Oliver, Kelly. *Womanizing Nietzsche: Philosophy's Relation to the "Feminine."* New York: Routledge, 1995.

O'Meally, Robert. *The Craft of Ralph Ellison*. Cambridge: Harvard UP, 1980.

Porter, Carolyn. *Seeing and Being: The Plight of the Participant Observer in Emerson, James, Adams, and Faulkner*. Middletown: Wesleyan UP, 1981.

Read, Herbert. "T. S. E.—A Memoir." *T. S. Eliot: The Man and His Work*. Ed. Allen Tate. London: Chatto and Windus, 1967.

Ryan, Michael. *Politics and Culture: Working Hypotheses for a Post-Revolutionary Society*. Baltimore: Johns Hopkins UP, 1989.

Said, Edward W. *Culture and Imperialism*. Random House/Vintage, 1994.

Schaub, Thomas Hill. *American Fiction in the Cold War*. Madison: U of Wisconsin P, 1991.

Schmitz, Neil. *Of Huck and Alice: Humorous Writing in American Literature*. Minneapolis: U of Minnesota P, 1983.

Shakespeare, William. *Coriolanus*. Ed. Harry Levin. *William Shakespeare: The Complete Works*. The Pelican Text Revised. Ed. Alfred Harbage. Baltimore: Penguin, 1969. 1212–54.

———. *Hamlet, Prince of Denmark*. Ed. Willard Farnham. *William Shakespeare: The Complete Works*. Pelican Text Revised. Ed. Alfred Harbage. Baltimore: Penguin, 1969. 930–76.

Sigg, Eric Whitman. *The American T. S. Eliot: A Study of the Early Writings*. New York: Cambridge UP, 1989.

Silverman, Kaja. *Male Subjectivity at the Margins*. New York: Routledge, 1992.

Simmons, William. "Cultural Bias in the New England Puritans' Perception of Indians." *William and Mary Quarterly* 38.1 (1981): 56–72.

Smith, David L. "Huck, Jim, and American Racial Discourse." *Satire or Evasion? Black Perspectives on "Huckleberry Finn."* Ed. James S. Leonard, Thomas A. Tenney, and Thadious Davis. Durham, N.C.: Duke UP, 1992. 103–20.

Stave, Shirley. "Toni Morrison's *Beloved* and the Vindication of Lilith." *South Atlantic Quarterly* 58.1 (January 1993): 49–66.

Steele, Meili. "Metatheory and the Subject of Democracy in the Work of Ralph Ellison." *New Literary History* 27 (1996): 473–502.

Stepto, Robert. *From Behind the Veil: A Study of Afro-American Narrative*. 2d ed. Urbana: U of Illinois P, 1991.

Sundquist, Eric. *To Wake the Nations: Race in the Making of American Literature.* Cambridge: Belknap/Harvard UP, 1993.

———. Ed. *Cultural Contexts for Ralph Ellison's Invisible Man.* A Bedford Documentary Companion. Boston: Bedford/St. Martin's, 1995.

Tompkins, Jane. "Sentimental Power: *Uncle Tom's Cabin* and the Politics of Literary History." *Glyph* 8 (1981): 79–103.

Trilling, Lionel. "Introduction." *Adventures of Huckleberry Finn.* New York: Rinehart, 1948.

Twain, Mark. *Adventures of Huckleberry Finn.* Ed. Walter Blair and Victor Fischer. Berkeley: U of California P, 1985.

———. *Mark Twain's Autobiography.* Ed. Albert Bigelow Paine. 2 vols. New York: Harper and Brothers, 1924.

Warren, Kenneth W. *Black and White Strangers: Race and American Literary Realism.* Chicago: U of Chicago P, 1993.

Weinstein, Philip. *Faulkner's Subject: A Cosmos No One Owns.* Cambridge: Cambridge UP, 1992.

———. *What Else but Love? The Ordeal of Race in Faulkner and Morrison.* New York: Columbia UP, 1996.

Werner, Craig Hansen. *Playing the Changes: From Afro-Modernism to the Jazz Impulse.* Urbana: U of Illinois P, 1994.

Wonham, Henry B. *Criticism and the Color Line: Desegregating American Literary Studies.* New Brunswick: Rutgers UP, 1996.

INDEX

abjection, 39, 82, 90–91
Adams, Henry, 166
African American literature and
  culture: and living with others,
  16–21, 47, 54–55, 65–66, 100,
  103–4, 142–43, 154–55, 188,
  198 n. 4; as oppositional, 27; and
  power, 30–32, 133, 142; as
  rhetorical, interactive, 6–14, 108–
  11, 135; as separate, 26–27, 110–
  11, 198 n. 4, 202 n. 4. *See also* blues;
  double consciousness; jazz
alliances, activist, 67
American literature, teaching of. *See*
  teaching
antiwar movement, 15, 22
Anzaldúa, Gloria, 205 n. 8
Arteaga, Alfred, 108, 109
autocolonialism, 108

Baker, Houston, Jr., 7, 109
Baton Rouge High School, 15–16, 21,
  199 n. 9
Baym, Nina, 17–18, 108, 132, 141
Bedient, Calvin, 157
Beidler, Peter G., 77
Benjamin, Jessica: on destruction, 144,
  203 n. 12; on domination, 13, 17,
  20, 24; on maternity, 54, 200 n. 2,
  201 n. 5; on transference, 29, 54,
  189, 197–98 n. 1
Berger, James, 201 n. 9
Bersani, Leo, 69
Bhabha, Homi, 7
Bigsby, C. W. E., 105
blindness, 34–35, 100–143, 151–52,
  170–71
blues, 128–29, 135, 141–43, 204 n. 2
Breitwieser, Mitchell Robert, 154,
  204 n. 2

Brenkman, John, 82
Budick, Emily Miller, 198 n. 4

canon: debates, 17–19, 79, 100, 113,
  194; dominant, 23, 26, 29, 33–36,
  41, 64, 145
Chase, Richard, 19
Chinitz, David, 159
civil rights movement, 15, 21–22
class, 24, 44, 46, 67–68, 158–64,
  183–86
Clemens, Samuel L. *See* Twain, Mark
Clover, Carol, 194
colonialism, 148, 150, 153, 158–60,
  169–70, 177, 180, 188
community, 42
Conrad, Joseph, 139–40, 150
control, 185–86
critical hermeneutics, 82
Crusoe, Robinson, 16–17, 20, 85, 175
cultural studies, 68

Davidson, Harriet, 157
decolonizing cultural resistance, 26–28
Deleuze, Gilles, 16, 20, 85, 124, 152,
  175, 200 n. 4
democracy, 2–4, 6, 15, 17, 19–21,
  120, 125, 190, 195; as myth,
  102–5
Demott, Benjamin, 199 n. 10
depression, 55–57, 60, 201 n. 6
difference: disappearance of, 34, 162,
  166; fear of, 145; incommensurable, 109–10, 116; learning from,
  192–96; negotiation of, 120, 203–
  4 n. 12; projected, 123; tolerance
  of, 118
distraction, 157–65
domination, 2–4, 6, 13, 17, 19–21,
  29, 81–83, 195

Jay, Gregory S., 1–2, 3, 8, 193,
198 n. 3, 203 n. 7, 205 n. 6
jazz: as cultural resource, 109, 188;
eclecticism of, 7; as interactive,
improvisational, 5, 15, 115, 117,
154, 202 n. 1, 204 n. 2; as style of
The Waste Land, 35, 101–2, 167;
suspended possibilities of, 98
Jehlen, Myra, 44
Joyce, James, 167

Kearns, Cleo McNelly, 154, 205 n. 6,
206 n. 10
Kristeva, Julia, 89–90, 97, 189, 195,
201 nn. 5–7, 2

language, 201 n. 6, 56
Lawrence, D. H., 19
learning, 138–39; cross-cultural, 17,
26, 47, 101, 117, 131, 139, 143,
194–96; failed, 26, 32, 183–88;
from others, 3, 28, 94, 192, 194–
96; of roles, 44, 78; in transference,
89, 126
lies, 75–77, 84–85, 87–88, 91
Lind, Michael, 199 n. 10
literary vs. historical study, 3–4
loneliness, two kinds of, 39, 57–58, 82
Long, Huey, 20
Longenbach, James, 154
Lott, Eric, 7, 65, 67–68, 73, 77–78,
95, 199 n. 4, 200 n. 11
love, 10, 30–32, 34, 38, 43, 58, 90,
107, 112, 136–37; and
intersubjectivity, 170–71, 205 n. 5
Lyne, William, 202 n. 4
Lyotard, François, 171

Marx, Leo, 25
maternity, 42–43, 90, 197 n. 1,
200 n. 2, 201 nn. 5–8
Melville, Herman, 112

metaphysical, the, 148, 169, 178
minstrelsy, 31, 65, 67–68, 73, 123,
200 n. 11
misogyny, 166, 203 n. 11
mixture, fear of, 166, 205 n. 4
modernism, American: Eliot and,
144–88; Ellison and Morrison and,
33–35, 100, 103–7, 113, 117, 139–
40, 143; as ironic disillusionment,
25, 28; in tradition of romance and
realism, 16, 24, 33–35, 189–90
moralism, 15–16, 21–25, 44, 70, 96,
104, 117, 191, 199 n. 10
Morrison, Toni, 4, 6, 7, 8, 9, 16–21,
26, 98–99, 198 nn. 2–3; *Beloved*,
27–29, 34, 37–63, 92–94; *Jazz*, 4–
15; *Playing in the Dark*, 29, 64, 83–
84, 85, 112
Mouffe, Chantal, 6, 125
multiculturalism: democratic,
transformative, 6, 8, 35, 125, 168,
195; oppositional, 1–2, 8, 35, 118,
125, 193; pluralist, 1–2, 8, 18, 27,
35, 110, 118, 125, 192–93; and
shared political ethos, 3
myth, 102–5, 148

names, 99
Narcissus, images of, 89–90, 92
nationalism, 26–27, 109–10, 191
nature, 147, 177–78
North, Michael, 167–68, 194, 199 n. 4,
204 n. 2, 205 n. 3

Oliver, Kelly, 200 n. 2
O'Meally, Robert, 109

paternity, 89–92
patience, 176–82, 186–87
pedagogy, 117
phenomena, a-signifying, 152, 154
plans. *See* plots

transformative encounters: in
American literature, 100, 189–90,
196; cross-cultural, 29, 45, 131; in
democracy, 125; in Eliot, 34–35,
145, 149, 152, 153, 157, 167–72,
174–76, 205 n. 6; in Faulkner, 11; in
Morrison, 8, 12; in reading, 3–5,
121, 193, 196; vs. revelations, 119
Trilling, Lionel, 18, 19, 25
Twain, Mark, 5, 7, 17, 102–4;
Adventures of Huckleberry Finn, 15–
16, 21–26, 29–33, 37–39, 43–44,
64–99, 101, 112, 116, 133, 141,
145–47, 187, 194

undifferentiation, 168–70
unities, false, 145, 148, 168, 188,
191–92
unmaking identity, 9–11, 23, 34, 100

Warren, Kenneth W., 199 n. 4
Weinstein, Philip, 9, 198 n. 2, 199 n. 5
Werner, Craig Hansen, 198 n. 4,
202 nn. 1–2, 203 n. 11
Whitman, Walt, 205 n. 6
women's movement, 15, 22
women writers, American, 17–18, 27
Wright, Richard, 104, 203 n. 11